D1602853

THE WANTON
CHASE

THE WANTON CHASE

CHASE

PETER QUENNELL

AN AUTOBIOGRAPHY
FROM 1939

COLLINS
St James's Place, London
1980

Williams Collins Sons & Co Ltd
London · Glasgow · Sydney · Auckland
Toronto · Johannesburg

First published 1980
© Peter Quennell 1980

ISBN 0 00 216526 0
Set in Garamond

Printed in Great Britain by T J Press (Padstow) Ltd, Padstow, Cornwall

To M.Q. and A.Q.

ACKNOWLEDGEMENTS

For his kind permission to publish extracts from letters written me by Henry de Montherlant I am indebted to M. de Montherlant's literary executor, M. Jean-Claude Barat. I must also express my gratitude to Sir John Gielgud, who has allowed me to quote from his recent book, and to Messers George Allen and Unwin, who have authorised me to reprint eight lines of a poem by my friend Arthur Waley.

P.Q.

'Pursuing is the business of our lives . . . Every
arising difficulty, that for a while attends and
interrupts the pursuit, gives a sort of spring to the
mind . . . Intricacy in form, therefore, I shall define
to be that peculiarity in the lines, which compose it,
that *leads the eye a wanton kind of chase*, and from the
pleasure that gives it the mind, intitles it to the
name of beautiful . . .'

William Hogarth *Analysis of Beauty*

I

During the summer of 1939, accompanied by Cyril Connolly, I embarked on a long expedition across Central France towards the Mediterranean coastline. It was a calamitous holiday; the skies were always clear, and many of the landscapes through which we passed, particularly the great tawny uplands of the desolate volcanic Auvergne, as beautiful as we expected; yet peace and happiness eluded us. Cyril, though preoccupied with a new love – his beloved, a very young girl, wearing a French schoolboy's hooded cloak and carrying all her luggage bundled into a large red spotted handkerchief, had joined him at an earlier stage of the journey – was still much concerned about his absent wife, whom he had generously but incautiously left behind to amuse herself in Paris. Again and again he telephoned her far-off hotel, and usually received the same answer: '*Madame n'a pas rentré . . . Non, monsieur, madame ne répond pas!*' These enquiries he continued every hour; and next morning we watched him descend the stair-case hollow-eyed and woebegone, to spread around him an atmosphere of nervous gloom that slowly overcast our spirits.

I, too, was suffering a secret anxiety. My own companion, I noticed, as soon as we had reached a halt, would pay a hurried visit to the local post-office where, evidently, she hoped to find a letter, and on one occasion dashed off an elaborate reply, which she then repented of and tore up, scattering revelatory fragments around the room. A minor catastrophe was the loss of the newcomer's bundle. While helping us tie our bags on to the roof of the car, she had hitched it to a bumper; and by the time she recollected its existence, after twenty or thirty miles' motoring, all that remained was a wreath of dusty shreds. She and Cyril were obliged to turn back, and search the roadside for her treasures; but us they temporarily deposited in a small sun-smitten town named St. Affrique[1]. A desolate place; the streets

---

[1] St. Affrique, I afterwards learned, had a tragic link with Byron's family; for Medora Leigh, believed to be the poet's love-child by his half-sister Augusta, after many vicissitudes had married a French private soldier, Jean Taillefer, whose family owned a farm at Lapaeyre, a neighbouring village, and died of smallpox there among her peasant relations on August 29, 1849.

were torrid and narrow; and dominating every doorstep sat an aged black-shawled woman, who muttered sharply hostile comments. The immodest brevity of G.'s English shorts especially offended them. '*Honteuse!*' they exclaimed; and a crowd of inquisitive, aggressive children presently took up the cry. Stones flew skimming past; and, when we ventured into the church and sought to examine the gilded ironwork of its finely moulded altar-rails, from the sacristy emerged an indignant priest who ordered us out into the noonday glare.

We escaped at last; but our relief was short-lived. Neither the disappearance of Cyril's new friend nor the reappearance of his wife — she was far too candid on the subject of her recent gaieties — did much to ease the situation; and I returned home feeling a good deal more exhausted than when we had begun our journey. War was now imminent; and my employers, having first announced that they had no choice but to cut my salary by half, decided that they must move from the threatened metroplis and take makeshift offices in Brighton. Later, they changed their plans. But I remember the malaise and discomfort of the depressing days that followed — darkened train-journeys, lonely hotel-rooms and a general sensation of harrowing incertitude. Then, in May, 1940, not long after my firm had returned to London, I heard my brother Paul was dead. How he had been killed I did not discover at the time; his colonel's message of condolence gave us little information; and it was only by hazard, through an officer who recognised our surname when I met him in the country, that I learned the details of my brother's end.

His company had set up their headquarters at a concrete pill-box, built during the First World War, at Nieuport on the Belgian coast just beyond the French frontier. It was a period of utter confusion. Although the German army had nearly enveloped Belgium, their exact whereabouts were not yet known, until an advance-guard reached the neighbourhood of the pill-box, inflicted some casualties but very soon withdrew. To an unmilitary mind it might perhaps have occurred that one of their main objectives had been to fix the range of their opponent's strong point. Paul's company, however, had stood firm; and the massive bombardment that quickly followed the thrust blasted and blotted out their whole position. During the holocaust my brother had met his death — in a slit trench, running for cover, or beneath a pile of concrete debris.

Paul was an admirable young man, gay, vigorous and hard-working. Far less puritanical than any of his older relations, he had thoroughly enjoyed his youth; and my mother, while they shared a London flat, seemed always ready to excuse, and even occasionally approve Paul's escapades. Sometimes, it is true, his adventures strained her patience — for example, when she had left him alone in their flat, and he had brought a girl to stay. Her return was unexpected; and Paul and his mistress, she noted, like the Mad Hatter's guests who moved regularly around the tea-table, had shifted day by day from room to room, abandoning a bed as soon as it was thoroughly rumpled, and heaping successive pieces of furniture with a pile of unwashed dishes. Then she was indeed astonished and offended; but she bore my brother no enduring grudge. Despite his amorous vagaries, in so many other traits he displayed a close resemblance to my father. Besides his energy and pertinacity, he had the same straightforward disposition, C.H.B.'s loud and penetrating laugh, and his bright, unclouded eye. In Paul's nature there was nothing morbid or perverse, nothing dark or introspective. My mother herself had a pronounced neurotic strain, which she had transmitted to my sister; and I, too, had evidently inherited some of her phobias, anxieties and fears. Paul alone, the future planner and builder, had reproduced the true paternal type, and died at twenty-four under the nicely focussed barrage of a distant, unseen enemy.

Many months earlier, Paul had joined a Territorial regiment. A military life appeared to suit him well; and he looked his best when he came home on leave in his Fusilier's uniform. But, being ten years older and far more slothful and sedentary, I did not attempt to follow him; remembering my brief but ignominious experience of the training-corps at school, I doubted if I should ever make an effective modern soldier. It was the parade-ground, I think I can honestly claim, rather than the battlefield I really dreaded; and I argued, somewhat speciously perhaps, that, as London, we were often told, would be bombarded from the air, I might take a civilian job without undue discredit. Thus I had added my name to a list of middle-aged, or nearly middle-aged men, writers, editors, journalists, artists and executives, who believed that their training qualified them for some pacific kind of war-service, and presently found myself a hard-worked press-censor at the Ministry of Information. There I remained through the long-awaited Blitz, seated in an immense but overcrowded room, behind a wooden office-desk, applying the point of a worn-down blue pencil to countless slips of flimsy paper.

When I entered the Ministry, I had imagined that I might one day develop into a master-propagandist, whose diatribes, scattered across Europe, made Dr. Goebbels wince with fury. I was never so honoured. My friends John Rayner, originally features-editor of the *Daily Express*, and the gifted cartoonist Osbert Lancaster were both attached to the Bedfordshire country house where the Ministry conducted its most secret compaigns to undermine the enemy's morale. But, although Osbert, who was producing a leaflet to be dropped among German troops in Russia, once suggested I should re-read Sergeant Bourgogne's memoirs describing Napoleon's retreat from Moscow, and pick out some particularly grim passages, which he could then illustrate with pictures of the horrors of frost-bite and lively comic sketches of mortified noses and fingers just about to drop off, I was not otherwise consulted; and I soon accepted the laborious daily task of editing, releasing and often suppressing news.

Every piece of tape that a messenger brought to our desks demanded very careful scrutiny; and a set of rules, entitled 'Stops and Releases', varied almost every day, each change being loudly proclaimed to the room by a brisk young female assistant seated on a central chair. No reference to a certain type of bomb! No mention of the latest raid! Numbers of lives lost during the last twenty-four hours required particularly close attention. The numbers themselves were suppressed; instead, according to the latest rules, we removed '35' and substituted 'some casualties', reserving 'considerable casualities' for a genuine disaster. Accounts of damage, too, were invariably edited; we must eliminate the slightest hint of the place in which the bomb had fallen. The report, cut beyond recognition, was then handed back to a disgusted journalist; and I thought of my days as an easy-going copywriter, when I had been concerned not with suppressing facts but with enlarging and adorning them. It went against the grain to pick up my blue pencil, and reduce a dozen ominous sentences to a few mangled and comparatively meaningless lines.

The Ministry of Information was housed in a huge white hulk, designed as the headquarters of rebuilt London University. Though unquestionably solid, it was also exceedingly conspicuous, and attracted many bombers. Somewhere in the building, until Japan had entered the War, hid my friend and mentor Arthur Waley, censoring the telegrams sent off by Japanese journalists; and a poem he then wrote, based on a T'ang model, gives a graphic impression of our ministerial life:

> I have been a censor for fifteen months,
> The building where I work has four times been bombed.
> Glass, boards and paper, each in turn
> Have been blasted from the windows . . .
> The rules for censors are difficult to keep;
> In six months there were over a thousand 'stops'.
> The Air Raid Bible alters from day to day;
> Official orders are not clearly expressed . . .[2]

I am not sure if Arthur worked after dark; but for me worse than the tedium of our days was the squalor of our restless nights. Now and then we enjoyed a brief vacation, when we could leave the Ministry and sleep at home; but very often we were required to work in shifts — so many hours in a stifling subterranean dormitory under hairy much-used blankets; so many above ground crouched at our usual desks or, during a lull, asleep upon the floor, ready to be woken up by an elderly office-messenger, who brought some hideous piece of news — say, a direct hit on a crowded bomb-shelter — from which we had to draw the sting.

Yet it is odd how quickly a habit forms, how easily we adapt ourselves to an unfamiliar way of life, and how often supposed necessities are revealed as superfluities! During the first eighteen months of the War, many of the belongings I had accumulated were dispersed or lost for ever. A day-time bomb that fell opposite the Chelsea flat to which I had moved when I left South Audley Street, besides smashing windows and fissuring walls and roofs, had partly broken down the front door. Though a Levantine middle-man arrived at the wheel of a Rolls Royce and puffing a stout cigar, to announce that he had the use of some bomb-proof cellars near Park Lane, where, for a reasonable remuneration, he was prepared to shelter all my goods, the fee he asked was well over a hundred pounds; and, with a brief contemptuous glance about my devastated flat, he almost immediately took his leave. Thus, before I could clear the place, a host of objects had vanished; and, later, those I had entrusted to friends were frequently mislaid or stolen. What became of the small red box I stored away in a certain Mayfair lumber-room? It included — no great loss, I admit — a quantity of early manuscripts; but, among them, were two long letters written to me by T.S. Eliot and Edith Sitwell; a collection of eighteenth-century bronze medallions representing the

[2] See *Madly Singing in the Mountains*, edited by Ivan Morris, 1970.

family of George II; a pear-wood statuette of Kwannon (bought on the eve of saying goodbye to Tokyo) in a gold-flecked lacquer shrine; and, far less valuable, yet equally loved and admired, a small glass cube I had purchased in a Peking street-market, that enclosed the miniature effigy of a snarling Chinese lion-dog.

My memory preserves pleasantly vivid impressions both of the pensive goddess and of the green black-spotted beast; but all it retains of T.S. Eliot's letter is that, commenting on a critical essay of mine, in which I had suggested that the author of *The Waste Land* was still a Puritan at heart, he had asserted that he was proud of his Puritan ancestry, and that a long line of studious clergymen and judges had firmly fixed his mental pattern[3]. I missed these relics; sometimes I miss them today. Yet I did not greatly regret the loss of other household goods, and found there was much to be said for travelling light and, if need be, sleeping where I dined. At one period, I shared a curious *ménage-à-trois* with a bohemian young married couple in their roomy basement flat, whither I hurried – as the sirens ululated and the rumble of the Blitz approached, often trying not to run – from an adjacent tube-station. My visit was brief, but full of emotional dramas and dramatic episodes. Strange personages appeared and disappeared; and once we were roused by a handsome drunken young man, usually a gentle, good-natured character, who, preparatory to knocking on our door, had kicked his boon companion down the area-steps.

I have forgotten my next refuge. When I look back, whole long passages of my early war-time career seem completely to have slipped away. Beneath those bloodshot heavens the business of daily life was casual and haphazard; but, as often as we could leave the Ministry, we ate at an Italian restaurant, conveniently underground, not very far along the street, which before the War had been part of a small hotel used by foreign dancers, jugglers and acrobats, and now provided us with enormous portions of *pasta* and flasks of rather rough chianti. We also drank at the Ministry's own bar, a crowded, hot and noisy place; and there I remember unexpectedly sighting a celebrated modern poet. A trim, discreet and sober-suited figure, he had a romantic attachment, I knew, to a no less famous woman novelist; and I assume that she had recently bidden him an expansive farewell. Across his shirt-front, under his bow-tie, I noted the butterfly-image, printed in fresh rouge, of a pair of female lips. It added an amusingly surrealist touch to his otherwise reserved demeanour.

[3] I cannot date this letter; but it was written when Eliot's religious and political position was much less clearly defined than it became at a somewhat later period.

Meanwhile, having learned my rôle at the Ministry, I had once again begun writing. Three or four reference books attracted little attention among the papers on my table; and I resumed the habit I had already acquired in the long days at my copywriters's desk, of carrying on my own work, and scribbling by fits and starts. Just before the War, I had published a new biography, a portrait of Caroline of Anspach, consort of George II and, since Elizabeth I, certainly the shrewdest and most cultivated woman ever to occupy an English throne. I had a magnificent caste – the sovereign himself, an explosive martinet, who, said Lady Mary Wortley, regarded the rest of mankind as creatures he might 'kick or kiss for his diversion'; Sir Robert Walpole, that herculean cynic, who governed his master with the Queen's connivance; the brilliant, self-destructive Bolingbroke, and the fascinating, effeminate Lord Hervey; besides a long array of fine subsidiary personages, Pope and Swift and Lord Burlington, and Burlington's aide, 'The Signior' William Kent. My book was not, nor did I mean that it should be, a lasting contribution to the study of the early eighteenth century; but I like to think that it reflected the period's ethos, which I believed I understood; and my researches into the character and genius of Pope encouraged me to compose a detailed portrait of the noble Augustan that appeared during the 1960s.

At the Ministry my subject for the second time was Byron; and I rounded off *Byron, the Years of Fame* with an account of his Italian life. Better written, I think, than its predecessor and inspired by a much more adult point of view, it came out in 1941; and, although my study of Caroline had had larger sales — books on royal personages invariably appeal to the English taste — it received some generous notices, my kindliest critic being Desmond MacCarthy, who, as he had never completed his own work, might well have been the most severe. It was a book I enjoyed writing; to follow the rapid evolution of my hero's fluid personality — at Venice a promiscuous man of pleasure, surrounded by his raffish favourites; at Ravenna, a chief of the local patriots and shawl-carrying *cicisbeo* of a young Italian married woman; at Genoa, seen through Lady Blessington's eyes, a somewhat faded and superannuated survivor of the London great world; but in every mood and at every stage of his progress, alert and keenly self-aware — was an absorbing occupation; and the fact that I had often to work by stealth, and hide my manuscript behind a heap of office files, did not make it less enjoyable.

Meanwhile, Duty, wearing the neat uniform of a retired naval officer, surveyed the censors from his dais; and the Commander must have suspected that the defensive wall of documents I had raised around my manuscript concealed some undertaking that had very little to do with the official war-effort. At the same time – another form of escapism that I no longer feel demands apology; the shock of terrible events repeatedly drives one back into the microcosm of one's own immediate concerns – I began a love-affair, which, if it could scarcely have been called a grand passion, touched the heart and warmed the senses. Of Astrid I remember nothing but good. She had blue-green, slightly prominent eyes, sleek fair hair, a well-shaped sensuous body, and a lively, amiable disposition. She laughed a great deal, appreciated laughter in others and, although she knew I was supposed to write books, and hoped I might one day have a 'real success', seldom extended the scope of her reading beyond the fashion magazines and new detective stories. Rimsky-Korsakov's *Chanson Hindoue* was among her favourite compositions; and today, if I pass a certain door and the glass-vaulted entry that approaches it, I remember the morning after the first happy night we spent beneath the same roof. It was Sunday; a record of Rimsky-Korsakov's song was revolving on the gramophone; snow was falling outside. We had forgotten the Ministry, and almost forgotten the War, despite the damp pages of a Sunday newspaper that contained dreadful reports of disaster and defeat, scattered carelessly across the pillows; and behind a heavy curtain of descending snow-flakes our refuge seemed doubly secret and secure.

Later, Astrid exchanged her ground floor flat for a little house off Curzon Street. Love-affairs often benefit from an element of social intrigue and a touch of low comedy; and these were provided by the presence of an elderly Canadian millionaire, who was then pursuing Astrid, and who had decided that, as a preliminary move towards seduction, he would set her up in style. Luckily, during the grimmest period of the Blitz, he often retreated, before the sirens sounded, to his Surrey manor-house, and did not appear again until next day; and it was at Culross Street that I made an important discovery about the close relation between fear and pleasure. My earliest experience of an air-raid had been ridiculously unfortunate. A friend, with whom I stayed in the country, had asked me to call on his invalid wife – she had just suffered a crippling motor-accident – as soon as I regained London, and give her any help she needed. I found her in bed, helpless and almost immobile, pinned to a solid wooden frame until her broken bones recovered; and, although the German aircraft that crossed the Channel had done so far comparatively little damage, that evening they released their whole strength. Bomb after bomb came fiercely whining down and shook the room in which she lay; I could no more have transported my charge to a place of greater safety than I could have moved a grand piano; and, since the room itself, built out into a Chelsea garden, lacked the protection of an upper storey, every plane that passed above our heads sounded monstrously close. I listened to the throb of desynchronised engines; not a single British gun replied. Beyond the windows sprang up lurid lights; all Chelsea seemed to be ablaze. I held my charge's hand; it remained cool and steady; mine, I knew, showed signs of trembling. My original purpose, of course, had been to bring her calm and comfort. But by the time day had dawned and peace at last descended, though broken gas-mains were still blazing along the street, we had totally reversed our rôles.

Fear, I soon learned, obeys no fixed law; in the effects of courage and cowardice there are endless variations. That night I experienced acute alarm; during a later raid, which was not less terrific, my emotions took a very different shape. 'Perfect fear casteth out all love', Cyril Connolly exclaimed about this time; and once at least I proved him wrong. I was visiting Astrid when we sighted a tremendous glow that rose against the southern sky; and thither we travelled in Astrid's dashing sports-car, her admirer's latest gift. Its source was a gigantic woodyard on the Embankment, not far from the Tate Gallery; and few more splendiferous spectacles of its kind have I ever witnessed or imagined. It recalled Turner's picture of the destruction of the ancient Houses of Parliament, and Pepys' record, early in September 1666, of how he had watched the Great Fire as it rushed up the hill of the City, 'a most horrid malicious bloody flame, not like the fine flame of an ordinary fire', but instinct apparently with fiendish life. Even birds it engulfed. Pepys had the sympathetic eye that distinguishes a true-born writer; and 'among other things (he observed) I perceive the poor pigeons were loathe to leave their houses, but hovered about the windows and balconies till there were some of them burned their wings, and fell...'

This fire, however, appeared not malicious or bloody, but a gay and genial conflagration. No lives were endangered. Only Chinese and Japanese painters and, among English artists, William Blake, have done full justice to a tongue of flame; and the flames that leapt from the woodyard had a peculiarly sinuous grace, dividing and subdividing in wonderfully intricate streamers, and breaking up again in fiery particles and drops that eddied and drifted away beneath the clouds. A wood-fire on so huge a scale threw off a heavy pungent fragrance; its warmth was agreeable, too; and we almost regretted the efforts of the busy firemen who struggled ineffectively to damp it down. Then, after we had enjoyed its beauty for some time, we heard the engines of returning raiders. German planes, the British press reported, having launched their incendiary bombs, would presently revisit the target, and blow fire-fighters into the molten centre of the blaze with the help of high explosive; and, as the throb of their engine rapidly grew louder, we hurried back to Culross Street. Astrid's house was an old and fragile building; but that night fear and pleasure combined to provoke a mood of wild exhilaration. The impact of a bomb a few hundred yards away merely sharpened pleasure's edge; and next day we wandered, agreeably bemused, around the shattered streets of Mayfair, crunching underfoot green glaciers of broken glass strewn ankle-deep upon the pavements.

Astrid had strong nerves and, perhaps because she was of Scandinavian descent, an extremely strong head. I should have done well, no doubt, to preserve her generous affection. But, at that period of my life, I was still restlessly inquisitive, and thought that to refuse a new experience, if it were presented under some odd and stimulating guise, was a craven act of self-betrayal. One afternoon Astrid proposed we should call on her 'rather dotty little friend' Julia, who was then living with a middle-aged French colonel, said to be lynch-pin of the Free French Secret Service, an independent unit which obeyed its own laws and, its critics alleged, conducted its private interrogations by means of regrettably 'un-English' methods. The Colonel I afterwards met both in London and in Paris – a small, grey-faced, lizard-like man, hollow-cheeked and bald-headed; and at the moment he occupied a modest flat somewhere above Shepherd's Market.

When Astrid and I paid our visit to Julia she was sitting all alone, on the end of the bed but fully dressed, as though she were a good little school-girl waiting to be taken out. At first, the conversation flagged. It was dull, dead-quiet afternoon; until suddenly an isolated bomb, jettisoned no doubt by a lost raider, slid shrieking down and made the windows tremble. The explosion immediately raised our spirits; Julia opened a bottle of champagne; and I began examining our hostess. She might have had Eastern blood; there was something about her slightly slanted eyes, her prominent cheekbones and smooth olive skin that suggested the youthful concubine of a legendary Mongol chieftain; while her narrow-waisted, rather wide-hipped body recalled the figures of the celestial dancing-girls I had once admired at Angkor Wat. Julia was young – certainly not more than twenty-two – still shy, and now and then, youthfully gauche; but she had an air of secret self-possession and, illuminating her face in rare flashes, a half-provocative, half-malicious smile.

We contrived to meet again; this time we met alone; and Astrid, since she had recently developed a passing affection for a dark, curly-haired young lieutenent, whom she called 'the Black Lamb', though ruffled and annoyed, was neither much surprised nor passionately hurt. Thus I gave up an unromantic but thoroughly amicable relationship to set sail on far more dangerous waters. Just why I did so – through curiosity, restlessness or sheer stupidity – today I cannot quite be sure; and perhaps I had better postpone the question until I have described the sad results, and filled in the untidy background of my life during the later part of 1942. The Blitz continued to drive me back and forth; and, finally, I came to rest at a studio occupied by Cyril Connolly, where a fellow tenant was Arthur Koestler, whose extraordinary novel *Darkness at Noon* had already earned him wide acclaim. As a novelist, I greatly admired Koestler; as a human being I sometimes found him a little touchy and suspicious; and an absurd squabble presently broke out, followed by an irate correspondence, because I was alleged to have told a girl we both knew that in bed he wore a hair-net; and he protested that I had gravely injured his chances of securing her affections. 'Like every civilized Continental', he said, he wore a hair-net only when he was going to his bath.

On Cyril's next move I followed him across London, and shifted my luggage and books and a few somewhat battered chairs and tables into a flat that he had leased in Bedford Square. A couple of rooms on the topmost floor of the house gave me all the space I needed; and there I stayed while the fury of the Blitz declined, and the first guided missiles, the so-called 'Doodle-Bugs', began to pulsate through the sky. Cyril's household, in these war-time surroundings, was a constant source of wonder. He kept the War at bay more effectively than any other man I knew. Being the director of a magazine, he was exempt from military service; and even 'fire-watching', after a single night's duty – I well remember how I saw him leave the house carrying a case of cigars, a hot-water bottle and a heavy tartan rug – he had managed to escape. About his own existence he drew a magic circle, within which he pursued his personal affairs and employed his native power of charming.

To describe his charm is a by no means easy task. Cyril was not a regularly handsome man; and, as he grew middle-aged, a circumference of double chins slowly encompassed his keen observant features. Though he liked to please, nobody, if the company were uncongenial, seemed less afraid of displeasing, and he would retreat into a deathly silence – a silence that could almost be felt, so strong was the effect it made, and such was the paralysing check it imposed on ordinary social gossip. Given an agreeable companion, however, preferably a sympathetic young woman or an appreciative older friend, he became a different character. The alert face appeared to absorb his jowls; his spider-eyes would dance with fun and malice; and he might even execute one of his famous knock-about 'turns', which were sometimes all the more rewarding for being wholly unexpected, as when he entertained a rather serious-minded duke and his family, gathered round the tea-table, by giving a brilliant impersonation of the Chimpanzees' Tea Party he had witnessed at the London Zoo. Cyril's rendering of the senior chimpanzee, his air of stern authority and bursts of petulant rage, is said to have been a histrionic masterpiece.

At Eton Cyril was a fierce misogynist – that is obvious from his letters[4]. But his early marriage having converted him to women, he soon assumed the rôle of *homme-à-femmes;* and his adult life was passed in a protracted series of heterosexual relationships, which caused him endless joy and misery. Not only did he love women and frequently arouse their love; but he had acquired an invaluable knack of persuading them to run his errands. Thus, at Bedford Square and the small adjacent office from which he edited *Horizon*, he was attended by a pair of devoted female acolytes, whom he had both taught to sub-edit a magazine and instructed in the art of cooking. They also served his food; and Evelyn Waugh, a notably critical guest, was shocked when he attended an alfresco dinner party, to find himself waited on by two bare-legged and bare-footed girls. Their feet were cracked, he said, like those of an old camel – a comparison that his host, though well-accustomed to Evelyn's savage quips, declared offensively inaccurate.

Another duty Cyril's attendants undertook was typing the manuscript of *The Unquiet Grave;* and, as one, at least, was romantically in love with the author, and, among much else, the book

[4]   *A Romantic Friendship: The Letters of Cyril Connolly to Noel Blakiston.* edited by Noel Blakiston, 1976.

contains a moving lament for the wife who had deserted him, his choice of amanuenses struck me as singularly strong-minded. The text, he tells us, was based on a private journal kept 'between the autumn of 1942 and the autumn of 1943'; and he then devoted a second year to giving it a literary pattern. The result was set and re-set; and eventually it consisted of 'thirty long galley-proofs scissored into little pieces like a string of clown's black sausages... and spread out on the floor to be arranged and re-arranged...'[5]. The chair he occupied, while he conducted his labours, no doubt deserves a place in history. I had lent it to him from the store of salvaged possessions that heaped the larger of my rooms; I had had it built by a Japanese carpenter according to my own design. I am a poor designer; and the massive chair I had planned, with its wide low seat and huge flat arms, was exceptionally ill-proportioned. But it suited Cyril, who preferred a semi-reclining pose to sitting upright at a table; and, having placed a board across the arms which carried papers, books and pens, he strengthened the stout defensive enclosure — at a distance only the crown of his head was visible — that protected him against intrusion.

Safely established there, he could follow his train of thoughts through the landscapes of the past and present, evoking 'a private grief...for which he felt to blame', expressing his hatred of war-time propaganda and of the squalid gloom that had overwhelmed London, and voicing his poignant sense of being cut off from France, where his happiest recollections now lay buried. The celebrated lemurs had long since died; at Bedford Square he harboured no favourite beast; the last I remember, a lithe, beautifully spotted African genet, which had an awkward trick of refusing to relieve itself unless it was provided with a bowl of water — such a bowl the Connollys always supplied in their sitting room or bedroom — had vanished about the same time as their marriage broke down. But a white sulphur-crested cockatoo temporarily sat behind his chair. A ferocious bird, whenever it left its cage it would descend like a snow-white thunderbolt, a whirlwind of savage wings and talons, on any newcomer who crossed the threshold; and no less violent than its detestation of strangers was the passion that it showed for Cyril, at whose approach it would immediately sink to the ground, pinions extended, crest thrown stiffly back, bubbling and gurling an insensate song of love.

Cyril's rooms had a pleasantly occupied look and, thanks to his acolytes' patient help, numerous domestic comforts. Mine, on the

[5]   *The Unquiet Grave;* introduction to the edition of 1950.

23

floor above, afforded a drab spectacle of bohemian laissez-faire. I was always meaning to arrange a decent interior, unstack the various pieces of furniture, now piled up as if they belonged to an abandoned restaurant, unfold a table and hang some of the prints and pictures that had survived the ruin of my Chelsea flat. But I was too hurried in the morning; when I got home, usually far too tired. I had developed nocturnal habits; and Cyril remarked that he saw me seldom nowadays, since I went out before he was yet awake, and very often returned long after he had gone to bed. How did I spend my leisure? That I have nearly forgotten. But many of the blacked-out hours I suppose I passed at night-clubs. These institutions had sprung up and flourished all over the metropolis; and in the diary I began to keep on January 1st, 1943, I record having visited both the *400*, a vulgarised relic of the fashionable pre-War world, and a far more bohemian place, the *Jamboree,* whither I again resorted on the 15th – a 'tipsy good-tempered evening (I wrote) which faded out into a blur' – and yet again on the 29th, when I found the scene repulsive; 'the whole room wrapped in a hot clammy grey fog that seemed to be rising from the floor: in all directions prostrate drinkers; a woman with cascading blonde hair...being carried from a table...'

It was their total lack of charm, elegance and even the most commonplace amenities that gave these war-time night-clubs their attraction. They were invariably crowded and hot; and the atmosphere was dim and dense – so dense that, towards the end of the night, one felt that it was becoming semi-solid; and the entertainments they offered were strikingly monotonous. At the *Nut-House,* for example, the proprietor and a macabre young negro waiter each stood up to sing a song; and the fact that their repertoire never varied, and that the proprietor's ditty had a weird and meaningless chorus –

> You push the damper in, and you pull the damper out,
> And the smoke goes up the chimney all the same!

in which his audience loudly joined, gave one the impression that one was attending some barbaric tribal ceremony or primitive religious rite. If the Blitz drew near, the black-out curtains that masked the doors would occasionally sway and rustle. Otherwise reminders of the War were few; though gallant fighter-pilots, stationed at Biggin Hill, who only half-a-day earlier had been sweeping the skies over the English Channel or 'hedge-hopping' across the fields of northern France, might arrive to join our celebrations. Here servicemen amiably associated with civilian castaways; and I remember seeing a pale young naval lieutenent stretched full length upon a sofa, while he allowed the contents of a bottle of gin he held up high above his head to trickle down into his open mouth. Soon afterwards I learned that the submarine on which he served was reported lost or missing.

My friends and I also frequented the *Gargoyle*, a comparatively civilised club in Soho. Founded before the War by David Tennant, a rich and restless dilettante, it had a huge Matisse among its decorations; its clientèle was part suburban, part outrageously bohemian; and beneath its gilded roof I once watched Dylan Thomas, immensely drunk and wildly jovial, gulping the wine he had snatched off a stranger's table from his own dilapidated shoe. If I wasted much of my time in night-clubs, that, I imagine, must have been largely due to the powerful influence of habit. I form habits easily and cherish them determinedly; any habit, once established in my life, acquires a superstitious value. I appreciated the ritual development of those long expensive evenings, and welcomed the reappearance of the rather suspect bottle I had bought the night before, which the honest waiter had scored with a pencilled tide-mark to show the quantity of alcohol not yet consumed.

All around familiar human shapes could be distinguished through the fog — abandoned dancers, talkative drinkers and silent, unmoving amorous couples, the last often so closely interlaced and fused into such a complex pattern that they resembled the Runic figures of the Book of Kells, and one asked oneself whether, as dawn broke, they could ever quite be disengaged. In a certain night-club, at a certain hour of the morning, I left my table and retired behind the scenes to a brightly lighted washroom, where an attendant awaited me carrying a big glass of some mysterious foaming mixture. A central-European refugee, he invariably put the same question: 'Everything *under control*, Mr. Quenr.ell?'; to which I answered that I thought it was, and, having knocked back the prickly restorative potion, produced the tip that he expected.

Another soothing ritual was my visit next day to a chemist's shop in Piccadilly, either Perkins (today unluckily changed) opposite the Green Park, or Heppells (now, alas, defunct) near the corner of St. James's Street. Heppells furnished an especially wide range of powerful morning pick-me-ups, some reputed to possess not only nerve-steadying but strongly aphrodisiac properties, which ranged from an 'American', the draught I usually favoured, to an 'Amber Moon' or 'Green Flash'. Behind Heppells' counter, in a spotless white coat, a square, short-necked, broad-shouldered assistant, with an air of unshakable savoir vivre and a quiet understanding smile, greeted each of his customers by name and, like a good barman, was never unduly loquacious, though prepared to talk if talk were needed. He had his regular clients — an elderly retired general, who sat glaring into space and gripping a large half-empty tumbler, his long, sad, time-furrowed bloodhound-mask stooped over the handle of his stick; and a more raffish personage, who, on dismounting from the taxi that had brought him to the door, could seldom immediately find his balance, but often executed a series of eccentric turns and pirouettes as, fur-collared coat flying and bowler hat askew, he headed blindly for his goal.

I remained an addict of night-clubs throughout the last two war-time years; and, oddly enough, the exhausting life I led seemed to do me very little harm. Meanwhile, I had left my desk at the Ministry of Information. During the latter months of 1942, the sharp-eyed naval commander I have mentioned on a previous page began to adopt an attitude towards my work that grew slowly more and more abrasive. No doubt he suspected I was writing a book; and it may be that my affectionate relationship with my fellow-worker Astrid had provoked some hostile gossip. One day I was ordered by the Commander to present myself before the Admiral, revered headmaster of the whole department; and the Admiral, a smallish, wizened, beetle-browed sea-dog, delivered a stern official telling-off. I was both 'lazy' and 'unenthusiastic' the Commander had informed him; and, although I refused to admit that I was ever lazy — at times, perhaps, I might feel sleepy — I protested that blue-pencilling endless newspaper reports of bombs and bomb-damage and deaths and fires was scarcely calculated to arouse enthusiasm in any reasonable human mind. These protestations the Admiral, folding his hands and lowering his shaggy brows, evidently considered he could disregard. I must choose, he said, between leaving the Ministry and — now came the really important point — accepting a similar post in Belfast, where a censor happened to be badly needed. I gave way and, having bidden Cyril goodbye and closed my Bedford Square rooms, I climbed into an army plane. It was a desperate leave-taking; and my desperation increased when I had obtained a first glimpse of that dark and unfamiliar city.

Belfast seemed even grimmer than London, and twice as ugly and bereft of hope. Its gloomy late-Victorian streets included not a single decent building; the biggest hotel alone, a fairly expensive place, would supply a meal much after six o'clock; and most of its inhabitants depended on 'high tea', accompanied by an enormous black tea-pot and a reeking pile of buttered toast. Only the Belfast pubs offered a measure of comfort; they were lined with the cubby-holes called 'snugs', in which mackintosh-clad drinkers sat behind swing-doors, downing pints of stout and wiping the yellow froth off their blunt impassive faces. Never have I felt so lonely. The exiled censors among whom I worked had brought their families to Ireland; I had solitary lodgings; and my spirits reached their nadir when night fell, we locked the filing cabinets, extinguished the gas fire, and I was obliged to make my way home. Tramlines, that shone beneath the rain, divided ranks of curtained villas. I arrived at my own villa – the front-door I opened had a decorative stained-glass panel – turned off the gas-jet that flickered in the hall and tiptoed up the stairs to sleep. On the bed my good-natured spinster landlady had heaped a huge and heavy quilt; and my dream-life under that oppressive weight was haunted by disturbing visions.

Before I left London, I had addressed an urgent appeal to my ministerial friend John Rayner, and begged him, if he could possibly find the means, to devise some method of escape. He took immediate action; and, after three or four weeks at Belfast, I received a brief telegram, which announced that I was being transferred from the Ministry of Information to the Ministry of Economic Warfare. Thus I returned to London and entered another office. In my youth, the eastern side of Berkeley Square was still lined with eighteenth-century houses – Horace Walpole's old house occupied a corner-site. But, since those days, they had almost all been demolished by a money-grubbing modern firm, which had substituted a gaunt commercial block. That block the Ministry now occupied, and had filled to over-flowing. There my departmental chief was Leonard Ingrams, who, at a considerably earlier period, was said to have attracted Cocteau's notice, and to have inspired the portrait of an unscrupulous Oxonian dandy in his brilliant short novel *Le Grand Écart:*

> *Peter Stopwell eût possédé la beauté grecque si le saut en longueur ne l'avait étiré comme une photographie mal prise. Il sortait d'Oxford. Il en tenait sa fatuité, ses boîtes de cigarettes, son cache-nez bleu marine et une immoralité multiforme sous l'uniforme sportif.*

Time had changed him, destroyed his pretensions to beauty and, if

Stopwell is indeed a portrait of Ingrams, quenched his Anglo-Saxon immorality. Between his reddened eyelids glimmered weary eyes; and his rough hair was brindled white and brown. But, unlike Stopwell, he had a generous heart and a sympathetic disposition, which, after my experiences with the Admiral and the Commander, quickly put me at my ease. As to the exact nature of my official duties, however, or the part I should play in the economic blockade of Europe, he did not give me many hints. Still, I had a separate office and a large bare polished desk; and now and then papers marked 'Secret' were dropped into my wire tray. Their importance varied; some might merely consist of extracts copied by a postal censor from intercepted correspondence, because it was supposed that they threw a revelatory light upon the economic situation; and I was amused to read fragments of letters exchanged by Lord Ivor Churchill and his American mother, Consuelo Duchess of Marlborough, about furnishing materials they had recently acquired.

Having joined a second ministry, I was determined I must do my best, and avoid any damaging imputations of professional idleness or private languor. But it was difficult to keep my wits engaged when I had no settled task; and, although I invented a series of occupations, for example, drawing up and memorising a list of what we called 'strategic metals', the executive mood would presently decline. Around me similarly displaced, or misplaced persons occupied equally unfrequented rooms, and often visited their neighbours. Thus I met Richard Llewellyn, author of that immensely popular book *How Green Was My Valley*, a small neat dark Celt, now wearing the elegant uniform of a captain in the Welsh Guards, whence he had been temporarily seconded into Economic Warfare, of which he knew almost as little as I did myself. His best-selling novel was only three years old; and he looked enviably smart and rich. From a trouser-pocket at the end of a thick gold chain he drew a conglomeration of miniature golden objects – pen-knives, watches, compasses, tooth-picks, swizzle-sticks and clustered keys, even, I think, the bizarre instrument that every schoolboy used to treasure, meant for prising pebbles out of horses' hooves.

In our solitude we talked over literary plans, and decided to collaborate on the scenario of a film. Byron was the subject we picked out; I would supply the literary details, Richard the technical flair likely to attract producers. Of the information I duly provided, he made however, unexpected uses. Thus, having learned that, towards the end of our hero's life, while he was still lingering at Genoa, a young woman aboard an American ship presented her favourite poet with a single rose, Richard suggested that '*You Gave Me a Rose*' might be a suitably appealing title. He also wished to enlarge the part of Fletcher, Byron's stolid Nottinghamshire valet. In April, 1816, when Byron prepared to set sail, Fletcher must not immediately appear among his travelling companions. But, once the Dover packet had left the harbour, and the white cliffs slipped behind, a muffled stranger, leaning against a rail, would step forward and throw aside his cloak. 'Surely you didn't think *I* was going to desert you, my lord?' Fletcher would exclaim, as he choked back loyal sobs; and from that moment my hopes of developing into a prosperous script-writer gradually dwindled and subsided.

After my collaborator had returned to the outer world — presumably his regiment recalled him — I had very few associates. But, now and then, an unknown visitor, having filled in the necessary form and passed the official guardians of the hall below, might tap upon my office-door. Among the strangest was a tall, thin bearded man, the kind of hatless, rapidly moving vagrant, who, wherever he goes and whatever the season, besides a bundle of papers beneath his arm, is always carrying a heavy knapsack. Geoffrey Pyke flitted around London from ministry to ministry; though not an accredited scientist, he was an imaginative inventor; and some of his ideas had been taken so seriously by personages in or near the War Cabinet that he had drawn up detailed plans. The most extraordinary of his many ambitious projects concerned an aircraft carrier built of solid ice, the sea-water he intended to freeze, and keep permanently frozen, being mixed, I think, with wood-pulp[6]. Such a carrier, he declared, would prove virtually unsinkable, yet thanks to a heating-system that — just why I could never quite grasp — failed to melt the ice itself, perfectly inhabitable. Years later, I consulted a war-time expert about Z.'s cherished scheme; and he told me that he believed it might *nearly* have worked — Lord Louis Mountbatten had displayed some interest; but the plan was ultimately shelved.

So, alas, was an even stranger project for the conservation of surplus human energy. Pyke pointed out that we were perpetually wasting our strength by our vague, unnecessary actions; and he proposed, therefore, to instal in every household a simple piece of light machinery on which the citizen would take a daily turn, revolving a

6   For detailed descriptions of this strange craft, which was to be named *Habbakuk*. and of Geoffrey Pyke himself, see *From Apes to Warlords. 1904-1946* by Solly Zuckerman, 1978.

wheel or raising and lowering a crank, and thus generating energy that would somehow be stored away and canalised, and then devoted to the war-effort. Pyke had burning eyes; he inhabited a remote plane between the real and the fantastic, and strove passionately to give his visions substance. But the fact that, during his calls at the Ministry, he seldom got beyond my room, suggested that he had already lost the battle; and, soon after the war, I learned from a newspaper paragraph that the poor inventor had taken his own life.

Meanwhile, his occasional visits ceased; and again I sought out Leonard Ingrams and, for the first and probably the last time in my career, begged to be allotted a larger share of work. Ingrams smiled, shook his piebald head and told me that I must not fret. 'We like having you around', he murmured sympathetically, 'and before long, no doubt, you'll come in useful . . .' But my petition must have had some effect, since towards the end of 1942 I was shifted to another post, where my duties were far less ill-defined. D., my immediate superior, had reached the Ministry straight from the library of a famous Cambridge college. Long, lean and bespectacled, he was five years younger than myself, but considerably more austere. He seemed (I remember grumbling) to have neither vices nor engagements; and at the end of the day he showed a perverse reluctance to leave the office and return home. We had little in common. I did not then suspect that he was a learned Latinist, destined to produce a scholarly edition of a Roman Elegiac poet. But on English literature he rarely expressed a view, although I remember he once mentioned Byron and praised the ingenious double rhymes with which, particularly in *Don Juan,* Byron was fond of rounding off a stanza. Above all else, he had an exact mind; and his task at the Ministry called for the highest measure of exactitude. It was to balance the claims of economic strategy against those of unofficial charity, and to determine what private relief-supplies should be allowed to pass into occupied Europe through the rigorous Allied blockade.

Suppose, for example, that the Red Cross, or some other charitable body, wished to despatch a consignment of surgical boots to a clinic in the Channel Islands, was there not a danger that the German authorities might then rip away their rubber soles, and divert the precious material they had gained to a panzer division on the Eastern front? I doubted myself whether even the most methodical bureaucrat would find such a transference worth making. But my superior scrutinised the problem from half-a-dozen different angles, before he finally delivered a verdict, which was very often negative. No surgical boots for Jersey, Guernsey, Alderney or Sark! Not a single tooth-brush or clinical thermometer. Only when he was temporarily called away, and I happened to be left in charge, did the Channel Islanders receive an unexpectedly generous allowance of crutches – despite their valuable rubber tips – infants' clothing or condensed milk. D. also enjoyed drafting the elaborate answers to parliamentary questions that our Minister demanded; and Mr. Dingle Foot, a zealous stickler for facts, needed very careful briefing.

Visible from the Ministry's windows was a lonely marble nymph. Stationed at the bottom of Berkeley Square, opposite the disfigured remains of Lansdowne House (which Robert Adam had built in the 1760s for Lord Shelburne, afterwards 1st Marquess of Lansdowne, whose descendant, Henry 3rd Marquess, had given the statue to the public) she was the work of Alexander Munro, an early Pre-Raphaelite sculptor. There she stood and, happily, still stands – a pensive naiad drooping above a fountain that has long since ceased to flow, her smooth shoulders and gracefully moulded breasts worn by years of London rain, her bowed neck, the twist of her body and the line of the arms that hold the urn, forming a harmonious fluid curve. While classical art was being rediscovered, enthusiasts would frequently fall in love with, and now and then, we learn, make love to statues. The affection that the nymph inspired in me was a good deal more platonic; but she symbolised all the charm of peace, all the graces and virtues that a modern war destroys. Since parks and squares had lost their railings – pieces of delicate eighteenth-century ironwork were often carried off as scrap-iron – they had become refuse-littered dust-bowls[7]. The ruins one passed every day had at least a tragic and heroic look; and burned-out City churches, their steeples scorched and discoloured by fire, possessed a kind of dreadful beauty. Far worse were degrading minor details – telephone boxes that stank of urine, scrawled over with obscene inscriptions; the heavy sickening stench of crowded underground platforms where one picked one's way through lines of corpse-like figures asleep among their household goods. My nymph, though eternally silent and aloof, spoke a language I could understand. Even the rough graffiti that disfigured her marble flanks could not spoil her air of deep repose.

[7] Bloomsbury was luckier than most districts; for there the chief landlord, the eccentric Duke of Bedford, refused obstinately to give up his historic railings.

2

A particularly depressing aspect of my life at Belfast was that Julie had
been left behind. None of the letters she had promised to write me
ever found its way across the Irish Sea; and I often speculated, with a
twinge of jealous alarm, about her pastimes in my absence. Since our
first encounter, unwisely arranged by Astrid, she had gained a subtle
hold upon my feelings; and, as had happened only a few years earlier
when I grew more and more attached to Isabelle, a physical luxury was
now becoming an emotional necessity. Back in London, re-instated at
Bedford Square, I saw Julia almost every day; though, if a storm blew
up — and she was fond of raising storms — she might temporarily
disappear. Towards the end of December, 1942, such a storm had
parted us; but, during January, the journal I had begun to keep
contains a brief account of our reunion.

1943 had opened dismally. I mention 'icy rain' and 'yellow mud',
besides an 'atrocious hangover', which aggravated 'unpleasant
memories of last night'. After my customary morning visit to
Perkins, I had reached my office rather late, and written a letter to
Julia, 'about whom I still feel anxious and despondent'. January 2
brought me no relief; and I found it difficult to concentrate on yet
another bureaucratic problem — whether layettes and tins of
condensed milk should or should not be permitted to leave England.
The 4th, however, produced a dramatic change; Julia miraculously
re-emerged; and my text explains that I heard the hoped-for voice at
the moment I was half-way through a line:

> Sensations of flustered helplessness as I turn over files docketed
> with threatening little flags 'Action Here'. No news from J.,
> which perhaps is just as— I was going to add 'well', and report that
> my convalescence was proceeding slowly but regularly, when J.
> telephoned, unabashed and (apparently) affectionate.

We then agreed to meet at the Ritz that evening; but, once I arrived, I received 'a telephone message from J. putting herself off'; and not until twenty-four hours had passed did she finally materialise, 'looking rosy and innocent, with a disarming (if not entirely convincing) story of what she had been up to'. The lull that followed, my diary informs me, lasted a whole sunny week, despite occasional reminders that 'Julia *can* be very difficult'. 'Beautiful nights' were succeeded by 'friendly mornings'; and at our rendezvous she might even meet me 'in radiantly good mood'. My diary, or the part that concerns Julia, extends from January 1 to July 17. Its record of those troubled months seldom does me much credit; and, before attempting to narrate their events, I have carefully re-read a famous book, Hazlitt's *Liber Amoris*, as an example of the dangers that, should he seek to analyse an ill-omened love-affair, every auto-vivisectionist must run.

I do not pretend, of course, that there is a valid literary resemblance between myself and William Hazlitt, or any close personal similarity between Julia and Sarah Walker. But both Hazlitt and I, on our different planes, suffered ignominious reverses; and both the young women we loved had an inexplicable attraction. Hazlitt first caught sight of Sarah during August, 1820, when he took rooms at the house of a tailor named Micaiah Walker in Southampton Buildings, near Holborn. Sarah, Micaiah's young daughter, used to carry up the lodgers' breakfasts; and Hazlitt, whom she immediately attracted, would sometimes bid her stay and talk. That she was indeed a strange girl — all the stranger because she might have seemed so commonplace — is evident not only from Hazlitt's book, but from the recollections of a friend. The playwright Bryan Walter Procter (best-known under his pseudonym 'Barry Cornwall') often saw her at the lodging-house. 'Her face', he wrote, 'was round and small, and her eyes were motionless and glassy'. Hazlitt, too, describes those blank orbicular eyes; but for him they had an oceanic charm; and surely, he thought, through their 'glittering motionless' crystal, he might have divined 'the rocks and quicksands that awaited me below'. Her way of moving was also noticeably strange: 'she went onwards', Procter observed, 'in a sort of wavy, sinuous manner like the movement of a snake. She was silent, or uttered monosyllables... Her steady unmoving gaze upon the person she was addressing was exceedingly unpleasant'; and he adds that a German story-teller might have made her the heroine of a wild, ghost-ridden modern novel, endowing her perhaps with supernatural attributes.

Although Hazlitt developed a lunatic passion for Sarah, which increased whenever she entered his room, watched him at his urgent request while he ate his breakfast, or allowed him certain 'familiarities', such as perching on his knee, the emotions that she aroused in him were always cruelly divided. She had 'primrose-pale' cheeks, framed by dark curls – she chose usually to show her profile; and a 'little obstinate protrusion' marked the centre of her brow, and revealed her quietly stubborn spirit. She did not protest if a lover urged his suit, but murmured 'Let me go, Sir', then smoothly slipped away again. Hers was an 'equivocal face'. How much in Sarah was equivocation, how much was maidenly innocence, Hazlitt often asked himself. Was she no better than a 'lodging-house decoy' whom her vulgar and designing mother had instructed to amuse the clients? The chief weakness of Hazlitt's book – unquestionably the worst he ever published – is that he wrote it before he had quite emerged from the trance that numbed and almost paralysed his faculties until the end of 1822[1]. He was still too close to his subject; as he recollected them, the minutiae of Sarah's conduct each retained a separate sting; and the result was a 'case-history' of his spiritual sickness rather than a reasoned narrative. At the time, his friends suspected that he might be 'sinking into idiocy'; he would discuss no other subject; and the tone of his conversation, like the tone of the book itself, was embarrassingly maudlin.

The absurd misadventures I record in my journal are now over thirty years old; and here I must repeat that my own unaccountable beloved was not a second Sarah Walker, except that she had much the same gift of beguiling and perplexing, and employed it with the same readiness and the same instinctive skill. Did Sarah and Julia secretly despise men? In Julia's attitude towards the men she captured there was usually a touch of ridicule, which, having passed through various stages of derision, at the outset more or less good-natured, might afterwards sharpen into keen contempt. She needed love, yet resented being loved; and her resentment was apt to assume an unexpectedly aggressive guise. As I have already noted, she was fond of raising tempests; and, under January 11, I see a revelatory phrase in the pages of my journal. I had asked her, no doubt, exactly why it was she often made our life so difficult; but all I have preserved is her curious response: 'I *like* things to be difficult'; and I believe she spoke the truth.

[1] The *Liber Amoris*, which scandalised all Hazlitt's friends, first appeared in May 1823.

Was she a natural anarchist? And, if that be an accurate guess, how did her anarchism originate? Among Julia's memories, as among those of Isabelle, there lurked a disappointing father. Isabelle's parent had been proud, reserved and cold; Julia's, so far as I could learn, was weakness and amiability personified. A retired soldier, he had married a young woman who, his middle-class relations considered, was definitely 'not out of the top drawer', and whose short-comings, they frequently declared, his elder daughter had inherited. Her childhood was stormy— she developed some of the nastiest traits of the child that lacks love; and her father had retired into a state of self-pitying decrepitude. As she grew up, many attempts were made to complete her education; and she was eventually packed off to stay with a military uncle, her father's more successful brother, at an Indian cantonment. She had Isabelle's habit of telling stories about her juvenile vicissitudes; and one tale she told, presumably based on fact, described the poignant termination of a very early love-affair. She and a young officer had fallen wildly in love. He hated the service; when Julia's holiday ended, and she was about to sail home, he had stowed away aboard the ship; and somehow she had managed to conceal him until the liner reached Port Said. Discovered, arrested, taken ashore and transported back to India, he was then given the choice, she said, of facing a court-martial or being posted to an Indian border-station. He had chosen the latter course, and soon afterwards had shared the fate of one of Kipling's tragic heroes, dropped 'like a rabbit in a ride'[2] by an ancient native musket.

To substantiate her story, Julia produced a photograph of a handsome young man, and another of herself wearing elegant jodhpurs, a half-grown leopard at her feet. As with Isabelle's stories, I sometimes felt that her narrative had somewhat too literary a turn to seem altogether credible; but again I reminded myself that fact may imitate fiction; and Julia's voice, when she related it, and described how from the rail above she had watched the young man leave the ship, was muted, wistful and remotely sad. She was ostracised, of course, by all her fellow Anglo-Indian passengers; they intimated that she had 'let the side down'; and during the next few years she

[2] 'A scrimmage in a Border Station
A canter down some dark defile
Two thousand pounds of education
Fall to a ten-rupee jezail
The Crammer's boast, the Squadron's pride
Shot like a rabbit in a ride!

'Arithmetic on the Frontier':
Departmental Ditties

developed into the persistent foe and determined letter-down of every 'side' she had to join. This tendency and her low opinion of her father may well have determined her attitude towards his sex, whose affection she despised yet needed, and felt at times ashamed to need. Love for Julia was a deliberate exercise of power; and the difficulties that she provoked and welcomed only made the conflict seem more real.

Our conflicts never entirely ceased; they chequer the pages of my diary. Hazlitt's main rival at Southampton Buildings had been a fellow lodger, Mr Tomkins. My own Tomkins, an ambitious and adventurous young foreign artist, inhabited the opposite end of London; but Julia, although she had quarreled with him, still refused to give him up; and it was Tomkins' shadow, cast across our meetings, that often caused our bitterest disputes. During these clashes, my behaviour, I can now see, was neither sensible nor strong-minded. I would allow the dialogue to 'spiral wearily about familiar subjects', or adopt 'my usual practice of ... egging her on to say things that I didn't want to hear. A faint smile crept round the corners of her mouth as she dug home her more painful points'. For so young a woman, Julia had a sharp wit and a mordant sense of the ridiculous. She was extraordinarily quick at detecting one's limitations and exposing one's pretensions, and always adroit at holding up a glass where one saw one's silliest face reflected.

Yet she had another side; Julia's character appeared to embody two completely different selves — the hostile self she often revealed in London and the friendlier, warmer self that unfolded in the country. Yet even in London she could be spontaneously affectionate; among all my troubles I had moments of vivid pleasure, followed by the spells of halcyon calm that remembered pleasure brings. 'There is no one', I wrote on January 8, 'I like sleeping with more — or with whom I find it more agreeable to wake up'. Julia fell asleep as swiftly, and slept as calmly and deeply as a young cat, and awoke emitting the same gentle yawn. Her strongest attraction, however — she had few claims either to classical beauty or to photographic prettiness — was her exquisitely smooth and supple skin; and in the country, under the mild radiance of an English summer day, no longer bored, resentful and sulky, she became a gay and active figure.

For Julia going to the country meant returning to a lonely cottage, which she herself had bought and furnished — how she had raised the purchase-price I do not know — in an unfrequented part of Southern

England. It was a marvellously quiet place – so quiet that, when I looked out over the wide airy fields just beyond the garden-hedge, I sometimes imagined I could hear the clover springing. The cottage itself blinked from low-browed windows beneath a broad-backed tile roof; and its only immediate neighbours were the church, a small farm and another slightly larger cottage down a narrow grassy lane. The last building had a curious decorative trait; a range of bleached and weathered ox-skulls, nailed up at regular intervals around the eaves, gave it an odd resemblance to an early Greek temple, where the heads and horns of sacrificed kine often decorated the entablature, until, reproduced in carved stone, they became a stylised architectural motif. As for the church, it was sufficiently small and plain to have escaped Victorian restoration; and its sole monument was the unpretentious bust of a simple eighteenth-century squire. He had a kind old face, wrinkled and wizened, yet notably alert and shrewd. Such was Squire Honeywell's dislike of urban fashions that he did not wear a wig, but had insisted that the sculptor should depict him in a homely velvet night-cap; while the commemorative inscription, nicely cut below, dwelt on his domestic virtues, his devotion to his family, his care of his servants and tenants, and the sound example he had set his friends, rather than on his distinguished ancestry or his matrimonial alliances.

The Honeywells' manor, its garden, paddocks and park, had vanished many years earlier. For miles around Julia's cottage there remained no big estates; but, deep in the valleys, we glimpsed large prosperous farms, sheltered by heavy belts of woodland; and in the warm months, the coppices were thick with flowers like a medieval *mille fleurs* tapestry. At the end of a hilly path, two or three miles from the cottage, stood a solitary public house, which we had affectionately nicknamed 'The Fox-Hole', kept by a Mr and Mrs. Fox. Why should I remember their name, when far more important details now unaccountably elude me, or preserve so distinct a mental portrait of the aged Mr Fox himself? As he sat close to the fire that burned brightly in an antique 'basket-grate', his huge stony-looking, work-worn hands were always folded on his knees; and his thin steel-grey hair was neatly parted down the middle. Once perhaps he had been a gardener or a groom, pensioned off a quarter of a century ago. Sitting statue-still in an upright wooden chair, he seldom spoke and never smiled.

Of two visits we paid to 'The Fox-Hole' I have particularly moving recollections. One night – the season was late Spring – a heavy snowfall transfigured the whole landscape; and, when we left the cottage, we saw around us groves of fully-leafed trees that carried dazzling white cloaks and cowls. On the second occasion, August was nearly over; and, during our walk home, we descended a steep path between a field of barley and a field of wheat. The sun shone; but a vigorous breeze was blowing; and as it rushed from the wheat across the barley, the music of its passage changed. Among the Greek epithets of the ancient Corn-Goddess is '*Chalkokrotos*', 'bronze-rustling'; and the wheat-field, swept by the wind, gave forth a shuddering brazen murmur, while the bearded barley hissed and sighed. To these pagan harmonies Julia responded in her own impulsive fashion, and pulled off and threw aside her shirt. Wading bare-breasted through the corn, she made an admirable young Demeter.

The London flats that Julia occupied were temporary resting-places, and showed little care for her surroundings. But at the Cottage she adopted the rôle of energetic house-keeper, and diligently brushed and scrubbed and painted. She loved the house a good deal more than she loved or liked most human beings; and it assumed an almost sacred significance in her life and eventually, I found, in mine. She felt safe there; I shared that sense of safety; I was free from the obtrusive Tomkins and the dangers that he represented. Or so I thought, and foolishly continued to think long after we had said goodbye. La Rochefoucauld, who has provided a summing-up of so many grave emotional problems, devotes a well-known maxim to the theme of jealousy, which, he observes, 'though invariably born of love, does not necessarily die when love expires'. This is true enough; 'curses on Rochefoucauld for being always right!' Byron once ejaculated. Yet, although jealousy may outlive passion, it loses something of its previous power to wound; and by the time I heard a diverting piece of gossip about a rival's sojourn at the Cottage, so far was I from retrospective anguish that I enjoyed the story's comic details.

While I was detained in London, a gallant young soldier had been asked to take my place, I learned, and had naturally accepted. Julia and he were quite alone. Then the gate creaked; footsteps approached the door; and a timid knock was heard. When Z., still wearing his dressing-gown, boldly threw the door open, he discovered the local curate, who said he understood that Mr. Quennell, an author, very often stayed there – no doubt he was confronting him; and he hoped that Mr Quennell would agree to sign the book, a biography of Byron, that he tentatively held out. Z. acted with military promptitude – he had campaigned in the Middle East – accepted the volume, took it into the sitting room, procured pen and ink, and signed my name, succeeded by a flourish and an appropriately courteous sentence, upon the virgin title-page. He returned the volume; they exchanged silent bows; and the grateful curate walked home.

There were presumably other stories, of much the same kind, that have never reached my ears. Julia attracted, and sometimes encouraged the unlikeliest devotees; and, if they were disreputable, eccentric, or perhaps a little grotesque, she found them all the more appealing. Thus, she formed an affectionate association with a gang of Balkan horse-thieves whom the British Foreign Office had recognised as an Allied government in exile, and who led a gaily riotous life at a confiscated house near the Brompton Oratory. They had many women friends; and their hirsute ruffianism evidently delighted Julia. I did not know that she sometimes kept a diary; but, when at a much later period, I was allowed to open it, I read a graphic account of how, one winter night, pretending she felt ill, she had successfully got rid of me, listened to my footsteps 'crunching off through the snow', caught a taxi and happily joined their revels. Here, and in similar entries, I cut a Chaplinesque figure of fun; and the self-portraits sketched in my own diary cause me scarcely less embarrassment. I am by turns argumentative and plaintive, expostulatory and querulous; and my neat pencil script brings out into sharper relief the sad confusion of my feelings.

Tomkins remained an obstinate spectre whom I could not hope to exorcise; and, if Julia telephoned him, which she frequently did, the result was often painful:

> Telephonings (I report early in February) and, at Bedford Square, again more telephonings. She then proceeded to enlarge on last night's theme and lucidly explained my rôle as *pis-aller,* with some animadversions on defects of my character . . . She has now concentrated against me in a tight knot of resentment and suspicion. Nothing can loosen the knot . . . I must either accept my rôle . . . or for once make a definite move and face another period of appalling emptiness. A pity I have not a little more of the self-sufficiency J. credits me with . . .

Though I was never as decisive as I should have been, from time to time our rows were violent; and, on February 4th, I wrote that 'the bruise on her nose has spread — giving her a darkly spectacled appearance which is not altogether unattractive'. Early next day, after a night spent fire-watching at the Ministry, I found that Julia had vanished; 'felt oddly calm — almost relieved . . . a load seemed to have dropped off. Independence. Clarity. More good resolutions . . . Then J. rang up — on platform at Waterloo where she had missed her train. Plausible excuses and a candid friendly voice.' Not until mid-March did I finally decide that 'a continuous record has become too depressing'; and from that point, so far as its principal subject is my relationship with Julia, I can put away my diary. This I am glad to do; it is an unedifying document. My original purpose had been to chart the course and — perhaps I had some literary plan in view — follow the complex pattern of an ill-assorted love-affair. But none of the questions an inquisitive critic might ask receives a satisfactory answer.

Why did I struggle so feverishly and, when my efforts failed, submit so tamely? The main reason, I assume, was that I dreaded solitude. Since I grew up, I have always needed some strong emotional preoccupation that, like a golden thread, runs through my days, and links the images of the mind with the feelings of the heart. Should I lack that thread, my existence loses an essential quality; and, if again and again I refused to call Julia's bluff (which might have earned me a certain respect, however grudging), it was because I feared to snap the link, and face the period of emptiness and loneliness that would inevitably follow. Another reason was a great deal more childish. During my early youth, I had had few luxuries, and had therefore developed a kind of primitive greed I afterwards named my 'Oliver Twist Complex', and that, even today, the sight of the last nectarine lying alone on a plate, or of an unfinished bottle of excellent claret being carried off the table, still occasionally arouses. This greediness extends to the rewards of love, and has very much the same undignified results. I *needed* Julia's company and, rather than let her go, I would resort to almost any strategem — to the crudest bribery, for instance. Financially, her standards were very modest; but she liked collecting objects, small pieces of furniture, fragments of bric-à-brac, well-bound and beautifully illustrated books. She also enjoyed transactions that included a tincture of the louche or faintly ludicrous; and I remember exchanging a complete Jane Austen, published by the Oxford University Press with some admirable plates, for the hour or two or warmth and happiness she might have otherwise refused me.

Finally, my stubborn infatuation was a tribute to her power of charming; and here, indeed, as I have already suggested, she resembled Hazlitt's Sarah Walker. I was not her only victim; nor was I the first; and my successors formed a long and various array. Afterwards, when we were merely old friends, she would entertain me with bizarre accounts of the wild extravagances they had committed. Thus, there was a minor film-star, a strong athletic young man, who, discovering that she and his rather effeminate rival were locked behind a bedroom door, had somehow vaulted through a third-floor window; at which the rival had thrown himself on to the bed — a position of safety he declined to leave, since his adversary, he knew, was far too sportsmanlike to attack a helpless target. Even more bizarre was the fate of a virile middle-aged Frenchman who had pursued Julia all the way from Marseilles, where he had both fought in the Resistance and earned his living in *le milieu*. Among his compatriots regarded as a redoubtable *dur*, a revolver-toting tough guy, abroad, under Julia's subversive sway, he had quickly lost his bearings and, once he threatened to show signs of truculence, had been reported to the police. After a series of demoralising London adventures, bullied at Scotland Yard, and bewildered and made fun of by Julia's intellectual friends, he had turned tail and regained his native city on the verge of nervous breakdown.

Julia's later exploits, though equally picturesque — among her war-time triumphs, she became the favourite night-club companion of a Middle-Eastern potentate, well-known for his anti-British views — have little bearing on the present narrative. What concerns me is the peculiar effect she produced. She had acquired a knack, perhaps half-unconscious, of distinguishing her lovers' weakest points, just as certain wasps, accustomed to paralyse their prey, know exactly where to sink their stings. With this gift she also possessed a high degree of physical attraction — the kind of attraction that, at least in retrospect, cannot easily be pinned down. Today, while her features remain distinct, her essential charm eludes me; I remember only a girl of middle height, shapely, smooth-skinned, slit-eyed, who sometimes bundled her graceful body into a 'blue horse-blanket coat', and her brown hair into 'an untidy poodle coiffure' secured by several ill-placed combs. Yet, in times past, even her bohemian untidiness seemed attractive and appealing.

I owed my escape chiefly to good luck. Having spent some months at a war-time factory, Julia secured a much more interesting post, which eventually took her abroad during the early summer months of 1943. As I expected, she had an adventurous voyage out; and, despite the fact that, before she left England, I had not been strictly faithful, I was still jealous enough to read a letter to Astrid, where she mentioned some midnight encounters in a roomy gun-turret, with a sudden stab of pain. Thereafter my emotional convalescence ran a fairly rapid course. Besides discovering new interests, I was making new friends; for, although the passages I have quoted from my diary may perhaps have given the impression that I could think of nobody and nothing else, it refers to many other subjects, among them noteworthy parties I attended and the strangers whom I met there, books I enjoyed and the book that, on February 26, I myself had just begun writing. References to the progress of the War are brief; but there is a single description of an air-raid, accompanied by 'terrific anti-aircraft fire: pink smudges of exploding shells, red curving tracks of tracer-bullets'. Then, on March 2, Julia and I witnessed a 'grim news-reel of German surrender at Stalingrad' (which had taken place exactly a month earlier) and watched General von Paulus emerge from his dug-out, against a background of tremendous ruins, a gaunt, solitary, tragic figure, 'a twitch over his right eye and a three-days' growth of beard'.

Meanwhile, in London's relative quietude – I would never be bombed out again – my humdrum office-life continued; and an additional form of war-service had latterly increased its problems. This is a story I have so far held back to leave more space for Julia's portrait; but, on January 4, I had been unexpectedly conscripted as a part-time fireman, and, on the 12th, when I was summoned to an interview, had

> wandered in not quite impenetrable gloom through vast blitzed areas and up and down muddy lanes between burned-out tenements. A fried-fish shop; only one pub. Smell of a brewery and rumble of an underground. Eventually reached my destination – ghostly, empty school-building with children yelling on the steps. Cockney firemen lecturers: the squeak of a chalk on the blackboard, and the snap of the chalk breaking.

Not until March 4, however, was I definitely called up, and presented myself at the Fire Station. During my first night as a fireman, I was 'embarrassed by my helplessness over equipment and bedding; but everyone was kind and helpful, if a little patronising'.

Thereafter I failed to note my attendances; but they were regular and numerous, and often disrupted the pattern of my private life. The Blitz had died down; there was never a fire to extinguish; and we firemen occupied a subterranean room, drinking tea in chipped enamel mugs, eating cheese-sandwiches and playing 'black-jack', a rudimentary type of *vingt-et-un*. A radio shrieked incessantly; but the card-players rarely followed a programme or commented on what they heard, unless, as sometimes happened, it was a piece of classical music, to which they immediately responded with shouts of 'Turn that fucking thing off!'

Apart from one clever technician, who, during the worst of the Blitz, would climb down into a bomb-crater and expertly rejoin the broken electric cables, they had few opinions on any general subject, and their conversation, with its unending string of sexual expletives, was strikingly monotonous. I seldom succeeded in liking them; and, so far as they were aware of my existence, I am sure they did not like me. But they exhibited a virtue, I soon discovered, not often found among more educated people – a respect for their fellows' privacy, derived from a complete uninquisitiveness and a natural tendency to keep their distance. Brought up in over-crowded homes, they had nothing of the awkward curiosity, the eager preoccupation with their neighbour's affairs, that usually distinguishes the middle classes, and carried the habit of minding their own business to the point of fine discretion. Nobody asked me what I did, or how, before the War, I had managed to earn a living. They merely accepted me; and, while at an orthodox English public school I should have been a conspicuous social butt, I was neither ridiculed nor criticised. Observing my insufficiency, they neither smiled nor sneered.

My only real friend was the aged Mr. Bassom, who began to sell newspapers, as soon as dawn broke, in front of Holborn Tube Station. At home he had an elderly invalid wife and 'the little girl', their daughter; and we frequently discussed his wife's ills, the cleverness that the little girl showed, and his anxiety about her prospects. Being the oldest of the group and the earliest riser, he was always treated with consideration. Our superiors were easy-going; discipline was far from strict; and, at an early stage, when I received the alarming news that I had been ordered to stand sentinel all night on the threshold of our quarters, my informant quickly added that, having done half-an-hour's duty, I could 'nip in again' and go to bed. There was no trace here, I saw, of the so-called 'public-school spirit'; though the rather malicious book that Edmund Wilson wove around his experiences of war-time Europe[3] includes an anecdote about two literary firemen, clearly Stephen Spender and myself, whom he had heard complaining that the proletarian Fire Service was notably deficient in 'the spirit of the school team'. I remember the occasion perfectly, and that we were saying just the opposite; one of the most engaging features of the Service, we agreed, was its complete lack of the bourgeois *esprit de corps*.

Among my fellow firemen, the influence of the team-spirit took a very different form. Now and then, we had official lectures; and I recollect a lecturer concluding his speech with a brief but revelatory reference to the profits of the fireman's job. Suppose, for example, we entered a warehouse that contained lingerie and silk stockings. Some of this precious merchandise we might be inclined to pick up; but we must do our looting properly. 'Shove the stuff down into your boots!' he urged us. 'Don't just go chucking it around the van! Otherwise, if an officer comes along, you might get the other lads into trouble...', Besides listening to lectures and drilling, we also practised scaling ladders, were taught to couple and uncouple hoses— 'this is known as the *male*, this as the *female* coupling, for reasons (an often-repeated joke) that should be obvious to you all!' — and tried to learn the art of tying knots.

The last proved entirely beyond my powers. Unable at school to roll my puttees so that they remained firm and tight, I found it equally difficult to join two ends of rope in a satisfactory conjunction; and one evening, on the parade-ground, I suffered an ignominious set-back. An officer, walking along the ranks, ordered me out and bade me display my skill. 'Start with a clove hitch'[4]. I was handed two lengths of rope, and stood helplessly examining them. Such situations are apt to occur in a nightmare; I felt semi-paralysed and horribly alone. But some move I knew I *must* make; and, assuming a determined frown, I wreathed them through a series of fantastic arabesques; then, as they promptly fell apart, registered the expression of a music-hall conjurer whose favourite trick has miscarried; began again, and again looked gravely surprised when the projected knot refused to hold. 'That fireman had better brush up on his knots!' remarked the tolerant officer before he strode away.

[3] *Europe without Baedeker*. 1948.

[4] The clove-hitch, an encyclopaedia explains, is 'a jamming form of two half-hitches, used for securing a small rope to a larger one'.

A redeeming feature of my war-time life was the curious contrasts it afforded. Now I was a civil-servant facing a heap of files that bristled with little tags marked 'Action Here'; now a prisoner of the Fire Service, eating cheese-sandwiches, and stopping my ears against the radio, while I tried to read a book; now Julia's often troubled companion at a restaurant or night-club; now a cheerful guest in the Dorchester Hotel of one of the most extraordinary of modern London hostesses. I have already attempted to describe the famous Emerald Cunard[5], the only woman whom George Moore had passionately loved, whom he adored until his death, her electric vivacity, inexhaustible gaiety and the coruscating blend of sense and nonsense that formed her peculiar conversational style. I had met her before the War, during a party given by Hugh Lygon's sisters to celebrate their brother Richard's twenty-first birthday; and I remember the night because, having just lost my tail-coat on a German transatlantic liner, where the steward had substituted a garment that must originally have adorned a circus dwarf, I had been obliged to hire my evening clothes, and felt unconscionably stiff and awkward. But there I was presented to Lady Cunard and received an invitation. She still occupied her original London house, No. 7 Grosvenor Square; and the luncheon party I found already assembled was far too brilliant to be reassuring — an ambassador, a brace of cabinet-ministers, various distinguished middle-aged ladies and, I dare say, 'Chips' Channon or some other fashionable gadabout.

Our hostess opened the conversation with a surprising flight of fancy. Edward VIII, long a favourite guest, had recently resigned his throne; she regarded the new sovereign as an epitome of the domestic virtues that she considered most distasteful; and she spoke of a revolutionary march to the Palace, in which she insisted we must all join, and which she meant to lead, another Théroigne de Méricourt, mounted on a snow-white steed. At this the ministers showed signs of vague alarm. But then, by the sudden twist that often diversified her conversation, she turned abruptly to the them of love and, noticing perhaps that I was rather silent, decided she would draw me out. 'What do *you* think of love, Mr. Quennell?' she demanded. Although, at the time, I thought a good deal of love, she caught me altogether unprepared; and, since I had so far drunk only two small glasses of insipid white wine, I felt that there was nothing that I had to say, and blushed — a deplorable adolescent habit I had not yet overcome —

[5] *The Sign of the Fish.* 1960.

stumbled and mumbled, produced a commonplace phrase and retreated into silence. My neighbour was Lady Anglesey (afterwards known to me as the mother of a great friend); and she completed my discomfiture. 'You didn't do very well at that one, *did* you?' she murmured in her faint melodious voice.

When Lady Cunard returned to London, however – she left it on the outbreak of war, but quickly tired of New York – we met again and soon developed a much more comfortable relationship. I was now proof against nearly any question that she chose to throw at me; and before long, a page of my diary records, she had begun to take an 'almost tender but rather embarrassing interest in my sentimental welfare'. Two days later, I see, just after I had been conscripted as a part-time fireman, I visited the Dorchester Hotel, 'where I dined with Emerald C., Diana C.,[6] a solemn Santayana-loving young American soldier and C.C', and we heard, among other things, a quantity of 'anecdotage about "poor dear G.M." etc. till a quarter to one'. Next comes a description of 'a very odd party', that, besides Diane Abdy, Clarissa Churchill[7] and her platonic admirer James Pope-Hennessy, included an ex-ambassador, Sir A., and 'a knowing little American naval officer who ogled both James and myself...and whom Emerald (without quite grasping the situation *vis-à-vis* Sir A., which nevertheless was pretty obvious) did not at all approve of. Sir A. friendly but extremely silly. Compared Diane to a fruit-eating bat. Related myth about seals and fishermen's wives... Ambassadors should not unbend ---The less one sees and hears of ambassadors and ministers *en intimité,* the happier one feels.'

Without this touch of the odd and unexpected Emerald's parties would have lost their charm. She preferred to mix her guests, applauded adventurous talkers and, although a moment might come when she sharply drew a line, seldom frowned upon an indiscretion. Astonishingly indiscreet, it struck me, some of her celebrated guests were; for, unused to such company, I had assumed that eminent public characters must have fairly strong heads, only to discover that they became as garrulous as ordinary men under the influence of champagne and brandy. Emerald's dinners were frequently exhausting, but they could never have been called dull; and she herself was not merely a source of endless diversion but a splendid social catalyst, who, once the United States had joined the Allies and American forces reached England, played a particularly valuable rôle. In a passage

6   Lady Diana Cooper

7   Sir Winston's niece, the future Lady Avon

quoted above I mention the 'Santayana-loving young American' I had met among her friends; and Emerald, being an American by birth[8], attracted many transatlantic visitors, and explained to them the mysteries of the Old World with her own distinctive comments.

Elsewhere, the great American invasion had temporarily transformed the London scene; our allies covered a wide range, from polished graduates of Yale and Harvard – notably the well-known 'Sergeant' – and the polysyllabic products of Middle-Western universities, to the ruggedest gum-chewing G.I.s, who, in search of a 'good lay' or a pub where the beer was cold, wandered dejectedly around the streets. Among his compatriots 'The Sergeant' occupied a privileged position; such was his sucess, both with elderly hostesses and with middle-aged intellectuals, that he acquired an almost legendary renown; and it was said that his fame had even reached the Palace, provoking King George VI, a somewhat irascible man, to exclaim that he 'didn't want to hear any more about that damned Sergeant!' when his name happened to come up at breakfast. As 'the Loot', he also earned a reference in Evelyn Waugh's excellent war-time trilogy *Officers and Gentlemen*. But his military situation remained ambiguous; though he wore an ordinary sergeant's uniform, he seemed to lead a life of leisure. After five or six o'clock at least, he was almost always free.

The Sergeant was not the only American to become a London legend; and, at the opposite end of the social and moral scale, I remember hearing the remarkable story of an unknown G.I., who, whenever he could leave his post, took up his stand in Piccadilly, smoking a cigarette, his shoulders and the sole of his left-hand boot propped against a certain wall, and asked every feminine passer-by, young or old, squalid or elegant, the same brief and rudimentary question. The point of his manoeuvre was that he excepted no one; as he muttered out his blank demand, he neither smiled nor changed his pose; and, although the response he received was often a furious glare or a look of deep revulsion, suddenly and unforeseeably, he said, his luck would change. During the course of a week, he assured a British acquaintance, he made a series of surprising conquests.

On a less primitive level, the war-time pursuit of pleasure, now that we had American boon-companions, war-correspondents as well as soldiers, continued more and more briskly; and it was then I noticed that the American attitude towards alcohol was very different from the English. Members of both races were inclined to get drunk;

---

[8]   She had been born in San Franciso on August 31, 1872.

but, while the English would plan a quiet, enjoyable evening, and drink far too much along the way, our American friends would start with the solemn announcement 'Tonight I'm gonna get plastered!', and suit their actions to their words. The result was exactly the same; only the intention differed. To generalise about national attributes has always been a dangerous pastime; but the sharp contrasts between the English and American characters make the temptation irresistible; and I have often noted the vein of *extremism* that apparently runs through transatlantic life — the individual's tendency to carry a pattern of behaviour to the furthest point he can achieve. There was something Dostoievskian about the expression of grim resolve with which our friends told us that they meant to get plastered; and, having fulfilled their promise, they accepted the after-effects in a sublimely unselfconscious spirit. Thus, at the entrance of the Café Royal, I observed a large young officer, who, having first informed his companion that he felt rather tired and what he needed was a little nap, then subsided on to the carpet and peaceably curled up, his two fists clenched beneath his face, like a child just put to bed. He nearly blocked a door; guests and waiters stepped across him or tiptoed gingerly around him; but, until he was lifted and dragged off, nothing could disturb his rest.

As the War gradually approached its end — or the end, if not yet visible, became definitely foreseeable — London began to assume the appearance of a gigantic caravanserai, through which a host of travellers moved, bound for known or unknown destinations. Sometimes pseudonyms disguised their true identities. Introduced at the Ritz to a tall distinguished Frenchman, who suggested an English 'gentleman-rider' with a pleasing touch of Don Quixote, I soon guessed that Monsieur Dubois or Monsieur Leblanc was probably his *nom de guerre,* and afterwards learned that his real name was Emmanuel d'Astier de la Vigerie, and that he moved regularly between England and occupied France, carrying important messages to and from the French Resistance. Not every hero completely looks the part; but Emmanuel's splendid *'tête de hidalgo'* — hollow cheeks, a finely arched nose, a lofty forehead and bright, deep-set eyes — seemed an accurate reflection of his bold and intransigent character. Once I had gained his friendship, I found him perfectly willing, even relieved perhaps, to be able to talk about his experiences beyond the Channel; and, when I asked him if he had often been deeply afraid, he described a single episode. The date was August, 1943; the background, an apartment in Montmartre, where a staunch old woman sheltered him. He had entered the main room early that morning to catch her peering — more inquisitive, he thought, than frightened — into the almost empty street below. '*Mes petits camarades sont là*', she whispered. What little friends, he had demanded. '*Ces messieurs de la Gestapo*', who had already questioned her. He saw that black car? The worst of them all was the big fellow, wearing the panama hat. She asked herself whether they were coming up here now…

As the employees of the Gestapo crossed the street, a balcony outside the window hid their movements. Emmanuel and his accomplice could only wait, though the room behind was piled high with Resistance pamphlets, far too bulky to conceal or burn. Then indeed, Emmanuel admitted, he had suffered agonising terror; he could feel beads of ice-cold sweat run from his armpits down his sides; and, while he stood motionless and expected the rumble of the lift that would bring '*ces messieurs*' to the door, he had passed the time working out multiples of three, a device he had employed on previous occasions to subdue unsteady nerves. The lift, however, had remained silent; clearly the panama-hatted man had been following another trail. Emmanuel's narrative so much impressed me that I begged him to produce a written record; and after the War he published a small collection of admirably vivid sketches[9], and gave me a copy, inscribed '*à Peter Quennell dont une phrase, au Ritz, a été à l'origine de ces sept fois sept jours…*'

Emmanuel was a naturally gifted writer; but just as interesting as his work and war-time adventures was his romantic personality. He was one of those members of the privileged classes who, obeying some secret law of their nature, move inevitably towards the Left. In August 1789, during the deliberations at Versailles, I feel sure that the baron d'Astier would have jointed the vicomte de Noailles[10], and voted for the abolition of seignorial rights; and I have no doubt that in 1830, 1848, perhaps even in 1871, he would have been prepared to man a barricade. About his previous life I knew comparatively little; but I heard talk of a disastrous early marriage, and of a bohemian period when, like many other Frenchmen of the period, he was said to have experimented with cocaine. In 1943 all that was behind him; he had become deeply attached to a charming Russian woman Kay,

[9]   *Les Editions de Minuit*. 1947; a section of the book, 'Sept Jours en Eté', had been published under my own editorship in the *Cornhill*. May 1944.

[10]   Modern members of the Noailles family, I was recently amused to learn, have not yet forgiven the vicomte Louis for his traitrous behaviour, and like to point out that he sprang from an inferior branch of their line.

offspring of a former Soviet diplomatist and a close and faithful friend of Julia's. It was through Julia I had first met him at the Ritz; and one night, since the lovers were temporarily homeless, and Emmanuel was leaving next day — benzedrine, morphine, cubes of condensed food and a cyanide capsule already packed into his bag — I offered Emmanuel and Kay the use of my sitting-room at Bedford Square. So absorbed were they in the joy and sorrow of the moment that they forgot to draw the black-out curtains; and I was soon aroused by thunderous footsteps on the stairs and excited voices from the room. When I opened my door, I found a posse of local air-raid wardens who were clamouring for admission, while Kay, scantily clad, both her long thin arms extended, with loud cries of '*Ils ne passeront pas!*' stood prepared to give them battle. It took some time to explain the situation and send the wardens away about their business. But peace at last was restored; and, before day had broken, Emmanuel once again had vanished.

De Gaulle honoured his war-time record. In May 1944, having joined the French Committee of National Liberation at Algiers, he became its Minister of the Interior, and, in September of the same year, was appointed French Ambassador to Washington. His feeling for the General, however — '*Le Symbole*', he nicknamed him — had by now become extremely complex, a blend of reluctant admiration and keen personal antagonism; and he hastened to resign his post. De Gaulle fascinated him — that he could never conceal; and *Sept Fois Sept Jours* includes a memorable account of dining alone with his chief at a London hotel, and observing the great man's gestures, 'slow and heavy like his nose', his waxen skin and slightly feminine hands, which, palms turned upwards, appeared to be lifting 'a world of ponderous abstractions'. He did not love men, Emmanuel concluded; 'what he loves is their history, above all else the history of France', particularly the latest chapter that he himself was helping to enact and inwardly chronicling as he went along. Some years after he had renounced his allegiance to De Gaulle, Emmanuel published an acute appreciation of the work and character of Saint-Simon.[11] His analysis is uncommonly shrewd; but references to De Gaulle, and comparisons between the Symbol and Louis XIV, and the principles that each incorporated, occur at almost every turn. De Gaulle, if not his King Charles' Head, remained a perpetually haunting presence; and my only glimpse of the General in London, as he stalked down Berkeley Street, closely followed by an aide-de-camp, helped me understand

[11] *Sur Saint-Simon*. 1962.

my friend's aversion. His whole appearance was imposing – but too imposing, too self-contained and self-enclosed, to be altogether sympathetic; and he resembled, I thought, a giant stick of asparagus, solid and elongated, thicker and larger than life, the topmost portion of his massive, grey-coated frame very slightly bent forward.

It was De Gaulle's apparent inhumanity, and his firm belief in himself as the destiny of France personified, that had antagonised Emmanuel d'Astier, the revolutionary humanist. I never saw him again; the symbol seldom went out into the world, unlike Gaston Palewski, his garrulous and amorous subordinate; and I spent most of my time, not with leaders and heroes, though Emmanuel, on his brief reappearances, I was always glad to see, but with civilian misfits of my own kind. Some I have already described; others I have left unmentioned; but one name – that of Isabelle, my second wife, who had divorced me five years earlier – evidently calls for notice. She must, I assume, have regained England some time in 1942; among the friends and enemies my diary lists she has become a well-established figure, who evokes no special blame or praise, except that I deplore her 'hacking smoker's-cough', and wonder why, during our brief marriage, she had made me quite so miserable.

Of her experiences since the German invasion she spoke in cool and almost casual tones. After escaping from Paris, where she had formed an attachment to a young French journalist, she had travelled slowly southwards and taken refuge at an isolated farmhouse near the line between occupied and unoccupied France. The proprietors seemed honest, kindly people; but the peasant's wife, having hidden her among the milk-churns on their cart and driven her across the line, had suddenly pulled up, ordered her to take off her expensive fur jacket and a brooch that she was wearing, pushed her out on to the road and driven away. Somehow Isabelle had reached Marseilles; and there, she told me in the same emotionless voice, she had discovered she was pregnant, and have given birth to twins. It was a cold winter; food was severely rationed; the hospital, managed by a few nuns, was entirely unheated; both the children soon died. Although she remembered the pain and misery she had suffered, she could not remember if she had ever seen their faces.

She had changed, of course; her fine transparent skin had grown opaque; she had lost her liveliness and youthful lightness; and the Teutonic side of her nature was becoming more apparent. As she still received the small allowance that L'Ami – now married and a decorated serving officer – had agreed to make her when they parted, she led a tolerably carefree life. Her most irksome problem was what she should do with her leisure. This was a problem she had long confronted; and, in the oppressive atmosphere of war-stricken London, it seemed increasingly difficult to solve. Alcohol provided, if not a complete solution, at least a temporary escape. Like many drinkers, she needed a regular routine to support her through the hours, and frequented an afternoon-drinking-club – such clubs were then to be found in almost every Mayfair back-street – run by a friendly serviceable woman, who smiled and talked and polished glasses, while Isabelle, rigidly upright on her stool, drank and smoked away the time. I am ashamed to admit that, should I pass the club and catch a glimpse of Isabelle sitting alone there, I was apt to hesitate, then hurry on.

Yet she had a few friends; and one of her cronies and daily drinking companions was the veteran man of letters Norman Douglas. 'Uncle Norman' loved the young, both platonically and passionately; and the young were drawn to him. He had none of the conceit, none of the pretensions and prejudices, that often go with literary fame; his natural cynicism had simplified his view of life, and left him infinitely tolerant. During my youth I had much admired *South Wind,* whereas today I prefer his travel-books; and I was curious to meet him. His work, however, was the only subject he would on no account discuss. 'I've shut up my little shop', he declared; and nothing would persuade him to re-open it. Let's forget my books, his expression implied, and proceed to talk of something else, something rather more vital, such as where, in this accursed metropolis – he had always hated London – he could find a bottle, even half a bottle, of honest Scotch whisky. Age and hardship had reduced his needs to a minimum – a bottle of whisky every twelve hours and occasionally, I suppose, an entertaining bed-fellow.

His passions, at this period of his life, though he once threw off a lewd hint about his relationship with Isabelle, were entirely paederastic. At an earlier stage, it was said that he had kept a juvenile harem that included boys and girls alike; but, having been severely 'clapped' (to use the eighteenth-century term) by the wife of an old friend whom he had visited and seduced on his way home from the races, he had abandoned adult heterosexual love. His subsequent pursuit of little boys had involved him, during his foot-loose middle age, in many dangerous situations – again and again he had had to break camp and slip across the nearest frontier. But these setbacks had neither scarred his spirit nor diminished his cupidity. When I knew him, he was a cheerful old Garden-God, staunch, resolute and undismayed, clumps of thick white hair and heavy eyebrows projecting boldy over a wrinkled, red-knobbed mask. I doubt if he had ever felt a regret; remorse or repentance, or, indeed, the *angst* that Cyril Connolly helped to popularise, would have been far beyond his comprehension.

I wish I enjoyed the same immunity myself; for all my determination to live in the present, I am a natural backward-looker; and, now that the war was ending, thoughts of the part I had played — or, rather, had not played — would occasionally prick my conscience. One intrepid friend had kidnapped a Nazi general; a second, penetrated a Greek airfield and affixed a series of plastic bombs to the under-carriages of German aircraft; a third, driven through Rommel's African lines and spent the night on the upper floor of a deserted Arab house, while German troops slept on the floor below, and Randolph Churchill's volcanic snores threatened momentarily to wake them. What had I done? Well, I had written a fairly solid book; that, I hoped, was to my credit. Otherwise, I had worked or idled in offices, attended night-clubs and dinner-parties, and proved a singularly incompetent member of the war-time Fire Service. I could not pretend that it was a very glorious record; or that I should be able to describe it for my descendants' benefit with a glow of satisfaction. Still, I had enlarged my scope, met some remarkable characters and — no doubt a salutary experience — now and then felt mortally afraid. Since the outbreak of war, in whatever else I had failed, I had kept my eyes open; and, like l'abbe Sieyès, summarising his achievement in the darkest period of the French Revolution, I could say *'J'ai vécu'*.

My last war-time job, after the Allied invasion of Europe, when the Ministry of Economic Warfare broke up, was by far the most congenial. I joined 'Radio News Reel', a junior branch of the British Broadcasting Corporation, which provided the latest newspaper-reports with an appropriate local background. Should the Russian forces, advancing through Eastern Europe, be poised to take a certain city, we would furnish a brief account of the place, its history, its strategic and economic value, and its pre-war population. If we were at a loss, we telephoned another department and asked for Mr Weidenfeld, an authority on Middle Europe, who soon arrived and, scarcely drawing breath, poured out a copious flood of details — not only the basic facts, but rapid, picturesque sketches of the city and its people, the names of its best-known families, of the cafés they frequented and their theatres, restaurants, *boîtes de nuit,* winding up with a vivid resumé of their political ideas and sexual habits. It was an extraordinary display; and I must admit I sometimes wondered if an aptitude for brilliant improvisation was not among the young man's gifts. But, whatever his sources, the material he supplied we hastened to accept and use.

George Weidenfeld, during the far-off 1940s, was an already plump, yet brisk and agile figure. Having been educated at an Austrian university (where he had fought a successful duel against an insolent Nazi bravo) and, later, escaped from persecution by struggling through the Alps on foot, once he had crossed the Channel, despite the rather reluctant welcome he originally received as an unknown and penniless refugee, he had taken England to his heart. At our office we soon became friends; and, when Cyril's landlord decided to cut short his lease now that the European war was almost over, George suggested we should share a house. A naturally resourceful man, he had discovered an early-nineteenth-century cottage, designed by John Nash after the completion of Regents Park, on the grassy verge of an extinct canal. The stucco-faced building was two-storeyed; George occupied the ground floor, and I moved into the rooms above. Park Village East and its companion, Park Village West, were secluded enclaves, which Nash had planned as a minor addition to the noble squares and terraces that lie beyond. Here, we were told, a hundred years ago, officers of the Albany Street barracks very often kept their mistresses; and there was an air of surreptitious gaiety about these little withdrawn houses, each constructed in a slightly different style, classic, Gothic, even vaguely Swiss. George's manner of life was more hospitable than mine; he launched the long round of crowded festivities that have amused him ever since. But, at this stage, the guests he entertained were, for the most part, writers, publishers and journalists; no ladies of quality or distinguished political figures had yet crossed his threshold.

George's polyglot guests, and their habit of using my bath-room if I failed to lock the door, provoked some slight domestic clashes; but, as a rule, we co-existed smoothly; and the only disturbing incidents of our stay were caused by strangers or intruders. Once, when I returned from the country after dark, I met George looking pale and shaken. The bell had rung, he said; and there, on the garden-path, stood a substantial wicker basket, which contained beautifully laundered bed-clothes and a neatly tucked-up baby. 'What did you do,

George?'; 'My dear, my dear', he replied, 'I thought I should *not* intervene'. He had, therefore, hastened to telephone the police-station; and the police had arrived, and taken the child away. Both George and I denied any connection with the unknown foundling's parentage; and the mystery of its origins was never solved. More alarming was a crime committed in the Village, just beyond our furthest lamp-post. Some vagrant sadist murdered a middle-aged woman and, before he abandoned the corpse, trampled underfoot her spectacles, savagely grinding them to splinters. Though a suspect — the caretaker of a neighbouring block of flats — was sharply cross-examined at the inquest, he could produce a fool-proof alibi, and was allowed to leave the court. Finally, we suffered a ludicrous invasion. My old friend Julia, back from her adventures abroad, carrying a single heavy bag and a massive sheep-skin coat, persuaded me to give her shelter and, having borrowed my key, entered the house one night, accompanied by David Tennant, always a glad abetter of mischief, and pillaged and laid waste the kitchen. They must have enjoyed themselves; our indignant house-keeper complained that her shelves were ransacked, and that gouts of chutney smeared the walls and ceiling. George's opinion of Julia would presently change; but then, almost on bended knees, he implored me to remove my friend.

This invasion must have taken place late in December 1944, or early in the following January, while I still performed a fireman's duties. They were abruptly and dramatically cut short on January 24, 1945. The last German plane had long since come and gone when I was present at my first fire. Every previous call had been a false alarm; but that evening, as I clung to the flanks of the engine, my helmet awry, my rubber boots, which I had not had time to secure, hanging in elephantine folds, my tunic half-unbuttoned and my belt undone, I thought we were bound upon some serious mission. Our objective was a Victorian office-building, next to the Law Courts, opposite St Mary-le-Strand, which showed not the slightest signs of the blaze we expected. We were told, however, that a fire had broken out somewhere in a central courtyard, and that our business was to gain the roof and subdue it from above. Carrying weighty rolls of hose, we climbed a dark and narrow staircase, reached a vantage-point and peered down five or six storeys into a many-windowed court. Behind some windows, or so we imagined, shone a faintly threatening gleam. As no officer had followed us up the stairs, we rankers used our own discretion and, aiming the nozzles of our hoses at various sheets of plate glass, immediately demolished them. It was a delightful exercise. As the windows crashed in and puissant jets of water shot through, we heard the sound of a miniature tidal wave surging round an empty office.

Our fun was too good to continue; a messenger soon arrived, who informed us that, far from extinguishing the fire, we had nearly drowned our colleagues on a lower level, and must instantly desist. We, therefore, rolled up our hoses — a long, back-breaking job — and prepared to join our friends. A roll of wet hose makes an awkward burden; I had one beneath each arm; and an unusually good-natured acquaintance lighted a cigarette, which he shoved into my mouth, remarking 'Have a fag, Quenn!'. When, at length, I had cleared the ground floor, I was unlucky enough to come face to face with an exasperated officer. A sharp little man, bearing gloves and stick, he fiercely reprimanded me. 'To smoke on a fire', I learned, was among the most atrocious offences in the British fireman's code. Since it was difficult to eject the smouldering stub, I was temporarily speechless; but, once I had recovered my voice, I was moved to shout back, and told him what he could do with his fire and with the Fire-Service in general. He then ordered me to report at the fire-station; and there I gave up my uniform, helmet, belt and boots, and was summarily cashiered. I also heard that, as a result of my recent behaviour, I need not expect a Fire-Force medal. That was the severest penalty I paid. Three months later, peace returned to Europe.

3

My recollections of the first days of peace are summed up in a single image. One radiant morning I saw Winston Churchill, perched on the hood of a large open car, drive along Piccadilly past the Ritz, bound for the French Embassy where he and the Ambassador, M. Massigli, would exchange congratulations. Around him, their horses' hooves ringing over the tarmac, mounted policemen slowly cantered. Although his cherubic face shone, and he waved his hat and his cigar, he had a remote and visionary look, an air of magnificent self-absorption, as he rode in triumph high above the crowd.

Otherwise I have almost forgotten how that memorable day progressed. Bonfires were lighted beneath the trees of Hyde Park; and some of my friends – among whom was the middle-aged Baroness Budberg, once H.G. Wells' beloved companion, a woman of abundant gaiety and charm but uncommon size and weight – spent the night dancing about them and wildly leaping through the flames. I fell asleep myself after a dinner party, and did not stir again for many hours; and, when I awoke, my fellow guests had vanished, and the fires had died down. An inescapable sense of anti-climax pervaded the next few weeks and months; but my own transition from war to peace was, on the whole, comparatively smooth. My habit of simultaneously writing and performing my official duties now proved to have been very useful. I had recently completed a new book, *Four Portraits,* a quartet of miniature biographies, which emerged the same year; and, some time before the War ended, I was offered two rewarding posts. In the autumn of 1943 I had become the *Daily Mail's* book critic; and, in 1944, I had undertaken the editorship of the venerable *Cornhill Magazine.*

They were remarkably diverse jobs; and that the *Daily Mail* should ever have engaged me may perhaps appear surprising. I was not an established daily journalist; nor were the books I had written likely to attract its editor. The explanation lay in my personal and social, rather than in my literary life. During the earlier part of 1943, I had met the press-lord Esmond Rothermere. His friendly rival Lord Beaverbrook I had already once encountered; and I had been struck by his wrinkled saurian features, his hoarsely crackling voice and needle-sharp eye. Much more benevolent was the impression that the owner of the *Daily Mail* produced. He was as handsomely tall as Beaverbrook was diminutive and gnome-like, as mild and urbane as the proprietor of the *Daily Express* was uninhibited and rough in speech. Some of Beaverbrook's opponents have alleged that, besides spoiling and over-protecting his favoured employees, he occasionally destroyed them. There was nothing destructive about Esmond's attitude towards mankind; and, if his benevolence might sometimes be confused with indifference, it was none the less agreeable.

When we met at a country house near London, he was accompanied by Ann O'Neill, the stimulating *inspiratrice* he was to wed in 1945. I shall not attempt her portrait here; her interests are too various, her activities too numerous; and she has seldom sat still long enough to allow the portraitist to fix an outline. All I can offer are some preliminary sketches and a general tribute to her gift for living. No doubt the contrasted strains in her ancestry have had a strong effect on her development. Through her father she was born a Charteris, and is thus descended, collaterally at least, from the notorious rake-hell Colonel Francis Chartres, whom Pope satirised and Hogarth caricatured[1]; and, through her mother, allied to the plutocratic Tennant clan, offspring of the Victorian Sir Charles Tennant, an immensely rich and virile merchant prince. Her Charteris kin, since the death of the wicked Colonel, were imaginative, cultivated and often erudite patricians – her grandmother, Lady Wemyss, beloved by Arthur Balfour, had been a distinguished member of the 'Souls'; and each family contributed something to the formation of her adult character, the Tennants, her bold executive energy; the Charteris side, that romantic, impulsive spirit which has directed her adventurous career.

Among her chief assets has been the wonderful knack she possesses of discovering a new adventure, and recognising a fresh challenge, in every experience that comes her way. Her latest adventure, when we originally made friends, concerned the reformation of the *Daily Mail* and the lengthy list of improvements she thought the Northcliffe Press required. They were far-reaching; and stories of the changes she

[1] Pope mentions Colonel Chartres in his *Moral Essays*, Epistles II and III; Hogarth caricatures him in the first plate of *A Harlot's Progress*.

planned, and of a sinister feminine influence that stretched from the Dorchester Hotel into the labyrinth of Northcliffe House, soon circulated around Fleet Street pubs. They caused considerable dismay and alarm. First as Lady O'Neill, then as Lord Rothermere's wife, she acquired the status of a legendary monster, with whose name journalists in far-off suburbs were believed to frighten naughty children. But reforms took place. Stanley Morison, *éminence grise* of the *Times*, was commissioned to redesign the *Daily Mail's* somewhat antiquated front page[2]; and the dashing Frank Owen, who had edited the *Evening Standard* from 1938 to 1941, presently occupied its editorial chair; while Alastair Forbes, a brilliant young Bostonian, but more English than the English, was appointed political commentator on the pedestrian *Sunday Despatch*.

My opening review for the *Daily Mail*, which appeared in September 1943, was so incompetent that the Features Editor hardly dared to publish it, and suggested I should scrap the piece and try again. But the second was luckily less inept; and the proprietor himself sent me a message of approval. I held my ground on the *Daily Mail* until October 1956; and, during those thirteen years, I tried the patience of a series of editors and sub-editors, who hesitated, I suppose, to sack me because I had a friend, or friends, behind the scenes. But I had learned, meanwhile, that scrupulous punctuality was one of the greatest journalistic virtues, and made sure that my copy was never late, or needed rigorous correction. I received my reward when the current Features Editor, a cynical peace-loving man, to whom I had apologised for some mishap, told me that I needn't worry: 'Old boy, of all the *Dorchester Commandos*', he said, 'you give me much the least trouble!'

My main problem in writing weekly reviews was how I could persuade my editor to regard the publication of books as a really serious subject, no less topical than the result of a football match at Wembley or a tennis tournament at Wimbledon. Sporting journalists discussed a player's form. Why should not a modern writer's form, revealed by his latest work, be similarly dealt with? At the office, however, it was generally assumed that a book-review required a 'peg'; that it should tell a tale, have a provocative personal slant, or introduce a 'talking-point'. A book-critic must try to amuse his readers; having done so, and diligently levelled the ground, he could

---

[2] His efforts were blocked, however; and all that he managed to do was to redesign its coat-of-arms.

then discuss a book upon its literary merits. I attempted to satisfy these demands, yet only review books that I thought myself deserved attention, and that an experienced daily journalist might perhaps have put aside. During my efforts to preserve the correct balance, I occasionally fell between two stools; and, whereas Desmond McCarthy, who understood the difficulties I faced, gave me generous encouragement, another friend, an earnest young publisher, took a more unsympathetic line, and suggested that some of my reviews he had seen in the *Daily Mail* were possibly 'a little cheap . . .'

Cheap though they may have been, I did not produce my articles either easily or quickly. It might take me almost half a week to read the books I was reviewing and write seven or eight hundred words; and my superstitious respect for the English language, complicated by a variety of private quirks, such as my neurotic anxiety to avoid repeating prepositions, very often held me up. I lacked, moreover, an important gift that distinguishes the true journalist from the literary amateur — the gift of responding immediately to any subject that confronts him, and of translating his rapid response into brisk colloquial phrases. Cyril Connolly, for example, whose talents were both literary and journalistic, arrived at a definite opinion with enviable speed. Once when I carried him to the theatre, to see a new American comedy of which I had promised I would write a notice, I myself was vaguely amused and pleased; but Cyril soon began fidgeting so desperately, and uttering so many loud reproachful groans, that our neighbours protested and we were obliged to leave our seats half-way through the second act. Had he been the critic and I his guest, no doubt he would have dashed off a highly entertaining diatribe. In fact, *Harvey* (a somewhat too whimsical fantasia about the relations of a lonely drunkard and a huge imaginary white rabbit) is a rather poor play; and its English run was brief.

Having dwelt at some length on the difficulties of book-reviewing, I must not forget its satisfactions. I enjoyed the business of praising a praiseworthy book, which, I liked to think, at least in the columns of the *Daily Mail*, might otherwise have gone unnoticed; and I was not averse from mounting a full-scale attack against a thoroughly bad novel or slipshod popular biography. Among my finest targets was an historical romance that had achieved gigantic sales. The heroine, oddly christened Topaze, is shown romping around Whitehall Palace in the reign of Charles II, leaping into four-poster beds, reclining on anachronistic 'couches', or hiding behind brocaded curtains unfortunately called 'drapes'. Topaze's love-affairs, by present-day standards, would be considered remarkably innocuous; but at that period, when even the London Library still kept *Les Liaisons Dangereuses* under lock and key, this childish tale was accounted wildly daring; and its minimal erotic content appeared to stimulate a host of readers.

I mention it here because no other review I published had so pleasing a reception; but I was slightly perturbed to come face to face with the novelist, who was then making a tour of Great Britain, at a week-end party that we both attended. Our hostess, a violet-eyed beauty from Los Angeles, had apparently conceived the idea of founding an intellectual salon; and she had invited, besides myself and the celebrated novelist, the famous Ely Culbertson, author of 'the Culbertson System' and past master of the bridge table. Mr. Culbertson, a lively, if rather self-centred conversationalist, gave us a graphic account of a recent visit to Russia, where he had interviewed a high-ranking Communist official in charge of public sports and pastimes, and had explained how he hoped to popularise bridge-playing, based, naturally, upon his own system, throughout the Soviet motherland. The official, alas, had promptly trumped his ace by announcing that Soviet policy envisaged the gradual elimination of this bourgeois, crypto-Fascist game, with its aristocratic court-cards; and that, far from facilitating the issue of new packs, he and his colleagues were already hard at work quietly cutting down their distribution.

As a conversationalist, the authoress's scope was a good deal more restricted. She spoke seldom, and then in muffled tones; and her whole aspect was somehow curiously disquieting – liquorice bandeaux over a large pallid brow, and a tall bulky frame in which few of the ordinary physical features seemed to occupy quite the place that I expected; so that for a moment – perhaps it was after dinner – I entertained a weird suspicion that two separate midgets, one riding on the other's shoulders, might have been crammed into the same black satin dress. She frequently retired to her room; and I imagined that, as soon as she closed the door, the human edifice was dismantled, and the twin performers were temporarily set free. Next day, our hostess suggested that the novelist and I should talk of literary concerns. But, when I maintained that George Eliot was the masculine pseudonym adopted by a woman writer, and she briefly yet obstinately disagreed, I felt our dialogue had lost its point. She did not guess that I had reviewed her book; and we parted upon civil terms. Of her later career I have heard nothing. *Topaze Triumphant*, I believe, was the novelist's only brain-child.

At the best of times, the relationship between authors and reviewers is apt to be a little strained; and, should he attend a literary party given by a bustling publisher, the critic is often conscious of eyes averted and of backs deliberately turned. A bad review is rarely forgotten or forgiven; and, although sometimes the author's chagrin may pass – despite an occasional half-joking reference to 'that horribly unfair piece you once wrote about my book (which incorporated so much original research) on "The Secret of the Pyramids", – there are also occasions when it begets a life-long enmity and, year after year, the reviewer is confronted with a frozen smile or overt scowl. Here I feel it my duty to explode a legend that I have sometimes heard repeated. Critics, in my experience, do not accept bribes. I must admit, however, that, many years ago, when I received a slim volume of verses, published by a local printer, no doubt at the poet's expense, I found enclosed a cheque for three guineas. I sent it back, and elicited a petulant reply. The poet was surprised and hurt; he had merely followed, he assured me, what he imagined was 'the customary practice'.

Meanwhile, my visits to Northcliffe House, unless I was collecting an armful of the latest books, were comparatively few; and I did most of my work either at home or, from 1944 to 1951, in the *Cornhill's* sheltered office. I had long been familiar with No.50 Albemarle Street, which then had the simple yet grandiose inscription 'Mr. Murray' painted on the right-hand side of the door; and again and again I had climbed the broad and graceful eighteenth-century stairs (past Thorwaldsen's marble bust of Byron that Isabelle had once so wantonly disfigured[3]) towards the drawing-room, where John Murray II had read aloud the poet's letters, even the most scandalous passages, to his assembled friends and clients. The *Cornhill* was lodged at the top of these stairs; and, having gained my editorial living-space, I enjoyed certain extra-territorial rights. I was allowed to smoke, a habit strictly forbidden in other regions of the building. At least, I could smoke cigarettes; but, having been given a particularly fine cigar – far too good to leave unfinished – I trailed its fragrance behind me while I walked upstairs; and Sir John Murray suddenly burst into my room and, remarking '*you're* the offender, I see!', ordered its immediate extinction.

[3] See *The Marble Foot*, 1976

Sir John, as the anecdote may suggest, was a formidable traditionalist, though, being at heart a just and generous man, he had given me a free run of his archives when I wrote my books on Byron; and I doubt if he wholly approved of some of the stories and essays we published in the new *Cornhill*. His nephew and heir, now John Murray VI, both from an editorial and from a personal point of view, proved a much more sympathetic host; and he, I imagine, had persuaded Sir John to resuscitate the *Cornhill* which, after a long spell under Lord Gorell's editorship, had been suspended in 1939. A hundred-and-sixty volumes of previous issues lined the wall beside my chair. Their presence encouraged me. Launched in January 1860 by George Smith, head of the publishing firm of Smith, Elder[4], 'the orange-coloured magazine', edited by Thackeray, had had an extraordinary début, and sold a hundred and twenty thousand copies. Such was its success that Thackeray had fled to Paris, and threatened to run wild among the *bijoutiers* of the Palais Royal. He could not sleep, he declared 'for counting up his subscribers'.

The *Cornhill's* triumph had been well-deserved. The first issue contained both the opening sections of two popular serial novels — Thackeray's *Lovel the Widower* and Trollope's *Framley Parsonage* — and a long and memorable poem by Tennyson, his poignant threnody 'Tithonus', which evokes the mood of pagan doubt and despair that haunted his earlier poetic life:

> The woods decay, the woods decay and fall,
> The vapours weep their burthen to the ground,
> Man comes and tills the field and lies beneath,
> And after many a summer dies the swan.
> Me only cruel immortality
> Consumes: I wither slowly in thine arms,
> Here at the quiet limit of the world . . .

Other contributors, during the course of the Victorian Age, had included Charlotte and Emily Brontë, Matthew Arnold and John Ruskin, George Eliot, Mrs. Gaskell, Elizabeth Barrett Browning, Dickens, Meredith, Stevenson, Swinburne, Richard Burton, Wilkie Collins and (at a later period) Thomas Hardy and Henry James. With this background, I was naturally inclined to disregard the fashions of the present day, and determined merely to satisfy, so far as I could, the public's taste for good writing. *Horizon,* on which Cyril Connolly and Stephen Spender had set sail in 1939 — Stephen obtained

[4]   From whom John Murray acquired the magazine in 1917

shore-leave after two years' co-direction – pursued a very different course. It was a modernist magazine. Cyril had become a devotee of contemporary art and thought, and rightly saw himself as an active member of the intellectual avant garde. He felt perfectly at home, and received the respect he deserved, amid Parisian *cénacles,* cliques and côteries, whose doctrines – the philosophy, for example, of Jean Paul Sartre – he propounded with the greatest ease. My own mind is far less well-equipped; Existentialism (like Logical Positivism and seventeenth-century Jansenism) is a system of ideas that I am always convinced I have grasped so long as I am listening to an explanation, but that, after a few weeks or days, imperceptibly escapes my hold. The courageous modernity of Cyril's journal, and his efforts to keep his readers in touch with the latest trends and movements, helped to carry it throughout the war-years, and made it the favourite magazine of many youthful British servicemen[5]. *Horizon* continued its excellent work from 1939 until 1950. My editorship of the *Cornhill* lasted just a year longer.

At no period were our papers literary rivals. *Horizon* was dedicated to the spirit of the age, to new ideas and new discoveries, some more valuable, I think, than others; while in the *Cornhill* I merely assembled whatever I considered worth printing, irrespective of the author's birth-date or the ideology he represented. Mine was an individual, perhaps a dilettante choice. But among our contributors were Louis Aragon, Max Beerbohm, Clive Bell, Isaiah Berlin, John Betjeman, Elizabeth Bowen, Maurice Bowra, Truman Capote, Kenneth Clark, Patrick Leigh Fermor, André Gide, Harley Granville-Barker, Margaret Lane, Rose Macaulay, Somerset Maugham, Harold Nicolson, Anthony Powell, Steven Runciman, William Sansom, Osbert Sitwell, Freya Stark, Francis Steegmuller, Robert Trevelyan, Hugh Trevor-Roper, Arthur Waley, Evelyn Waugh and H.G. Wells – not, it strikes me, a discreditable list. At the same time, I was able to put on record an interesting piece of social history – a letter from Jane Austen's best-loved niece, Fanny, the daughter of her third brother, Edward, who had been adopted by a rich cousin[6], in which she informed her sister that 'Aunt Jane's

---

[5]   'During the summer of 1940 . . . we received letters from pilots fighting in the Battle of Britain, often saying that they felt that so long as *Horizon* continued they had a cause to fight for'. Stephen Spender: *World Within World,* 1951.

[6]   Mr Knight of Godmersham Park in Kent and Chawton House in Hampshire. Through Edward's marriage with Elizabeth, daughter of Sir Brook Bridges, he became the father of Fanny, who herself married her cousin, Sir Edward Knatchbull, and whose son took the additional name of Hugessen and ascended to the peerage. The letter was first shown me by my

immediate domestic circle was not everything that they themselves esteemed:

> Yes my love (wrote Lady Knatchbull) it is very true that Aunt Jane . . . was not so *refined* as she ought to have been from her *talent,* & if she had lived 50 years later she would have been in many respects more suitable to *our* more refined tastes. They were not rich & the people around them . . . were not at all high-bred, or in short anything more than *mediocre* . . . Aunt Jane was too clever not to put aside all possible signs of 'commonness' (if such an expression is allowable) & teach herself to be more refined, at least in intercourse with people in general. Both the Aunts (Cassandra & Jane) were brought up in the most complete ignorance of the World & its ways (I mean as to fashion) & if it had not been for Papa's marriage . . . & the kindness of Mrs Knight, who used often to have one or the other staying with her, they would have been, tho' not less clever and agreeable in themselves, very much below par as to good Society . . . If you hate all this I beg yr. pardon, but I felt it at my *pen's end* & it chose to come along & speak the truth. It is now nearly dressing time . . .
>
> I am ever beloved Sister your most affec.
>
> F.C.K.

I enjoyed my unexpected find for a variety of reasons — not only because it added something to our knowledge of Jane Austen's background, seen through prejudiced Victorian eyes, but because it threw fresh light on a close relation of whom she was particularly fond. Cassandra Austen's sketch of Fanny Knight shows a graceful, slender girl, her dark hair neatly cut short in the fashion of the day, herself sketching or painting at a small domestic card-table. She looks fresh and delicate. Yet this very same girl would become the rich and snobbish married woman, mother of a future peer[7], who hinted that, even though her famous 'Aunt Jane', either by good management or good luck, might have 'put aside all possible signs of "commonness"', she had lacked the distinctive social polish that glorified her nieces' milieu. Apart from 'August 23', Lady Knatchbull's letter is undated; but I assume that she performed her painful task some time

old friend the late Edward Rice; and with his permission and that of Lady Knatchbull's descendant Lord Brabourne I published it, during the winter of 1947/48 in No.973 of the *Cornhill.* It is quoted in Jane Aiken Hodge's *The Double Life of Jane Austen,* 1972. The manuscript, I am told, has now been lost.

[7] After a distinguished career of public service, Edward Hugessen Knatchbull, b.1829, was created, in 1880, 1st Baron Brabourne of Brabourne.

after 1850. Why did she perform it with such relish? We know that she had consulted her sympathetic aunt about her early love affairs – most of her suitors had been 'sensible rather than brilliant', perhaps decidedly 'below par'; and a modern commentator[8] suggests that the recollection still rankled. Whatever the origins of Lady Knatchbull's spite, her character had undergone an odious metamorphosis; but this may be partly attributable to the age in which she lived. Aunt Jane was a child of the Regency; Fanny belonged to a very different era; and the moral and social bias of the new age made her Jane's instinctive foe. Jane had often laughed at English 'Good Society'; Fanny, since she had wedded an eighth baronet[9], was now its fiercely loyal guardian.

The spirit of an age and the effect of the time-spirit upon individual human beings are among the literary biographer's chief concerns. In my biography of Caroline of Anspach I had attempted to establish the ethos of the period that had engendered Swift and Pope; and in *Four Portraits* the epoch I had chosen was the second half of the eighteenth century, which, like the Victorian Age, considered itself immensely superior to the decades that had preceded it. Though I admired the seventeenth century, and in 1933 had edited a selection of seventeenth-century verse, I surveyed it from a certain distance. Much as I enjoyed its splendid devotional poets, I could share neither their strong religious faith nor their violent sectarian passions; and only when I reached Pepys and John Evelyn and other founding fathers of the Royal Society did I feel completely at my ease. But there was nothing archaic or remote about the later Georgian epoch. 'Whether we acknowledge or ignore them', I wrote in my new study, 'Boswell, Gibbon, Sterne, Wilkes are ancestors to whom every educated citizen of the modern world is more or less indebted . . . I have attempted to refresh their portraits, to suggest similarities and dissimilarities, and the relation that they bear to a wide historical background. Each is the portrait of a man obsessed by an idea – an aim . . . that gained definition and acquired momentum thanks to the conflict waged between circumstance and the individual ego'.

Four Portraits, published in 1945, was the most satisfactory book that I had yet written, and still compares favourably, I believe, with many books that I have written since. Besides underlining their sharp

[8] Jane Aiken Hodge. Op.Cit.

[9] Her aunt's jokes about the baronetage in *Persuasion* may have struck her as particularly offensive.

dissimilarities, and the clashes of opinion and taste that frequently divided them – James Boswell, with whom my studies began, abominated Gibbon, condemned Sterne and distrusted John Wilkes – I endeavoured to unite my four heroes in a single literary pattern, which would serve to illustrate the broader pattern of the age. I respected them all – Gibbon for his fidelity to his own genius; Sterne, for his imaginative scope, his command of language and his romantic sensibility; Wilkes, for his dash and courage and gusto and unconquerable love of life. But to Boswell I grew particularly attached. When I studied Baudelaire, sixteen years earlier, I had noticed how an artist's strength and his weaknesses were often closely interwoven, and how from the failures of his personal existence sometimes sprang his greatest triumphs. Before he died, Boswell was so inveterate a drunkard that the unsteadiness of his hand made it difficult for him to correct a proof-sheet; he had lost his health and ruined his reputation; sadder still – he had valued his popularity – he was now regarded as a downright bore. An obituary notice in the *Gentlemen's Magazine* summed up the wretched tenor of his last days: 'his joke, his song, his sprightly effusions of wit and wisdom . . . did not appear to possess upon all occasions their wonted power of enlivening social joy . . . Convivial society became continually necessary to him, while his power of enchantment over it continued to decline'.

Yet Boswell's faults – his excitability, his childish impetuosity and his desperate vulnerability – were another aspect of his high creative virtues. Had he been better balanced, more dignified in his behaviour and more quietly reasonable in his emotions, he could scarcely have produced his accepted masterpiece, the *Life of Johnson,* or the lesser-known journals and memorabilia that he called his 'curious archives'. Boswell had a consuming appetite for truth, and hankered after knowledge as eagerly, and at times as indiscriminately, as he lusted after women. During his pursuit of experience, he was ready to sacrifice both decency and dignity, and never hesitated to lay his heart bare. He had 'a kind of strange feeling,' he announced in the 1770s, a decade when his personal behaviour was at once absurd and scandalous, that he, 'wished nothing to be secret that concerns myself '; and he encouraged, rather than sought to control or disguise, the chaotic agitation of his thoughts or the wild confusion of his moods. 'You have told me', he reminded his friend Temple in 1789, 'that I was the most *thinking* man you ever knew . . . I am continually *looking back* or *looking forward . . .'* Through the experiments he had practised on himself he became a wonderfully acute observer and the author of the first modern biography in the history of English letters. Despite the gloom that surrounded his final period, he did not underestimate his great achievement. 'I am absolutely certain', he wrote, 'that *my* mode of biography . . . is the most perfect that can be conceived, and will be *more* of a *Life* than any work that has ever yet appeared.'

His 'curious archives', however, long lay forgotten in the Ebony Cabinet at Malahide and in many other hiding-places. When they were finally disinterred and assembled by the keen explorer Colonel Isham, and the publication of Boswell's *Private Papers* began over half a century ago, the self-portrait he had been drawing since his youth took its place among his finest works. His journals revealed the matrix of confusion from which his genius had emerged; and his descriptive sketches showed his talent for personal portraiture and his gift of critical analysis. Boswell constantly pursued famous men and did his best to gain their friendship, sometimes because he hoped that he could one day follow their example and, if he measured himself against them, could discover the secret of his own identity — as a young man, just who and what he really was he could seldom quite determine — sometimes because his acute historical sense kept demanding a fresh supply of themes.

Having once hunted down both Voltaire and Rousseau — exhausted by the young man's importunities, Voltaire had protested 'my head turns round' and sunk into an arm-chair — in 1776 he visited and closely questioned another 'mighty infidel'. David Hume, he learned, had contracted a mortal disease; but, although 'lean, ghastly, and quite of an earthy appearance', he remained obstinately good-humoured and said that he considered the notion of human survival 'a most unreasonable fancy'. His gay courage horrified yet fascinated Boswell; and, after a dramatic scene, admirably described in his archives, he left the philosopher's presence with strangely disturbing impressions that he found it hard to shake off. Boswell had few heroic personal qualities; Victorian moralists, headed by Macaulay and Carlyle, vigorously abused the man; and I welcomed the opportunity of depicting an 'anti-hero' who had turned his weaknesses to such excellent account, and of dwelling on the writer's merits. Boswell was no Gibbonian stylist, no imaginative fantast in the vein of Laurence Sterne. He had a plain and humdrum style; but it is repeatedly enlivened by some brilliant minor touch, comparable to the spark, illuminating the pupil of the eye, with which a portrait-painter brings a face alive. And then, while I admired my subject at his best, even at his worst and silliest he did not forfeit my esteem. Flaubert, describing Madam Bovary's end, claimed to have developed very much the same symptoms; and, as I followed his vagrant course, I occasionally suspected that I myself was becoming a little too Boswellian.

My quartet of eighteenth-century portraits made a handsome-looking volume, and received a series of extremely pleasant reviews, but had a rather modest sale. I could not echo the words of a well-known woman novelist who, when I asked her about the fortunes of her latest book, replied in contrite accents, 'almost *embarrassingly* successful, I'm afraid . . .' The economics of writing and publishing have a certain horrid interest; and this is the only book I have published of which I happen to have preserved accounts. Between 1945 and 1949, the first edition — a revised edition appeared in 1960 — earned me nearly £2760; and 18,210 copies of both printings were eventually sold. Later publications, I think, were somewhat less remunerative; and, when I entered my fourth decade, despite the regular income that the *Daily Mail* supplied, I was not by any means rich. A number of foolish idiosyncracies made my problem still more difficult. From my father I had inherited one of his unluckiest failings — his phobic attitude towards money. Total destitution was a prospect that had always haunted him; for he remembered the dark financial clouds that had overcast his parents' household; and those memories had implanted a horror of indebtedness, which he regarded as not only the worst of social misfortunes but a repulsive moral vice. The discovery that he was five or six pounds in debt would have made it quite impossible, he told me, to expect a good night's sleep; and although I had seldom been out of debt since the time I left Oxford, yet am apt to sleep soundly, my treatment of the problems of earning and spending is almost equally irrational. A bank-manager's letter may temporarily paralyse my ability to think or act; and I am inclined to put it away, both unopened and unanswered, while I gradually regain my nerve.

Verlaine wrote a book he entitled *Mes Prisons,* describing the gaols he had known; and I have thought myself of producing a similar book on my long unhappy struggles with the modern banking system and the managers whom it employs. One manager I met was called Mr. Skull, and another Mr. Hope. The former unquestionably deserved his name; it was he, I think, who, at a period when bank-statements were far more carefully detailed than they are today, would hold up a

69

sheet and run through the cheques listed, reading out their destination and enumerating the expensive night-clubs and restaurants in which I seemed to waste my substance. Mr. Hope, a white-haired man of the world, was similarly well-named; the strongest epithet he used was 'naughty', and the severest penalty he threatened to impose was 'a letter that I fear you might not like'. Alas, he died suddenly and left his official records, I heard, in a state of some confusion. He had granted loans with a magnificent generosity that disconcerted his successor.

Middle age should be a time of creative calm for the writer or the artist. Thus Gibbon, at the age of thirty-nine, having published the opening volume of *The Decline and Fall*, had placidly settled down near Lausanne to complete his noble project; till, 'on the day, or rather night, of the 27th of June, 1787', he 'wrote the last lines of the last page' and, after laying down his pen, 'took several turns in a *berceau,* or covered walk of acacias', high above the moon-lit lake. I cannot pretend that my middle years were either as tranquil or as consistently productive as I had hoped they might become; and, although time had modified the outlines of my character, I still exhibited certain Boswellian traits, which often warred against my peace of mind. But I had changed, and continued to change, both intellectually and physically. I was no longer thin and gaunt. During the war-years, through some mysterious metabolic process, I had grown a good deal heavier; and my complexion, greenish pale in youth, had acquired a far more sanguine colouring. The Georgian poet had largely disappeared; and the lock of hair that had bisected the poet's forehead, drooping down towards his right eyebrow, dear Astrid, who asserted that the look it gave me was both affected and effeminate, had severely pushed back and, by doing so, removed the last traces of my pensive adolescent self.

Even now, I was subject to moments of panic, spells of deep melancholy and long bouts of atrabilious gloom; but the last twenty 'restless and irregular' years had taught me many useful lessons; and I had learned, if not the art of pleasing, at least the knack of being pleased, and of establishing an amicable relationship with my fellow men and women. I had ceased either to mistrust them or to demand too much of them; my disposition was less romantic, therefore easier and friendlier; and enjoyment came more readily. In the past I had coveted social success, but, because it seemed beyond my reach, had pretended to despise it, and had made my Oxford rooms a kind of

70

Timon's cave where I sat alone and glowered or brooded. In those days I cultivated an air of cynical insouciance that I seldom really felt. I was absurdly thin-skinned; but among the benefits one receives in middle-age is the thickening and coarsening effect of time upon the emotional epidermis. As soon as I had overcome a tendency to shrink from hurts, I found that the world was losing half its terrors.

Meanwhile, I had discovered in my middle-aged temperament an unexpectedly gregarious strain. My second marriage had enlarged my view of the world; and the War, by jostling me to and fro, and removing most of my domestic comforts, had further encouraged me to quit my shell. Born under the Sign of the Fish, I now definitely exchanged my sullen hermit crab seclusion for a much more mobile way of life. I had few encumbrances; I was unmarried and destined to remain unmarried until the early summer of 1956; the places into which I moved after I left Regents Park – a small gimcrack house in South Kensington and a somewhat squalid flat off Baker Street, down a narrow cobbled mews – were untidily and sparsely furnished; and I spent very little time at home. I was seldom visited by friends of my own sex; I doubt if they knew exactly where I lived; and my mother, when she returned from American exile, having never been invited to cross my threshold – I thought that my meagre surroundings might alarm and puzzle her – assumed that I was probably 'keeping a girl', an idea she found it difficult to accept, though on this, as on so many other topics, she maintained an unreproachful silence.

Her suspicions were misguided; of that particular affront to her moral code I was, and always had been, innocent. True, Julia and her successor Perdita had spent days and weeks at Bedford Square; but they were in no sense 'kept' by me; and, had I offered them regular financial support, they would have thrown it back again. They valued their independence; for they belonged to a section of war-time society whom I called 'The Lost Girls', adventurous young women who flitted around London, alighting briefly here and there, and making the best of any random perch on which they happened to descend. Today they might well have joined a commune. But the feminine vagrants of that period were determined individualists; and, should they set up house, they frequently followed the example of Peter Pan's devoted Wendy, and played the part of substitute mother to a band of appreciative homosexuals. They were not 'lost' in the Victorian meaning of the term; often they had highly respectable families, with whom they sometimes corresponded; nor was their private behaviour always notably promiscuous. What distinguished them – and used to touch my heart – was their air of waywardness and loneliness. They were courageous, too, and seemed perfectly capable of existing without any thought for past or future.

The Lost Girls gradually dispersed once the European War had ended. But here, preparatory to bidding them goodbye and continuing the story of my post-war years, I must attempt a rapid sketch of Perdita. She first appears in my diary during the Spring of 1943, while Julia and her changes of mood were still my chief emotional concern; and for a while I oscillated between the two, deriving from Perdita's friendship, should Julia prove difficult, a kind of homeopathic solace. A pretty, fragile girl, she recalled a Pre-Raphaelite illustration for a book of German fairy-tales, and reminded me of the nixen or dangerous water-spirit, who haunted quiet pools and streams, and sometimes rose among the water-lilies to entrap a solitary mortal. I could see her as she might have been represented by a follower of Burne-Jones, breaking the surface of a pool, her wet hair dripping round her shoulders and her pale eyes faintly shining; and, when the image of Julia began to fade, Perdita's delusive features took its place.

In her own way, she, too, had a difficult, unruly nature; and her deceptions and perplexing evasions very often made me jealous. Life at Isabelle's side had implanted the habit of jealousy – a habit that, I must admit to my shame, I have never wholly conquered. Since jealousy is a disease of the imagination, its causes and agonising personal effects have been endlessly described by writers, from Catullus and the Elizabethan and Jacobean dramatists to the author of *A la recherche du temps perdu*. Shakespeare, Webster and Thomas Heywood (whose tragedy *A Woman Killed by Kindness* deserves far more notice than it usually receives) must have felt it at its deadliest.

> Talk to me somewhat quickly,
> Or my imagination will carry me
> To see her in the shameful act of sin

cries the Duchess of Malfi's half-demented brother; for, among the disease's most hideous and pitiable symptoms, is the tendency to conjure up images it then vainly struggles to obliterate, and make discoveries that, once made, become a further source of anguish. Proust's narrator, after his loss of Albertine, miserably delves into her hidden past; and with every detail he manages to bring to light his retrospective torments grow. His deepest troubles concern the association of Albertine and her lesbian friend Andrée, oldest and wickedest of '*la petite bande*'; and, during my attachment to one of the Lost Girls, I learned that she and another girl I knew had formed a passionate alliance. In jealousy there is a secret touch of envy; we suspect there may be a key to the Earthly Paradise, where every physical desire is fully realised and every emotional whim is gratified, that we ourselves have never grasped. How much more tormenting the idea of illicit pleasures upon entirely unknown ground! Mystery in any circumstances is a powerful aphrodisiac; and I broke the spell by following my friend's example and attempting to seduce her lover. An unworthy ruse perhaps; but, once I succeeded, a weight was lifted from my heart.

By now it may have become clear that none of the young women I pursued was conspicuously well-balanced; and why I should so often have plunged into situations that I might have guessed would cause me suffering I have never wholly understood. No doubt I had only myself to blame; the qualities I sought in the women I most admired were those least calculated to provide the basis of a reasonable relationship. Just as in the pictures I loved I had always welcomed a certain touch of ambiguity, in the faces that attracted me there was inclined to be something both elusive and secretive, even occasionally perverse, that suggested the existence, behind the face, of a discontented and rebellious spirit. '*Nous aimons les femmes*', Baudelaire once wrote, '*à proportion qu'elles nous sont plus étrangères*'.[10] The hero of my earliest prose book was still a much respected guide; and, although I longed – or thought I longed – for a quiet and sensible attachment, it was a woman's strangeness, her remoteness from my own life, that I usually found appealing. I was inclined to treat my beloved as a kind of wild pet, a creature of fantasy as well as fact, around whom I built a decorative literary cage.

Thus I developed a ridiculous habit of nicknaming my best-loved companions after favourite animals, likening one to a noble white horse, another to an 'obtuse' Australian wombat[11], a third to an elegant South-American monkey. My chief mistake, I was recently assured by a perceptive woman friend, has been to over-value women yet, simultaneously, underrate them, crediting the opposite sex with legendary attributes, and at the same time seeming to regard its members as a rare and alien species. In retrospect I cannot feel surprised that few of my middle-aged love-affairs ran an altogether

[10]   *Fusées*, in *Journaux Intimes*.

[11]   'One like a wombat prowled obtuse and furry': Christina Rossetti: *Goblin Market*

peaceful course. A moment came, however, when some genie, or good angel, suddenly set about my reformation, and offered me a chance of a steady happiness that I neither expected nor deserved. Clio was a gifted and graceful girl, nicknamed 'the long-stalked English rose' or, on occasions, '*rosa sine spina*', a blue-stocking yet possessed of an ardent nature and an instinctive aptitude for love, against which her social and moral beliefs sometimes fought a losing battle. Her photograph, I remember, captivated Desmond McCarthy, who praised her downcast eyes and thoughtful charm; but Cyril Connolly, through whom I had met Clio at a Bedford Square reception, sounded a slightly less appreciative note. As so often happened, his remark flew straight to the point, where it quickly stuck and rankled; 'she's just the sort of girl', he said, 'your mother wishes you would marry'. An accurate comment – my mother would have been among the first to applaud Clio's charm and sterling character; mischievous, nevertheless, since the idea that my mother might approve of a girl somehow slightly dimmed her fascination.

Clio, moreover, despite her gift for love, was an intellectual moralist. She belonged to the Labour Party, and had once, she admitted, carried a banner in a Left Wing march through London. About this episode and the earnest opinions she held I was much too fond of teasing her; while my cynical views and bourgeois misdeeds earned me many solemn scoldings. Could I not understand that by tipping a friendly guard who had helped me carry my luggage off a train, I had offended against his proletarian dignity? And why should *I* have felt entitled to disobey war-time restrictions by purchasing several pairs of inexpensive cotton pants – garments that I badly needed – from a dealer on the Black Market? Her seriousness accentuated my frivolity. Only after dark did we reach a complete accord; but fresh differences arose next day. A side of my character now emerged that grew more and more discreditable; I could not resist parading the weaknesses – snobbery, vanity, opportunism, greed – of which I knew I was suspected; and, oddly enough, having weathered so many storms, I found that I was beginning almost to regret my previous anxieties and tribulations. We parted sadly, though without a quarrel; and I was delighted, and not surprised, to learn that she had married soon afterwards. Our last encounter was in the London Library, where, besides ordering a book, she was trying to control the gyrations of two happy, noisy children.

Apart from Cyril, Clio met few of my friends; my existence during early middle age was divided into three sections which very rarely overlapped; my emotional interests, which had little effect on my work, though they wasted a good deal of time that I should have spent in writing; my professional life; and the various social amusements that good-natured hosts provided. I have already described my friendship with Emerald Cunard; and my link with Ann Rothermere, married to my employer since 1945, now brought me more and more enjoyment. She possessed both the gift of intimacy and a genius for entertaining; and even the darkest and gloomiest days of the War had not prevented her from giving parties. Usually they were held in a good cause, as when she organized a series of hospitable confrontations, gaily entitled 'Quiz the British', between our American allies and any native writers or politicians she could persuade to answer questions. The dialogues these odd encounters provoked were sometimes less conclusive than perhaps they should have been; but they were preceded by a large dinner and usually followed by a dance that lasted far into the night. The scene was often a theatre or a cinema; and the stage, once dancing had begun, displayed some curiously assorted couples. I remember Ann herself waltzing in the arms of that austere economist Lord Beveridge, author of the famous 'Beveridge Report' and main architect of the modern Welfare State.

With the support of the *Daily Mail*, in July, 1945, Ann also arranged a gigantic evening party, at which the results of the post-war General Election were to be heard and duly honoured. Churchill, the victorious war-leader, must undoubtedly emerge triumphant; and the *Daily Mail* had provided enough champagne to celebrate the Second Coming. It was needed, though not for the proper purpose; while results flashed on to the lighted screen, and one after another Tory strongholds fell, faces lengthened, jubilant voices sank, and the mood of a primitive wake submerged the atmosphere of carnival. Through the crowd stalked Lord Dudley, Ann's hot-tempered brother-in-law, furiously prophesying revolution; our host observed that now we were 'all finished'; and, with solemn tread, the grave Sir John Anderson, former Governor of Bengal and future viscount, strode silently towards the door, followed by his small devoted wife, who kept murmuring 'What *will* Johnny say? I can't *bear* to think what Johnny's going to say!' as she pattered just behind. Almost the only cheerful face I could see was that of Gavin Faringdon, the Labour Party's richest peer, who announced, wherever he could find listeners, that, under the new government, he expected to succeed Duff Cooper

– and how much fun we should all of us have!– at the British Embassy in Paris.

Ann's war-time refuge, like Emerald Cunard's, was the Dorchester Hotel. Warwick House, the Rothermeres' London home, near St. James's Palace, overlooking the Green Park, was not finally reopened until the autumn months of 1946; but during the previous year they had taken a country house close to Bognor Regis and the English Channel. Its name was Bailiffscourt; and it had been built by a fanciful member of a plutocratic brewing family. Lady M. adored the Middle Ages; and, although Bailiffscourt itself was a comparatively modern building, the walls were constructed of ancient stonework pulled from ruined cottages and barns. Light filtered into the raftered drawing-room and the dining-room, with its massive refectory table, through medieval arrow-slits; and, at their meals, her guests ate off pewter dishes and made use of archaic two-pronged forks. Nor did garden flowers ever decorate the rooms; Lady M.'s veteran parlour-maids – none was less than six feet tall – were trained to gather herbs and weeds; and gaunt bouquets of thistles and Old Man's Beard stood sentinel-wise here and there. At Bailiffscourt I passed the Christmas of 1945 – one of the most cheerful I can recollect. On Boxing Day festivities reached a climax, when two elegant young married sisters, whose husbands had gone off to bed, performed corybantic *pas seuls,* clad only in necklaces and grass skirts; while their septuagenarian father rode his grandchild's 'fairy-cycle' round and round the Knole sofas.

4

Our contracted war-time world was now gradually expanding; one could begin to think of foreign travel; and early in 1946 I was invited by Lady Diana Cooper (whom I had met before the War, but with whom my friendship had developed under Emerald Cunard's benignly catalytic influence) to spend a few days at the Paris Embassy. It was a delightful prospect, the only shadow being the discovery that Evelyn Waugh would arrive about the same moment. Since we had both left Oxford, though there had been a brief period when we had revived our former good relations, and had even contemplated sharing a London flat, our careers and interests had diverged. After the triumphant success of *Decline and Fall* and the breakdown of his first marriage, Evelyn had launched, writes the editor of his unfortunate *Diaries*[1], into 'new and fashionable circles'. He had adopted a fresh *persona;* the rampageous Oxford bohemian had become a self-elected representative of the British upper classes; and I remember the odd impression he once made on me as I saw him walking up St. James's Street, wearing a particularly glorious top hat, a small orchid in his button-hole.

During the War, when he joined the Royal Marines, and, with Robert Laycock's help, was afterwards transferred to Combined Operations, this novel image slowly hardened; and the truculent military man was added to his former row of masks. Naturally, he despised civilians; and from that point our meetings were seldom friendly, and very often grimly hostile. 'Evelyn Waugh appeared, pink, prosperous, aggressive', records my diary on January 8th, 1943; and, on the 27th: 'Drink with Dick [Wyndham] at White's. Evelyn in bar, giving a good imitation of military tough'. His welcome was characteristic: 'I always seem to be meeting *you* nowadays in the most unexpected places'; clearly his own club (to which he had belonged since 1941) was no place for a vague civilian

[1] *The Diaries of Evelyn Waugh,* edited by Michael Davie, 1976

outsider. He looked sternly contemptuous; but then, behind all the different rôles that Evelyn assumed there lurked a touch of self-parody; and he was often surprised, I think, and perhaps a little hurt, should the mask through which he had chosen to survey the world be taken at its face-value. The real face and the formidable mask, however, were not easily distinguished. He had a merciless sense of fun; and around those he had elected to dislike he built up strange, repellent fantasies. Nor did he spare his intimates. Though genuinely fond of Cyril Connolly, and well aware of Cyril's gifts, Evelyn found that his proud yet vulnerable character made him an irresistibly attractive target; and, while Cyril and I lodged under the same roof, we received equally opprobrious handling. We were supposed to co-exist with our sluttish concubines in a state of bohemian filth and squalor.

Having sighted me, for example, at a London restaurant and heard me say that we were quitting Bedford Square − I had omitted to explain that our tenancy had run out− he fired off a sudden query. 'For what reason?' he enquired. 'Financial? Sexual?' 'Neither, Evelyn', I replied. 'Oh, then, for *sanitary* reasons, I suppose'; and, brusquely waving me aside, he turned his attention to a plate of oysters. Such conversational kicks-in-the-stomach left his victim half-bewildered; and, because they were both unexpected and completely unprovoked, one could think of no riposte. But, if he were really astonished and disturbed, his method of assault was a good deal less effective; and, as I was preparing to start for Paris and happened to see him, on this occasion in a book-shop, we had a somewhat more evenly matched encounter. I said that I believed we should soon be meeting again. 'Where?' he demanded. 'In Paris, with Duff and Diana'. At this news, he registered a profound shock; his eyes goggled and his features bulged. 'Who introduced *you* to the Coopers?' he cried. I told him, and promptly repeated the question. 'Hazel Lavery'[2], he barked back, and stumped away into the street.

I was not surprised, therefore, when I opened Evelyn's diaries, and examined the passages that cover the early days of April 1946, to read a harsh report upon my conduct. 'Quennell arrived . . . and did badly'; by having sent a telegram, announcing my arrival, that included the words, 'Afraid Evelyn will not like it'; then, by wondering aloud 'if anyone ever reads Browning nowadays', at which the Ambassador had 'swelled, purpled' and recited several pages from

2   Beautiful widow of the well-known portrait-painter, Sir John Lavery.

Sordello; finally, by a random reference to a young woman I knew that, if Evelyn's reporting is accurate, was certainly unchivalrous. I am relieved by the thought that, as a diarist, he frequently distorted facts; for I notice that, the following Sunday night, I am said to have had 'palpitations of the heart brought on by sexual excess'. This malaise, I distinctly recollect, was due, not to the priapic exercises that Evelyn's imagination represented, but to sitting up till midnight, talking and drinking *fines-à-l'eau* at a café off the Champs Elysées.

Only the arrival of a scientific visitor did something to redeem my credit — 'an entirely bloody Professor Huxley[3] who put Quennell in the shade'. Meanwhile, I so much appreciated Paris, and the company of my host and hostess and their friends, that Evelyn's splenetic presence left me almost unaffected. I had had a difficult journey from London; at the Gare de l'Est there was not a taxi to be found; and I was obliged to walk across the city accompanied by an amiable porter carrying my luggage. Compared with London's dirty and ruinous townscape, the streets of Paris looked wonderfully intact and clean; and the British Embassy, when at last we reached it, in the rue du Faubourg St. Honoré, a fine eighteenth-century house *'entre cour et jardin',* had a splendidly pacific and patrician air. The Embassy has often been described. Its noblest feature, I suppose, is the succession of state apartments that occupy the first floor, the *salon jaune,* the *salon blanc et or,* the *salon vert* and, beyond them, the ceremonial bedroom that concludes the range. Their decorations are an engaging blend of Louis XV and Empire styles; but it is Empire that predominates; and winged sphinxes, gilded griffins and sharply-breasted caryatids uphold almost every chair or table.

For this period of French taste I have always had a deep affection; it was the product of a brief and brutal, yet vividly exuberant age —

> the time of the golden eagles, of high-flying plumes, of Greek coiffures, of glory, of great drum-majors . . . of official immortality (conferred by the *Moniteur*) of coffee prepared from chicory, of bad sugar manufactured from beet-root, and of princes and dukes made from nothing at all. But it had its charm . . . Talma declaimed, Gros painted, Bigottini danced, Grassini sang, Maury preached . . . the Emperor read Ossian; Pauline Borghese let herself be moulded as Venus, and quite naked too, for the room was well warmed . . .[4]

[3] Sir Julian Huxley, brother of the novelist.

[4] Heinrich Heine: *Florentine Nights, 1835*

The last words are said to have been Princess Borghese's response, when asked if she had not felt a little embarrassed on appearing naked in Canova's presence; and it was she who, soon after leaving the West Indies and becoming an Imperial Highness, had purchased the present Embassy, then the Hôtel de Charost, for 400,000 francs from the duc de Charost's heirs, but had sold it to the British government, for exactly twice that sum, during the year that followed her brother's defeat at Leipzig. The sale included much of her furniture, among other magnificent pieces the gigantic looking-glass, a present from the Emperor himself, decorated with Napoleonic bees, and the extraordinary *lit de parade*, where she received her courtiers and guests, flanked by reclining leopards and Egyptian caryatids, while overhead, surmounting the sweep of the curtains, an imperial eagle spreads its wings.

At night, the Princess retired to a small bed, draped with modest pink-lined muslin. In 1946, however, the new British Ambassadress preferred to sleep beneath the conqueror's eagle – a happy decision; for her morning receptions thus acquired the elegance of a royal *grand lever*, though she added a touch of gaiety and informality that seemed peculiarly her own. The room was apt to be crowded; her guests and members of the Embassy staff were perpetually arriving and departing; like Milton's Vallombrosan leaves, innumerable letters and papers lay scattered thickly all around; and the Ambassadress continued to distribute her attention between some half-a-dozen subjects, from a book she had enjoyed or a tour she recommended to an odd question of diplomatic protocol or the details of that evening's dinner. Clothes, too, were often brought out and inspected; but for the moment she wore the simplest of dressing-gowns and a net cap that tightly enclosed her features, fastened just below the chin. At the same time, a maid was preparing the tented alcove that had replaced the much simpler bathroom where Pauline Borghese had once washed in milk; and, having tapped on a hidden door, a minute yellow-skinned personage would silently slip across the carpet and, introducing himself as *'Pédicure Chang'*, move reverentially towards the bottom of the bed.

Napoleon's sister was not the only distinguished woman I remembered at the Embassy. Lady Granville, younger daughter of Georgiana Duchess of Devonshire and one of the most brilliant English female letter-writers, became Ambassadress in November 1824, and lived there altogether sixteen years. She is a marvellous subject for literary inquisition and, as a girl, often recalls the heroine of Henry James' tale *What Maisie Knew*. How much did Harriet Cavendish understand about the circumstances of her childhood, when her family at Devonshire House, besides the wayward mother she adored, her sluggish self-centred father, her beloved sister and Hart, her deaf delightful brother, included her father's fascinating mistress Lady Elizabeth Foster (whom Harriet detested and despised, though she was Georgiana's greatest friend) and Caroline St. Jules and Augustus Clifford, Lady Elizabeth's children by the Duke? Other illegitimate children lived on the fringe of the circle. Among her legitimate relations were her cousin Caroline Ponsonby and Lady Bessborough, her aunt; and, before she had grown up, she seems to have accepted the fact that Lady Bessborough had a long-standing liaison[5] with a handsome young man, Lord Granville Leveson-Gower[6]; and that Granville's honourable attentions to herself caused her aunt atrocious jealousy.

Yet somehow, with a blend of Christian fortitude and instinctive *savoir vivre*, she quietly threaded her way through all these problems, never losing either her worldly composure, even after her mother's death and her father's remarriage to the detested 'Lady Liz', or her own essential innocence. Harriet Cavendish was a plain girl; Granville Leveson-Gower, an extraordinarily good-looking man. But he knew from his early successes that beautiful girls are apt to make unruly wives; and, having married Harriet in 1809, he earned himself nearly forty years of happiness. I doubt if Lady Granville's admirable letters are very often read today. Yet they are as vivid and acute as those of Jane Carlyle (whom, given their difference social setting and very different married lives, she sometimes curiously resembles) and have the same neat epigrammatic turn, the same gift of fixing a scene or dashing off a portrait-sketch; whether she pays an obituary tribute to the charms of her brother's favourite Italian greyhound — 'I recollect all her ways, the sleepy affected *grande dame* manner' — describes an otherwise unknown Miss Crofton 'stepping about like a peahen', or discusses her relationship with two fashionable English guests who have just passed through the Embassy, and who esteemed her as much, she conjectured, 'as they can the person in the whole world who suits them least . . . I am sure we feel at moments equal remorse at finding our affection towards each other so cold and dead in the

[5] It had produced two children, christened George and Harriet Stewart, whom, after her marriage, Lady Granville affectionately accepted as her 'step-children'.

[6] A younger son of the Marquess of Stafford, he was raised to the peerage in 1815.

midst of so many efforts and acts of kindness. I would risk my life for them rather than spend a week with them . . .'

Although she had been brought up at Devonshire House, Chiswick and Chatsworth, and came straight to Paris from the Embassy at the Hague (after the Paris Embassy, the most beautiful in Europe) Harriet was duly impressed by her new home – 'a luxurious house, a delicious little garden . . . we have a *luxe* of rooms, all looking to the garden with the bright sun of L'Eté de St. Martin shining upon them . . .' Of the French themselves, however, she was less appreciative; they were 'pedantic and frivolous' she had decided, and showed an 'outrée consideration of rank . . . Now for a few of *les phrases d'usage,* which from their tone and manner give me a wish to hurl the cushions of their couches at their *crêpé* heads: *'Vous aimez Paris?' 'Vous-vous plaisez parmi nous',* neither as doubt or question. *'Lady une telle est bien: on ne la soupçonnera pas d'être une Anglaise'''.*

Revisiting the past through the present is an endless source of pleasure; for once I preferred intelligence to beauty; and it was the plain Cavendish, rather than the lovely Bonaparte, whom I should have liked to meet in the *salon blanc et or.* Harriet Granville and Diana Cooper would undoubtedly have made friends; they were similarly generous and similarly shrewd; and both were affectionate but prone to laughter. Both enjoyed the comic side of their ambassadorial functions. Soon after I arrived Diana informed me that she was organizing a 'poets' party', and that I, as the only poet in residence – a title I instantly denied – must preside over the gathering. I dreaded the occasion, until Stephen Spender, wearing a war-correspondent's battle-dress a little too small for him, from which his lengthy bird-like neck and long dangling schoolboy wrists protruded, suddenly arrived on an official visit. I knew then that I need feel no alarm; Stephen was both a master of 'public relations' and a genuine modern poet; and, while I retired to a comfortable sofa beside a pleasant Franco-Scottish lady, with a ready smile and an air of disarming gaucherie he darted to and fro about the room, greeting a succession of *chers collègues,* dropping the right word here and there, and generally promoting the atmosphere of intellectual good-fellowship that such difficult occasions need.

At the Embassy, in addition to poets, Diana received novelists and painters – headed by the genial opium-addict Christian Bérard – and the composer Georges Auric, as well as a host of English friends, some distinguished, some relatively obscure. The Coopers' liberal-minded choice of company did not always please the faction-ridden French, either contentious and ambitious politicians or representatives of the so-called *gratin*, the aristocratic inhabitants of the Faubourg Saint-Germain, whose *'outrée'* regard for rank, whatever they might pretend, had scarcely changed since Lady Granville's day. Among guests the French found most disturbing was a renowned Parisian *femme de lettres*. Louise de Vilmorin, poetess, story-teller, wit, had made the Embassy her second home, where she was admired and spoiled by her indulgent host and hostess, and by nearly every member of their household. Seen through their eyes, she possessed extraordinary charm; but it was a charm I never felt myself. Like Louise de la Vallière slightly lame, she had a hesitant yet rapid step, a sharp, intense profile and a shock of russet hair, on which, midway between crown and nape, perched a small black velvet bow. Her voice was husky; and, from the moment she entered a room, she very seldom drew breath.

Rather than lack an audience, she would hasten to provide some explosive indiscretion; and it was these fireworks that very often astonished her compatriots if they sat beside her at the Coopers' table. When War broke out, Louise had still been married to the Hungarian landowner Count Palfy; and, during that period, willingly or unwillingly, she had entertained Field Marshal Goering – an aspect of her past that, given the circumstances, no one wished to underline. Louise had decided otherwise; she kept a faithful pug called Bijou; and Bijou had the puggish habit of loudly snuffling and snoring. At luncheon Louise would reprove her favourite in her peculiar penetrating tones: *'Il ne faut pas renifler, Bijou! Le maréchal Goering a toujours reniflé comme ça. Tu sais, ce n'est pas gentil'* – an admonition that reverberated around the room and produced a sudden silence.

Just as annoying, though less embarassing, were the little tales she improvised. On the way to a dinner-party on the Left Bank in a huge ambassadorial motor-car, the Coopers begged her to tell us her famous story concerning the man and the giraffe. She quickly obliged: *'Il y avait un homme qui avait douze enfants; et ces enfants n'avaient jamais vu un girafe . . .'* This dreadfully whimsical piece of fantasy, having reached some unexpected climax, was received with loud applause; and she was asked to tell the tale again. *'Il y avait un homme'*, she began, *'qui possédait douze girafes qui n'avaient jamais vu un enfant . . .'*

I have a streak of physical clumsiness that fear, annoyance or embarassment very often brings out; and on that occasion, after I had listened for the second time to Louise's fairy-tale, it reappeared in full force. As we finally reached our destination, I rose from the *strapontin* I occupied and, forgetting that the story-teller was seated just behind me, allowed it to fall and catch her lame foot. She uttered a shrill scream and sank into a semi-swoon, while Duff and Diana, with indignant glances at me, did their best to lend her comfort. I offered earnest apologies; and, once Louise had been carried across the threshold and proved still capable of walking, she generously accepted them. We remained friendly acquaintances; and, several years later, she was kind enough to hint that I, too, found her irresistible. During a snow-storm I was battling through the blizzard as I left a London house, and passed her hastening in the opposite direction. We exchanged a couple of words; but, having entered the house, she delivered a vivid account of how, when she dismounted from her taxi, she had seen me waiting on the pavement, doggedly expecting her. I was thick with snow, she said, a snow-drift wreathed around my hat. *'On dirait le Père Noël!'* It was delightful to see a stolid Englishman displaying such romantic ardour.

I stayed in Paris from the 2nd until the 15th of April, and delivered a lecture — the ostensible excuse for my visit — to some kind of learned society on the literary relationship between France and England. The first Sunday we lunched at Chantilly, at the Château de Saint Firmin, the beautiful little house, belonging to the Institut de France, that the Academicians had lent to the British Ambassador as his country refuge. There could have been no better place for a diplomatist who was also the biographer of Talleyrand and a passionate devotee of literature. Saint Firmin and its immediate surroundings form the perfect late-eighteenth-century or early-nineteenth-century romantic landscape, with a weeping willow, the view of a distant cascade and, beyond it, a broad lake, large enough to be impressive, yet not so large as to have the melancholy, foreboding air that sometimes hangs about huge sheets of water. Across the lake rises the Château de Chantilly, built by Mansard for the Great Condé, but destroyed during the Revolution and rebuilt in pseudo-Renaissance taste by the descendant of the last of the Condés, the duc d'Aumale, son of Louis-Philippe. Only Mansard's magnificent stables remain. But the immense park recalls the last tranquil, dignified years of the Great Condé's prodigiously active life,[7] when he strolled beside his friends,

[7] Louis de Bourbon, prince de Condé (1621-1686); not only during the Fronde did he fight on both sides; but he distinguished himself both as a French commander against Spain and with the Spanish armies against France. His last descendant, the young duc d'Enghien, judicially murdered by Napoleon, had been born at Chantilly.

among them some of the noblest writers of his day, *'dans ces superbes allées, au bruit de tant de jets d'eau, qui ne se taisait ni jour ni nuit'*. Though he had left the battlefield and renounced the excitement of conquest and civil war, *'c'était toujours le même homme, et sa gloire le suivait partout*[8].*'

The idea of glory counts for more in France than it has ever done in England; and Chateaubriand, who had himself a romantic link with Chantilly, was its noblest literary exponent, and pursued it through all the vicissitudes of a long, adventurous career, as explorer, writer, minister, ambassador and indefatigable lover of women. Soon after editing Madame de Lieven's letters, I was allowed to open a big old-fashioned trunk that contained her personal and domestic archives — they included hourly accounts of Princess Charlotte's accouchement and death, secretly despatched by one of the royal physicians — and found there a small visiting card, *Vicomte de Chateaubriand*, beneath a tumbled mass of papers. How Madame de Lieven, I recollected, had disliked the newly appointed French ambassador, his airs and affectations, his moods and vagaries; and what spiteful fun she made of him! He had been preceded by a wave of publicity:

> The attachés (she writes early in April 1822) have taken it into their heads to advertise him as a romantic hero; and, yesterday, at a big dipolomatic dinner, M. de Marcellus told us that one duchess had died of love for him, that another had gone off her head, and a third had fractured her thigh. The whole table burst out laughing. The speaker was filled with righteous indignation that anyone could laugh about a thigh fractured in honour of the author of *Les Martyrs*. However, he tried to wipe out the accident by assuring us that his heart is of ice[9].

Later, he annoyed the sharp-witted Russian Ambassadress by declaring that he infinitely preferred stupid to pretentious clever women; and she informed Metternich that he spent his evenings at the Embassy with a singularly stupid favourite[10], talking for 'hours on end about glory, enthusiasm and, I fancy, also about virtue'. Chateaubriand's intense self-absorption, like Victor Hugo's, has a distinctly comic side. *'Tous les hommes d'esprit'*, observed his close

[8] Bossuet: *Louis de Bourbon: Oraisons Funèbres*.

[9] From *the Private Letters of Princess Lieven to Prince Metternich, 1820-1826*, edited by Peter Quennell, 1937.

[10] Madame Lafon, wife of the well-known tragedian.

friend and rival in love, the subtle aphorist Joseph Joubert, *'valent mieux que leurs livres. Les hommes de génie valent moins . . .'* But, if Chateaubriand as a man was often less imposing than his books, his genius enabled him to weave the records of his life into a vast symphonic composition, the posthumous *Mémoires d'outre tombe,* which he finished in May 1839, and used to read aloud, as the majestic work proceeded, to Juliette Récamier, his 'guardian angel', every afternoon when he visited her little drawing room above the garden of l'Abbaye-aux-Bois.

Chateaubriand's passion for Madame Récamier had begun in 1800 at the apartment of Germaine de Staël. The great woman had just left her bed; and, while her maid attended her and she played with the fresh green myrtle-sprig that she almost always carried, she poured out her customary flood of eloquence. Then Juliette entered, wearing a white silk dress, and disposed herself upon a blue silk sofa. Madame de Staël continued her discourse. *'Je répondais à peine . . . Je me demandais si je voyais un portrait de la candeur ou de la volupté. Je n'avais jamais inventé rien de pareil . . .'* Yet he was not to enjoy that vision again for another twelve years; and the virginal beauty, whose elderly husband had played the part of a devoted parent, and who had repulsed so many suitors, did not finally become Chateaubriand's mistress until October 1818. Thus we return to the Forest of Chantilly; for it was there she sacrificed her virtue; and I have often wondered, as I walked around the Forest, on which knoll, or under which miniature temple, one faintly misted autumn evening, that memorable consummation was at last achieved. The innocent odalisque, so deeply yet so gently voluptuous, whom François Gerard had painted thirteen years earlier, was now a middle-aged woman, near her forty-second birthday; but she still preserved much of the youthful grace of the bare-footed *sans-chemise.* Chateaubriand was neither young nor handsome; fifty years old, short and pock-marked, he had awkwardly hunched shoulders that gave him the appearance, said Madame Lieven, of a hunch-back without a hump, *'d'un bossu sans bosse'.* Yet it was a marriage of bodies and souls alike, despite the numerous transitory escapades in which the lover could not help indulging. Chateaubriand had sought to transform his life into a balanced work of art; and Juliette, too, his biographer reminds us, had always cultivated her own idealised image, a harmonious blend of beauty and purity and unassailable tranquillity. Perfectionist recognised perfectionist, and narcissist met narcissist.

Although I remember walking one hard bright winter day across the crystalline landscape of the frozen park as far as Mansard's lofty baroque stables, where braziers had been lit, and a graceful young woman in a tricorne was putting her no less graceful mount through the complex paces of the haute école, I associate Saint Firmin and the forest beyond its garden chiefly with the summer months. A warm afternoon beside the lake, for example, remains particularly vivid. On the way from Paris, Duff Cooper had been quoting the French sixteenth-century poets. We finished an excellent luncheon and, having left the house, spread out sleepily along the terrace; but Duff sat down cross-legged beneath the shadow of a clipped tree, produced book and pen and a single sheet of paper, and at once began to work. He wore a smart grey suit, a carnation in his button-hole and a pair of diminutive black-and-white shoes— he had unusually small feet; and, sitting there, he reminded me of a porcelain pagoda designed for an eighteenth-century chimney-piece, a little flushed, it is true, yet wonderfully trim and compact, while, very seldom pausing to make a correction, he rapidly filled up the page. He was translating a sonnet by Joachim du Bellay; and the completed version he read aloud to his guests — it had taken him about three quarters of an hour — was both scholarly and musical. I doubt if, that afternoon, anywhere else in the world, a British ambassador had been more creditably employed.

Duff Cooper belonged to a period of diplomatic history that passed soon after his retirement. In 1947 the Foreign Secretary Ernest Bevin (who had developed a keen personal affection for the Ambassadress) reluctantly replaced him. Duff's proper background would have been the Palmerstonian age or perhaps the Congress of Vienna, at which he would have waltzed among the best, and paid enthusiastic court to the beauties there assembled. He was a devoted lover of women; and women's friendship, he once told me, had provided the greatest joys of his existence. He had a sanguine nature; and doubt, anxiety and self-mistrust seemed entirely foreign to his disposition. As a host, his only drawback were his sudden violent bursts or rage. These tantrums his family called 'veiners', since, while they lasted, the veins on his brow would swell and his face grow darkly purple. Though I was luckier than some of his friends, I still remember an occasion when I received a fierce Johnsonian reprimand. I had said — harmlessly enough, I thought— that Dickens could not be compared with Balzac. But I had had no intention of denigrating either genius; my sole point was how much they differed. I have forgotten which of them Duff championed. He charged, however, to his favourite novelist's defence; and, before the storm had gradually blown itself out, or my hostess had extended a protective wing, I had been severely 'tossed and gored'.

I returned to Paris the following July; and, in my engagement-book, against Saturday the 19th, I find the pencilled word 'Groussaye', the name of a country house near Paris. One of my fellow guests, Diane Abdy, whom I had often met through Emerald, suggested that I should accompany her to that extraordinary house, the residence of Charles de Beistegui, a millionaire expatriate, Mexican by birth but cosmopolitan by education. During the War, he had remained in Paris, where he held a minor diplomatic post and, thanks to his official privileges, he had been able to protect and provision many distinguished members of his circle. He was an immensely rich man; and about the origins of his fortune curious stories were related. I have heard it said, for example — the story comes, I must admit, from a somewhat imaginative rancounteur — that his grandfather had performed a useful, if slightly undignified task in a Mexican provincial city. There, at the *paseo,* as aristocratic carriages rolled round and round the main square, and their occupants exchanged bows, a strange-looking personage, wearing a big parti-coloured cloak, glided to and fro amid the carriage-wheels and, should a lady beckon, would swiftly open the door and slip the silver pot that his cloak concealed underneath her crinoline, then remove the vessel and spirit it away again with the same unobtrusive sleight of hand.

A popular figure, he had managed to pick up lucrative financial tips, and had founded the fortune that his clever children had enlarged. Very soon they crossed the Atlantic; and Charles de Beistegui was sent to Eton. But he was no ordinary Etonian. A boy of his age, his father considered, undoubtedly required a mistress; and a suitable hetaira was installed nearby. English acquaintances remember meeting him, while they themselves were walking along the High Street to visit a book-shop or consume strawberries-and-cream, trudging off to do his duty— a prospect that, so far as they could make out, gave him very little pleasure.

Before the War he had built a fantastic apartment in Paris, of which the upper floor was unroofed, with windows, chimneypiece, marble furniture and a living carpet made of grass and daisies. That I never saw; but at the Château de Groussaye I passed a memorable weekend. The house itself was a plain Empire building; but it had been extensively altered and embellished, and the whole of one wing completely gutted to enclose a towering library. Twisted mahogany stairs, as in some Baroque fantasia, climbed the walls from stage to stage. Resplendent bindings glimmered on every shelf; and on the lower shelves I admired fine editions of the best-known classic French authors. As I ascended, however, the quality of books declined; and, reaching the fourth gallery, I found that it carried numerous volumes of the British *Annual Register,* which provided a long attractive strip of red.

Elsewhere, in the lengthy series of rooms that ran towards the dining-room, Beistegui had hung peacock-bright silks, specially woven for him at Lyons by a firm whom Marie-Antionette had once employed. The effect was oddly dazzling. In our imaginary pictures of the eighteenth-century we are apt to envisage faded hues — wall-coverings that long ago lost their radiance and Aubusson carpets that the sun has bleached. Here the décor was brilliantly, even loudly gay. Beistegui had always an adventurous taste; and, besides his affection for the eighteenth-century, he had a passion for Victoriana; though his drawing-rooms reflected the mood of Versailles, his bedrooms imitated Balmoral with tartan table-cloths and rugs, ink-wells in the guise of ram's-horns and archaic wash-stands, where morning and evening a folded linen towel was laid across a marbled metal can. Naturally, he employed a host of servants; and, on Sunday, as soon as he returned from Mass, whither he drove in a yellow-wheeled barouche, a regiment of liveried footmen invaded the lawn, carrying trays that bore little glasses of vodka and supplementary hors d'oeuvres. Like old-fashioned English footmen, they appeared to have been chosen for their size; and they had very high, rigidly starched collars that upheld their sweating chins.

Later, I visited Beistegui at the Palazzo Labia on the Grand Canal, home of the superbly imaginative frescoes in which Tiepolo depicted the meeting of Antony and Cleopatra. Having scaled a monumental staircase through a double file of gondoliers, we entered a smallish room and gathered round the circumference of a vast Renaissance table, entirely covered with a star-shaped array of English and American magazines, to await the Begum Aga Khan, who kept us standing more than half an hour, but at length arrived, a jewelled wax-doll, all smiles and charm and regal grace. We were then free to dine and, after we dined, examine the Venetian painter's masterpieces. What a contrast between the artist's grandiose vision and its present social setting! Tiepolo's hero and heroine have an air of exalted dignity. They are evidently engaged in a ceremonious, almost a religious rite, while musicians strum on the balcony above their heads and a dwarf postures on the steps below. Beside their feast the modern banquet seemed a sadly trivial affair; and it was difficult to imagine the Begum Aga Khan dropping an orient pearl into a glass of champagne.

That was the last time I saw Charles de Beistegui; but afterwards I heard that he had built a miniature private theatre in the gardens of his country house, and that, later still, once he had lost health, he became a restive malcontent, wandering to and fro across Europe, inspecting other people's houses and gardens, which he compared unfavourably with his own, and grumbling bitterly at the welcome he received and the miserable food and beds that he was offered. Groussaye I never wished to revisit; though he had exquisite taste and employed the finest craftsmen, there was something unsympathetic, even slightly unnerving about Beistegui's artificial paradise; and I felt happier, when I returned to Paris, in a more bohemian world. Here my cicerone was often Georges Duthuit, a critic who exercised his talents on both sides of the English Channel and, before the War, had given me my earliest introduction to the Parisian *vie de bohème*.

Saint-Germain-des-Prés and the Boulevard Saint-Germain were already favourite resorts of mine; and I had frequently sat at the *Café des Deux Magots,* hoping I should recognise some famous artist, but had so far always failed. Then I was taken by Georges and Marguerite Duthuit to the studio of the much-admired Rumanian sculptor Constantin Brancusi. Today his reputation has suffered a decline. Giacometti, for example, announced that, while he himself 'cut fat from space', Brancusi only 'made objects'; and the stern art-historian Douglas Cooper, according to the author of a recent study[11], had dismissed the sculptures he produced as 'hollow decorative artifacts' — an opinion in which the English expert appears to have concurred with the New York Customs Office, who had decided that one of Brancusi's large bronze birds was 'an object of manufacture' rather than a work of art.

At that period, however, the artist and his products equally delighted me. Between fifty and sixty years old, he was shortish, muscular and broad-built, his long beard heavily grey-streaked and his thick hair darkly grizzled. His studio, spacious and well-swept, resembled a magician's cave. Here was none of the squalid confusion that surrounds so many artists; but his works were stationed against

[11] *Brancusi* by Sidney Geist, 1968

the walls like a band of magic servitors, ready to take off, as soon as he uttered the word, on any errand he demanded. Everything gleamed or shone. Brancusi detested shadows, and the crevices where shadows lie; he favoured a smooth and highly polished surface; and among his 'Birds in Flight', reduced to a needle-sharp form, and his bronze and marble fishes – it was not a fish, he said, that he had attempted to capture, but a spark of the essential piscine spirit – were ranged a multitude of stony eggs, from which a woman's head, the pensive face bent a little to the side, seemed to be gradually developing. He was a generous host, and loved alcohol; his taste for wine, his biographer tells us, eventually became excessive; and he smoked so many cigarettes that, towards the close of his life, nicotine-poisoning set in. He also adored music, and had invented a gramophone of a remarkably original type. It possessed two separate tables; one played a record from the beginning to the end, the other the same disc from the end to the beginning. The result was an extraordinary chaos of sounds; but it excited and inspired Brancusi; and he broke into a vigorous dance, as David danced before the Ark or, in the Romanesque church at Souillac, Isaiah treads his solitary measure, pointing to an unfurled scroll that prophesies the Virgin Birth, and allowing the wind to rush through the skirts of his robe and comb out the tendrils of his beard.

The sculptor dancing amid his works had a similarly prophetic air. Meanwhile, Georges, a large handsome man with the chest of a Percheron horse, who could seldom resist an invitation to take the floor or, indeed, any kind of social gaiety, soon sprang up and joined the artist. I think I followed them – I had drunk a good deal of Pernod, for which I suffered next day; but Marguerite, Georges' wife, remained patiently upon a sofa, now and then protesting, in her gentle whispering voice, that it was really time to go home. Her pleas were disregarded; Georges had a vigorous, dominant character, and liked to live at a dramatic pace, travelling, courting women, composing articles and reviews, and plunging headlong into the explosive controversies that he waged with other critics, particularly with André Malraux, de Gaulle's Minister for Cultural Affairs and, in that rôle, Georges' dearest foe. Through him I learned something of the frenetic savagery that pervades French intellectual life. Our avant-garde British art-critics, like Roger Fry or Clive Bell, might call their adversaries crude and vulgar; Georges announced that they were totally obscene, and suited his vocabulary to his views. Thus, asked his opinion of the fashionable painter Pavel Tchelitchew, he said that the Russian's colour-schemes recalled 'pus oozing from an ulcer', a comparison that in modern art-criticism I had never heard employed before.

If he scarified artists of the present age, he was not inclined to spare the past. In his earlier years he had sat at the feet of an American named Pritchard, the çi-devant curator of a provincial museum, from which he had thrown out every work of art except a few Byzantine coins and statues, and who, since he had moved to London, would perambulate our national collections heading a little band of eager students, and loudly assuring them that some reputed masterpiece, say a Bellini or a Mantegna, 'could have been done by any boot-boy!' Georges had inherited Pritchard's passion for the Byzantine achievement; and his critical standards were no less strict. But Matisse – Marguerite, incidentally, was the artist's elder daughter – he continued to revere; and even the grand old man's tremendous egotism, the complete self-absorption of creative genius, he would mention half-admiringly. During the War, while Georges was in New York and the artist at his studio in Nice, Marguerite and her step-mother had remained in Paris, and had worked for the Resistance. The Gestapo presently arrested them; it was believed they might be tortured; but Matisse, on hearing the news, uttered an indignant exclamation: 'Those two women', he was said to have complained, 'would do *anything* to stop me working!'

Though I did not necessarily share his critical opinions, Georges' friendship, until the last sad days of his life – suddenly immobilised by a stroke, he was condemned like Heine to a 'mattress-grave' – afforded me unending pleasure. He was one of those Frenchmen who especially charm the English because they so closely resemble the Anglo-Saxon idea of what a Frenchman ought to be – tempestuous, high-spirited, eloquent, irascible, demonstrative. He made many conquests; but his admirers' attempts to please him were not invariably well received. He was easily offended and, if he took offence, was inclined to retaliate with some grandiose and sweeping gesture. Thus, when a rich and fashionable Parisian lady handed him the key of an apartment she had secretly furnished for his benefit, he tossed it out into the courtyard; and, when a more guileless young English woman offered him an expensive set of hair-brushes, which she had hopefully intended as a birthday present for his beloved only son, she saw him hurl them through a taxi window, and watched them go tumbling and skidding away across the greasy tarmac of a London street.

Georges was an author himself, and now and then he would ask me to translate an essay on some Byzantine masterpiece — a difficult commission; his prose-style and the critical approach he adopted were often strikingly oblique. But his chief allegiance was to the visual arts; and most of my glimpses of the Parisian literary world I obtained through other friends. Diane Abdy, for example, took me to visit the house of Paul Valéry, who had died a year earlier, and, somewhat against my will, presented me to Gertrude Stein during the last few months of her existence. I was presented under an assumed name. Not long before I had written a critical review of a perplexing volume she had just published; and both Diane and I thought that, under my own name, I might receive a chilly welcome. So it was as Mr Courtney — my mother's surname — that I was introduced on our arrival. A borrowed name is no less awkward to wear than a hired or borrowed suit; and Miss Stein, I soon noticed, regarded me with slight suspicion. She had a penetrating eye; and, although I detested her peculiar prose style — her 'mental stutter' (to quote Wyndham Lewis' phrase) and her strangulated repetitions — I was impressed by the weight of her personality and by the Hebraic grandeur of her face and movements. Many canvases, usually unframed, had been hung around her walls — Picasso's naked girl carrying a flower-filled basket, and his portrait of a younger Gertrude Stein, already large and square and solid, sitting, her fist against her thigh, like a Biblical prophetess about to deliver judgement. Beside the Picassos, she had some agreeable landscapes, the work of her protégé Sir Francis Rose, a young artist she greatly admired and considered our most distinguished British painter. Choosing me as her scapegoat, she attacked my whole nation for having wantonly neglected him.

Our pilgrimage to Valéry's house, however, has left behind it only rewarding memories. Since I first opened *Charmes*[12] at Oxford — Cyril Connolly, I think, gave me a copy of the book — I had reverenced the poet's genius. His prose-works, I must admit, I could not always penetrate; his early essay on Leonardo da Vinci I found more impressive than informative; and I was not quite sure that I should have had either the patience or the intellectual resolution to sit through an evening with *Monsieur Teste*. But his verse, particularly, of course, *Le Cimetière Marin*, the *Ébauche d'un Serpent* and the *Cantique des Colonnes*, still dazzled and delighted me. Here I recognised the crystalline compression of images I had appreciated in Mallarmé,

[12] The volume appeared in 1922, after more than twenty years' poetic silence.

reinforced by an element he must have owed to his birth – his father had been a Corsican, his mother an Italian – a sensuous lucidity and warmth of feeling that recalled Catullus and Horace and the Roman Elegiac poets. Ideas of life and death, alternating moods of passion and reflection, combine in *Le Cimetière Marin,* derived from his memories of the cemetery at Sète[13], to hold an almost perfect balance. Mediterranean sunshine dances over the tombstones of a graveyard high above the sea, where so much wit and beauty and transient passion lie sunk beneath its flowering grasses:

> *Ils ont fondu dans une absence épaisse,*
> *L'argile rouge a bu la blanche espèce,*
> *Le don de vivre a passé dans les fleurs!*
> *Où sont des morts les phrases familières,*
> *L'art personnel, les âmes singulières?*
> *La larve file où se formaient les pleurs.*
>
> *Les cris aigus des filles chatouillées,*
> *Les yeux, les dents, les paupières mouillées,*
> *Le sein charmant qui joue avec le feu,*
> *Le sang qui brille aux lèvres qui se rendent,*
> *Les derniers dons, les doigts qui les défendent,*
> *Tout va sous terre et rentre dans le jeu!*

Paul Valéry had died in 1945, a discreetly eminent, highly esteemed and carefully protected figure. But Diane Abdy, having met him through Madame de Béhague, the cultivated Jewish lady who employed him as her honorary librarian, had painted a vivid likeness of the poet, straw-hatted with a drooping grey moustache, and reported that, although amiable and worldly-wise, he was not a ready conversationalist. By Diane I was now presented to a member of his family; and – a rare privilege – she arranged we should visit the house that his descendants still shared. A tall, blank house in the quiet rue de Villejust, which Berthe Morisot and her husband, Manet's brother, had built during the 1880s, it was an extraordinary poetic shrine. The furniture itself was commonplace enough, and the dining-room perfectly suited to the needs of a prosperous middle-class French family. Above the large oval mahogany table a glass *suspension* hung from chains; and a multitude of Delft plates, blue and white, had been let into the walls. But elsewhere pictures by the great Impressionists and the charming canvases of Berthe Morisot covered

---

[13] Valéry himself is buried there.

every inch of space; and I was delighted to open the door of an old-fashioned *cabinet de toilette* and see Morisot's picture of a young modiste trimming a hat by golden-greenish artificial light, above a hundrum domestic array of basins, medicine-bottles, brushes, jugs and bathroom sponges.

Later, we were allowed to examine the poet's study, a small, constricted attic room, which overlooked a long row of the familiar metal chimney-points that revolve, with a whirring, whining sound, amid the roofs of nineteenth-century Paris. Valéry, our escort told us, had found more extensive views distracting. Nor, it seemed, had he much use for luxurious accessories. The only pieces of furniture his study contained were a roll-top desk, an office chair, a filing-cabinet and a life-sized bronze representation of his own starkly rendered head and shoulders. The poet, I knew, had led a somewhat social life, and very often dined out. Among Proust's favourite devices, once he has first portrayed a character, is to throw in, at a subsequent stage of the narrative, some unexpected scrap of information that, if it does not change the general effect, slightly modifies its outline; and, from an old French gentleman, bearer of a name that would have appealed to the historically minded novelist, I once heard that, when Valéry dined at his home, he and his contemporaries dreaded the moment immediately after dinner. As well-brought-up youths, they respected the man of genius, to whom they attributed all the austere wisdom of the philosophic Monsieur Teste. Valéry's conversation, however, struck a very different note; for, exclaiming *'Voilà une bonne histoire!'*, he would embark on the recital of an antiquated improper story, while they shifted uneasily, nodded reluctantly and did their best to conceal their embarrassment beneath a civil show of mirth.

5

At this period of my life, some fifteen years had gone by since I last produced a poem; and, although I still respected poetry as the sacred fount of literature from which every other form had sprung, I was now chiefly concerned with prose-writing under all its different guises. For three French novelists – Colette, Gide and Montherlant – I had a particularly deep affection; and each of them I was lucky enough to meet during the later stage of their existence. My brief impressions of Colette and Gide I have already put on record[1] – Colette, half-crippled by arthritis, yet extraordinarily alert and cheerful, who described her visit to London in 1900, London crowds celebrating the relief of Mafeking, and the '*assez aimable petite revîere*' that meandered past the country house at which she and her husband M. Willy stayed; André Gide, a strange, secretive figure, sharp-eyed, bald and beetle-browed, who reminded me of 'an elderly fallen angel travelling incognito'. Montherlant, it is true, I did not encounter until May 19, 1959; but he plays so important a part in my memories of Paris that I propose to tell the story here.

He seldom accorded interviews, and only suggested a meeting because I had recently undertaken the editorship of an English translation of his collected works. Montherlant had long occupied an *entresol* on the Quai Voltaire, exactly opposite the Louvre; and, having reached the door, I remember that I drank a glass of cognac at the bar of the adjacent Café Voltaire preparatory to entering. The stairs were dark; and, when I rang the bell, a middle-aged woman secretary led me through a sombre hall into a lengthy well-lit audience-chamber, a narrow room with a squeaking parquet floor and a high ceiling from which the paint hung down in strips. To left and right a range of planks and trestles supported fragments of Graeco-Roman statuary; and between them I moved towards a window that overlooked the Palace and the Seine. Beside the window stood a couple of Empire

[1]   *The Sign of the Fish*, 1960.

chairs, one slightly bigger than its fellow, and a marble-topped Napoleonic table. Otherwise the room was unfurnished. It included neither books nor pictures, and resembled the store-room of some modest provincial museum, where superfluous exhibits have been temporarily put away.

Then Montherlant made a quiet and rapid appearance — a short, spare man whose fine sharply-moulded features, below grey hair severely cut *en brosse,* were accompanied by large thin bat-wing ears. He was very much the Gallic *gentilhomme* — a type unusual among French men of letters — but had also the reserved and rigid appearance that French caricaturists attribute to the conventional Englishman abroad. His greeting, though perfectly civil, lacked any kind of human warmth; and, having motioned me towards the smaller of the two chairs, he immediately got down to business. Since we each of us understood the other's language, but spoke it with some hesitation, we agreed that I should address him in English, while he answered me in French, our subject being a volume of essays, the first of the series of projected translations, for which I had composed a preface. During the careful discussion we held that morning, at least on his side not a word was wasted. Nor, when he had settled the contents of his book and he had given me his imprimatur, could I divert him into casual talk. Before I bade him goodbye, however, I referred to the marble effigies that lined the room, and praised an almost life-sized nymph or goddess. He admitted that the figure had good qualities; *'mais il me semble',* he added in coolly considering tones, *'qu'elle a le pouce un peu disgracieux;'* and, as I looked, I saw that the gracefully modelled statue had indeed a rather ill-shaped thumb.

Such was our only meeting; but we continued to correspond; and of every book he published I received a presentation copy, with a courteous, even flattering *dedicace* scrawled across the title-page. Until his last days the letters he sent me generally concerned his work; for Montherlant, and, I assume, for many other French writers, *l'oeuvre* was the focal point of his existence; and there was no trouble he would not willingly take, no tiresome letter he would leave unwritten, if he felt that his literary cause required the effort. Thus, despite the fact that we had only once met, he would consult me at fairly regular intervals; and the correspondence I collected year by year runs to close on forty pages, sometimes type-written, sometimes in his own hand, which grew more and more illegible. Problems of translation always engrossed him; and, after an annoying false start, his English translators, John Weightman, who was responsible for the essays alone, and Terence Kilmartin, who handled other volumes, served his text exceptionally well.

Montherlant was delighted by the appreciations of his novels that he read in English papers, and developed a habit of contrasting English reviewers with his spiteful French critics. But he was doubtful about the presentation of his plays, and wrote anxiously enquiring, towards the end of 1961, whether Mr Peter Hall should be authorised to produce *La Ville dont le Prince est un Enfant*, Mr Hall, he learned, having recently staged Gide's *L'Immoraliste* in a dramatised version at the Arts Theatre, which made him fear that the play might be presented '*dans un certain esprit*', since Mr Hall appeared to display '*une prédilection pour les sujets de ce genre*'. Ten years later, the staging of *La Ville* was again causing him anxiety. A Mr Rattigan, of whom he had never heard – '*j'ignore, et j'ai toujours ignoré profondément, toute ma vie, la littérature contemporaine tant française qu'etrangère* – had been suggested by a theatrical agent as a suitable translator. Would I let him have my views?

I admire Montherlant's plays no less than I enjoy his novels. After the death of Gide in 1951, he became the greatest, if not the most influential, of twentieth-century French writers, though he stood apart from every modern movement, and the position he adopted on every issue – a lapsed Catholic who still respected his faith; an aristocrat who had ridiculed the nobility without losing his sense of inherited privilege; and a solitary who prized the virtues and sought the comradeship of his fellow human beings – seemed deliberately anomalous. Montherlant's prose style has an extraordinarily wide range, incorporating both the qualities of seventeenth-century French literature – the classic period of French prose – and some of the colloquial idioms of the current spoken language. Above all, it is vigorous and masculine; and an English reviewer once drew an unwise comparison between his earlier novels and those of Rudyard Kipling.

Two novelists could scarcely be more unlike; Kipling's survey of human motives usually passes over sexual passion, while Montherlant exalts desire and concentrates on '*les deux grandes affaires essentielles – l'amour et la création artistique*'. But love of a purely romantic kind he excluded from his scale of values: *:Tout ce qui est du coeur est inquiétude et tourment, et tout ce qui est des sens est paix*'. That was his personal maxim; '*c'est une de mes grandes forces, d'echapper à l'amour en connaissant, mêlées, le sensualité et la tendresse*'; and I recall a sentence that occurs in a letter he wrote me, dated April 25, 1966, referring to a preface I had written for the English translation of *Les Jeunes Filles,* where I had hazarded that the unscrupulous hero Costals, 'a rake and a misogynist, belongs to the same family as Richardson's Lovelace, Choderlos de Laclos's Valmont or, indeed, as Casanova'. *'Je suis surtout en sympathie avec Casanova* (he remarks) *parce que chez lui il n'y a nulle méchanceté et que j'ai toujours voulu mêler l'estime et l'amitié au sentiment de la sensualité'.* Even through his savage trilogy *Les Jeunes Filles,* as through a minor masterpiece, *L'Histoire d'Amour de la Rose de Sable,* run many strains of tender feeling.

No biography of Henry de Montherlant has been published since his death; and the veil of mystery that surrounded his life and loves has not yet been fully lifted. His attitude towards the women he described was always critical, sometimes sharply hostile; and he informed me that, if *Les Jeunes Filles* derided the sex as a whole, *'c'est que j'avais l'expérience de deux fiancailles pareillement rompues pour les mêmes raisons que j'ai prêtées à mon heros, et j'ai été assez exaspéré par ces fiancailles'.* His self-portrait — that of an uncommitted adventurer, *Montherlant, homme libre* [2] — may have included some fictitious elements proper to his literary legend; he did not give me the impression of being an altogether free and happy man; and his announcement that every day he needed a strong draught of pleasure, without which his vital spirits would decline, failed, I thought, to ring completely true. He was repeatedly photographed; and, among the pictures I have seen, very few display him smiling. There was something *voulu* about his resolute cult of enjoyment; and photographs of the young drawing-room hero his mother wished him to become, and of the amateur bull-fighter, footballer and cross-country-runner who represented his own juvenile ideal, look equally intense and stern. Though the Catholic novelist Georges Bernanos had voted him the most distinctively French of living writers, his compatriots, as time went by, especially Parisian literary critics, appeared to exasperate him more and more. *'Autrefois* (he told me in May 1963, after the publication of *Le Chaos et la Nuit) la méchanceté etait reputée donner aux Francais de l'esprit. Aujourd'hui, elle les rend idiots';* and he was struck, he added, *'par l'honnèteté tout anglaise — Je prends ce mot d'honnèteté dans son plus grand sens'* — of an English review that he had just read.

Meanwhile, the letters I received, though not more familiar, grew a little less impersonal. In my review of *Le Chaos,* I had pointed out that the novelist and his chief character were of exactly the same age, and that each confronted a somewhat similar crisis. This observation,

[2]   The title of an illuminating study by Michel Mohrt, 1943.

he said, had touched him deeply: '*Il est évident que ce roman a été écrit durant la traversée d'un tunnel, mais la prodigalité d'une nature créatrice fait qu'ensuite on n'y pense plus et qu'on écrit d'autres oeuvres "comme si de rien n'était", bien qu'il soit évidemment impossible de retrouver ce que vous appelez les enthousiasmes de ma jeunesse*'. Alas, he was too hopeful. As early as 1961, there had been references in his letters to physical infirmities; and I had ventured to suggest that the *vertiges* of which he spoke might perhaps be caused by Menière's Syndrome, the disease of the inner ear that had afflicted Dean Swift. He replied, however, that they were due to a sunstroke he had suffered in Paris during the tropical summer of 1959; and that they attacked him, should he leave his rooms, especially in crowded public places, such as a theatre, whence he was obliged to retire after only two or three minutes. Next, he lost the sight of an eye. The previous February, he reported in his own increasingly illegible hand, on July 8, 1968, that, as the result of a fall, '*j'ai perdu entièrement et définitivement un oeil*'; but that he was not disfigured, and could still write and read. This was the beginning of the end; the vertigo and falls continued; and in 1972 he learned that he must resign himself to total blindness. The penultimate book he sent me bore a splendidly generous inscription: '*A Mr Peter Quennell qui a écrit sur moi ce qui peut le plus encourager un auteur à être ce qu'il est . . .*' But the last contained merely a printed card: '*HENRY DE MONTHERLANT regrette de ne pouvoir dédicacer ce volume*'. The Romans and their cruel, voluptuous world had always kindled his imagination; and it was with Roman fortitude that, sitting in his room at the Quai Voltaire, he loaded a revolver and prepared his exit.

To my recollections of Montherlant, Gide and Colette I wish that I could add a sketch of Proust. But he had left the world when I was seventeen; and I saw him only through the conversation of one or two surviving friends, who remembered how he would briefly inspect a party, or wander through the passages of the Ritz, swaddled in mufflers and shawls, wearing a crumpled white tie and a buckled shirt-front beneath a long black, shabby greatcoat; or how, summoned to his bedside at midnight, they would find him pallid and unshaven, looking like a 'wounded crow[3],' yet ready to pour out a flood of marvellously entertaining gossip, or talk of literature, from Saint-Simon and Balzac to Meredith, Dickens and Dostoievski, far into the small hours.

Later, I heard of the effect he had made on a woman whom he

[3]   Jacques Porel: *Fils de Réjane*, 1952.

distantly adored. None of his characters is a straightforward portrait of any single human being; but Oriane de Guermantes embodies many of the traits he had observed in the comtesse Adhéaume de Chevigné; and her grand-daughter, Marie-Laure de Noailles, told me that Proust's incessant missives had bored Madame de Chevigné almost beyond endurance[4], and that, during her childhood, she had been employed by her grand-mother to pile them away inside a basket. *'Cet raseur de Proust'* was perpetually tormenting her; and she had seldom time to read his endless scrawls.

A much more appreciative correspondent was Prince Antoine Bibesco, a Roumanian domiciled in Paris, cousin to the celebrated poetess Anna de Noailles, and one of the brilliant young men for whom Proust had conceived the same romantic devotion that his Narrator feels for Saint-Loup. I had met him in London with Ethel Sands, protegée of Henry James, friend of George Moore and herself a gifted artist; and he had invited me to stay at his house upon the Ile Saint-Louis, where, he said, not only should I enjoy the series of pictures by Vuillard he had had framed around his salon, but, next to the bedroom I occupied, *'vous auriez même un escalier dérobé',* which would enable me to lead a completely independent life. Why he thought I might require a private staircase was a problem that I never solved; but the prospect of conversing with Proust's great friend I found irresistibly attractive; and, when I reached the tall old building, 45 quai Bourbon, planted on the prow of the islet that divides the river just behind the buttresses of Notre-Dame, it seemed fully to deserve its owner's praises.

He gave me a warm welcome; but his ideas of hospitality and of Anglo-Saxon habits, though he had long been married to an Englishwoman, Lady Oxford's daughter Elizabeth Asquith, were a little disconcerting. First, he summoned his *femme de chambre.* Monsieur was English, he announced; Englishmen were often thirsty; and every night she was to place on the table near my bed a fresh bottle of brandy and two or three bottles of mineral water. Other provisions he made for my comfort wers equally extravagant. Having been born six years later than Proust, he was then well over seventy; and the happiest period of his life, I suppose, had fallen between 1903 and 1913. That was the heyday of his friendship with the almost unknown writer; and Proust had liked and admired him both as an unusually virile and good-looking man and as a conspicuous member of the

---

[4] The comtesse Greffulhe, another of Proust's models for the duchesse de Guermantes, appears to have found him equally antipathetic. See Mina Curtis: *Other People's Letters,* 1978.

aristocratic côterie that included Bertrand de Fénelon (one of the prototypes of Robert de Saint-Loup) the marquis Louis d'Albuféra (lover of the young actress Louisa de Mornand, whom Proust affected to adore, and who may perhaps have provided certain details when he described Odette de Crécy) and the elegant Gabriel de la Rochefoucauld. In this rôle Bibesco frequently corrected his friend's minor social misdeeds, taught him just how he should shake hands — firmly, never flabbily — and warned him against his deplorable middle-class trick of attaching the *particule* to a surname without a Christian name or title[5].

The man of genius, however, seems to have valued the man of the world not merely for his social brillance or his dashing personal charm. From *Lettres de Marcel Proust à Bibesco*[6], it is clear that their friendship was also based upon what Proust himself must have regarded as an intellectual understanding. Thus, in November 1912, he confided the unpublished manuscript of *Du Côté de chez Swann* to Antoine and Emmanuel, Antoine's brother, begging that they would enlist the support of André Gide, Jacques Copeau and Jean Schlumberger, who made up the editorial caucus of the *Nouvelle Revue Française,* and attached a long explanatory letter, briefing them about the novel's plan. Proust's own introduction to the subject and style of the book is, I think, among the best yet written. Having outlined the whole complex edifice of Proustian beliefs and feelings — his view of Time, of conscious and unconscious memory (through which alone we can regain the past), of a Heraclitan world where everything changes and dissolves, and human characters, because our point of view shifts, rarely remain true to type — in his last paragraph he defines and justifies the peculiar style he has adopted. Style, he believes, is by no means a method of beautifying an author's prose, but 'a quality of vision, a revelation of the universe that each of us sees and that our fellows cannot see. The pleasure an artist gives us depends on his ability to reveal a second universe beyond the one we know.'

Proust had evidently trusted Antoine, although his diplomatic mission failed and André Gide returned the manuscript; but, when in 1949 I became his guest, I was astonished to discover how seldom Bibesco appeared to think of Proust, and how unwillingly he mentioned him. Perhaps it was an effect of age; I have noticed the

[5]   It was a grave solecism, for example, to speak of '*de* Musset'. In the world of the Guermantes the poet was 'Musset', 'Alfred de Musset' or 'M.de Musset'; and, having absorbed this lesson, Proust, after a visit to an exhibition of pictures by Van Dyck, informed Bibesco that he had greatly enjoyed the works '*de ce peintre que vous appellez si justement Dyck*'.

[6]   With a preface by Thierry Maulnier, 1949.

same reluctance in other friends of celebrated men and women – in the Marchesa Casati, that legendary *femme fatale*, now poverty-stricken, ghost-thin, black-veiled, from whom I sought to elicit her memories of Gabriele d'Annunzio; Ada Leverson, whom I often questioned about her intimacy with Oscar Wilde; and Antoine's mother-in-law, Margot Oxford, who, I had hoped, might be prepared to describe her early life amid 'the Souls'. I was always unsuccessful; the Marchesa would only talk of her cat, and complain that she found it almost impossible to feed him on her meagre war-time rations; Mrs Leverson's favourite topic was the beauty and intelligence of Osbert Sitwell; while Lady Oxford preferred to discuss bridge and her grim experiences at the second-rate card-playing club where she passed her afternoons.

As for Antoine Bibesco, he was far more concerned with the modern social world than with the literary *temps perdu*; and his attitude towards the present was resolutely frivolous. It irked him to look back; he was constantly on the move and, wearing an English suit, his straw boater – those were very warm days – tilted like an Edwardian top-hat, would rush in and out of the apartment, and from his bedroom into mine. What was I doing? Where was I going? And – I must forgive his curiosity! – I had left lying around a scrap of paper bearing initials and a telephone-number that he could not recognise. To which of my acquaintances did they belong? He also sought my opinion, even my advice, regarding various human problems, and usually baited his request with some far-fetched piece of flattery: '*Vous qui connaissez si bien les femmes . . .*' I must tell him, he said, whether, in my large experience, one might remain completely impotent for weeks or months at a time with a woman whom one passionately loved. When I said that I thought this quite possible, he would strike his hand against his brow, and affect to be astonished and delighted by my superior sagacity.

On the subject of Proust alone was he obstinately uncommunicative. If, for example, I referred to Proust's loves, he dismissed them as mere 'public lavatory affairs', and then dashed off in pursuit of some more interesting question. I learned very little; but, after I had returned to London, I received an essay of eight pages that he suggested I might publish. Despite misgivings, I accepted it; and it appeared in the summer of 1950, alongside articles by Hugh Trevor-Roper, Margaret Lane and Somerset Maugham. Entitled 'The Heartlessness of Marcel Proust', it confirmed my previous suspicions;

Bibesco had come to resent Proust, and the affection he had once felt for him had gradually dwindled and decayed. Yet the notes he attached to his collection of Proust's letters tell a very different tale. There he speaks of the *'preuves de compassion et d'amitié'* Proust had shown him when his mother died, and refers to *'la genérosité et la gentilesse incalculable'* that characterised the writer's attitude towards the persons whom he loved. The article even goes so far as to imply that the grief the loss of a parent had caused him may have been less acute than he declared; that Proust's heart was 'closed against the experience of love', in which he saw only a transitory, though a fascinating illusion; and that he was almost unacquainted with friendship's 'compensatory joys':

> Marcel, indeed, often reminded me of a banker who accepts one's money, but is perpetually weighing the coins and sending them to be analysed. He was never tired of measuring and estimating the quality of his friends' affection, and constantly demanding fresh evidence to prolong an interminable enquiry[7].

Thus, the essayist writes, he finally ruined 'both their friendship and the friendship to which he himself pretended'. Friendly association with Marcel Proust, in short, was 'wholly unlike association with a normal human being'. The novelist, he announces, was a sick man; and elsewhere he describes him as 'a neuropath . . . what a psychiatrist would call a "cyclothymic"'. Beneath his extravagant emotionalism lay a fairly cold heart; and, should a friend appeal to him in a moment of personal distress, he proved a 'somewhat cruel comforter'. On such an occasion, when Bibesco had asked for his sympathy, 'do not grumble', Proust responded; 'an unhappy love-affair is an unequalled acquisition'. Clearly, his *'petit Antoine'* attached far too much importance to the pleasure of possessing; in possession 'one possesses *nothing* . . . One can only truly love if one does not possess completely'.

Some of these criticisms, I was obliged to agree, may have had a solid basis. Proust's was a difficult, self-tormenting, greedily demanding character; but Bibesco appeared to separate his personal faults from the broader context of his genius, and to be indulging a secret antagonism that perhaps he had long felt but had previously disguised. Was there not a strange resemblance, I wondered, between

---

[7]   The article published in the *Cornhill* was, I think, translated by myself; and I have in my rendering of it altered a phrase here and there.

his attack on Proust and Proust's own destructive revaluation, in *Le Temps retrouvé,* of almost all the characters whom, in earlier volumes, he had lovingly, or at least admiringly depicted? There even the delightful Saint-Loup is revealed as a selfish husband and an inveterate paederast; and his most charming traits—his agility, grace and speed—have become the indications of a surreptitious vice:

> His life had not coarsened or slowed him down . . . Robert . . . had become slimmer and taken to moving more rapidly . . . This swiftness had . . . various psychological causes; the fear of being seen, the wish to conceal that fear, the feverishness that is generated by dissatisfaction and boredom. He was in the habit of visiting certain low haunts into which . . . he would hurl himself . . . like a soldier going into an attack.

Similarly, the elegant Madame de Guermantes is now an ageing, over-dressed woman, and the superbly insolent baron de Charlus a drivelling dotard in a wheel-chair; while the ancient social system of the Faubourg Saint-Germain has at last degenerated into an absurd and vulgar farce.

Should I have refused Bibesco's article? Well, although I considered it unjust, Proust, in a letter to the poetess Anna de Noailles, had declared that his little Antoine was 'the only man who understood him'; and Bibesco's evidence, however distorted by the passage of time, clearly called for some attention. But it did nothing to shake my own faith. Proust is one of those novelists who transform the world that they describe; and whose peculiar method of observing mankind we gradually adopt ourselves. As an undergraduate I had begun to follow the course of his books without always understanding them. Their effect was cumulative; and during middle age I studied the London background, and categorised my friends and acquaintances, from a distinctly Proustian point of view. Ann Rothermere's guests, for example, provided many splendid subjects. Before the end of 1946 she had re-opened Warwick House; it must have been almost the last big London house to be kept up in the affluent pre-War style; and the parties she held there were even more diverse than her crowded war-time routs.

Among Warwick House's faithful frequenters was a large array of English Guermantes, distinguished both by their intricate family relationships—everybody seemed to be somebody else's first or second cousin – and by the curious nicknames[8] that in those days denizens of the *grand monde* often wore. But Ann's guests also included painters, writers and gregarious journalists; and the fusion of these two elements produced agreeable meetings and, occasionally, a dramatic contretemps, as when Lord Dudley, a renowned hammer of the highbrows, watched Lucian Freud absent-mindedly munching a bouquet of expensive purple orchids and proclaimed his deep disgust; or when, at supper, Cyril Connolly was seated beside Princess Margaret, and she rose and, pursued by her Lady-in-Waiting, who murmured sotto voce *'Temper! Temper!'*, abruptly hastened from the table. Such explosions were few; though Ann did not dislike a spirited conflict, which she sometimes actively encouraged, Warwick House remained for the most part a calm and easy-going place; and the Rabelaisian maxim *'Fay ce que vouldras'* might well have been inscribed above the door.

Our host was usually present but, if the fun became too boisterous, taking a detective-story under his arm, he would recede and quietly vanish. Otherwise he produced an impression of tolerant good humour and detached benevolence; but, if a joke suddenly caught his fancy, he would emit a loud reverberating laugh which reminded me of Lord Palmerston's laugh as described by Henry Adams. Clearly Esmond was more concerned with politics and journalism than with literature or painting. Political personages frequently joined us; and one night, after a dinner party, I remember seeing Winston Churchill (whom from a distance I had already watched ride in triumph along Piccadilly) and being struck and somewhat daunted by his look of unselfconscious grandeur. The great man had no use for dialogue; women have often told me how difficult and exhausting it was to sit next to him throughout a meal. He would deliver a solemn pronouncement, accept a timid affirmation, and then relapse into a brooding silence. That night his mood was clearly grim. He was still in opposition; the cares of public business must have weighed upon him heavily; and he declined to be amused. But press-lords receive their newspapers early; and about eleven o'clock a solid sheaf was offered him. Immediately his face lightened; he spread them across his knees and began rapidly skimming through their pages. While he read, he uttered vigorous comments. The Socialist Prime Minister had unwisely seen fit to reprimand Field Marshal Lord Montgomery.

[8] 'Bobberty', 'Boofie', 'Buffles', 'Cardie', 'Chips', 'Cockie', 'Coote', 'Cuckoo', 'Deacon', 'Dot', 'Jubie', 'Mima', 'Mowcher', 'Scatters' are soubriquets that will immediately be recognised by a survivor of the period, but may no doubt puzzle a social historian in the year 2000.

Churchill's indignation was volcanic. Though I believe he himself sometimes made fun of the vain glorious Field Marshal, his references to 'that little rat Attlee' were exceptionally savage.

Later, I met Churchill only twice – at his son's house and in Lord Beaverbrook's garden. Randolph had recently married a friend of mine; and it had been arranged that I should take her to a film, and then return for supper with her husband and his parent. They had just attended some political rally; and during supper they were still deep in an important conversation. But, when the old statesman announced that he must go home and, dutifully attended by Randolph, ambled out towards the street, he could be heard enquiring who I was. 'An author', Randolph replied; 'he's writing a book on John Ruskin'. 'Ah, *Rushkin, Rushkin'*, responded the senior Churchill in his sibillant, sonorous voice that has been so often parodied; and, reflectively, as he bade his son farewell: '*Rushkin* – a man with a *shingularly* unfortunate *shex*-life . . .'

My last introduction took place at Lord Beaverbrook's ugly villa perched on the rocks of Cap Martin. I was then Esmond's guest near Monte Carlo; and one afternoon he informed me that we had to visit Max, who was entertaining Winston. I suggested I should stay behind; but Esmond amiably insisted; and we set out in rather formal garb, wearing coats and long-sleeved shirts and ties. At the door, an obsequious secretary appeared. 'Good afternoon, my lord', he exclaimed. '*My* lord awaits you in the garden'. Thither we descended, over concrete paths that imitated crazy-paving, past empty bird-baths, and under massive pergolas devoid of roses. Rounding a corner we sighted Lord Beaverbrook and his friends beneath a eucalyptus tree. He was naked except for a pixie hat, '*nu comme un ver*' as a Frenchman might have put it, entirely, unashamedly, indeed aggressively nude, his small lean, hairy torso exhibiting all the stigmata of incipient old age. His aide-de-camp, Captain Mike Wardell, a black patch covering one eye, had followed Beaverbrook's example; but Churchill, wearing a cowboy hat and a pair of embroidered slippers, had a bath-towel draped round his waist. He held a cigar, which he seemed to suck and mumble rather than continuously smoke, and a tall glass, half-full of whisky-and-soda, evidently much diluted.

They made an extraordinary group; and afterwards, when I reviewed the scene with Esmond and said that I hoped that I had managed to conceal my astonishment as we first caught sight of them,

he replied 'On the contrary. I saw your *jaw drop* . . . Once we had
been found chairs, a keen debate began – the year was 1951 – about
the election that was then approaching and Churchill's probable
return to power; and, since I was no politician and the youngest
member of the party, there was little I could say. Yet, suddenly and
altogether unexpectedly, Mr Churchill threw me a remark. 'It's likely
to be my last innings', he announced. 'So it had better be a good one!'
I warmly agreed, then again took refuge in silence, until
Beaverbrook, who must have felt that Tory battle-plans should not be
discussed before an unknown book-critic, at last decided to remove
me. Clapping his hands — his usual method of summoning an
attendant – he told his secretary, who arrived post-haste, that he
thought I should enjoy a swim; and I was led off to the pool, a large
turbid pool coated with dead leaves, into which I blindly stepped. I
had chosen the wrong end, and plummeted straight down, then
emerged and floundered to the nearest verge, spitting out leaves and
chlorinated water.

A view of Mr Churchill's latest canvases closed this memorable
afternoon. Asked his opinion of Mao Tse-tung's poems, Arthur
Waley observed that, in terms of aesthetic achievement, they were
not quite so good as Churchill's pictures; and the series of landscapes I
had seen around Randolph's London dining-room I had never much
admired. Thanks to the expert tuition of William Nicholson and Paul
Maze, he had lost his Sunday-painter's innocence; and the works he
showed us at Cap Martin, with their bold brush-strokes and heavy
splashes of colour, were more ambitious than appealing. While he
displayed them, however, I beheld the heroic verteran from an
unfamiliar point of view. Like all artists, good or bad, I suspected, he
was sometimes plagued by doubts, and felt the sad discrepancy
between what he had envisaged and the results he had produced. So
splendidly confident in everything else he did, here he needed our
support, and hovered about us almost anxiously, showing picture
after picture, while he awaited the words of appreciation that were
often difficult to find.

I did not see Sir Winston again. During his last premiership, the
Warwick House I had known underwent a sudden change, when the
hostess whose spirit had pervaded its rooms sought another field of
action. But, before this crisis occurred, her interest in the future of the
Daily Mail had remained extremely vigorous. Not only had she
chosen fresh contributors; but, at least according to Fleet Street

gossip, she had been largely responsible for the appointment of a new editor. Her candidate Frank Owen was already a member of the staff. A tall, flamboyant Welshman, described by *Time* as 'hard-handsome, hard-talking, hard-drinking', at a very early age he had edited Lord Beaverbrook's *Evening Standard* and, earlier still — he was then only twenty-three — had become the youngest member of the House of Commons; which caused Lloyd George, his aged compatriot, to remark that, if he played his cards right, he would presently, like William Pitt, be a youthful Prime Minister. Frank directed the course of the *Daily Mail* with immense gusto and somewhat erratic zeal, from 1947 to 1950; and, while he held the reins, a visit to the editor's office was invariably entertaining.

The previous occupant of his chair, Stanley Horniblow, had had a solemn, weighty presence. Frank often began an interview by offering me a glass of champagne; he had always an open mind; and, once a bottle was standing between us, he grew even more receptive. Where else, for example, could I have found an experienced editor who allowed me to attend and write a front-page account of a sensational murder-trial? Frank immediately agreed, although by granting my request he knew that would infuriate every crime-reporter on the *Mail*. So to Lewes assizes I went, and there watched the extraordinary criminal, John George Haigh, doze and fidget in the dock throughout a sultry summer afternoon. Haigh, as I have suggested elsewhere[9], provided a fascinating problem; an extremely commonplace man, to judge from his trim appearance, a neatly clipped brown moustache and small brown beady eyes, he had been the author of a long series of carefully organised, horribly grotesque and brutal crimes, which involved shooting his victims, then plunging their bodies into metal drums filled with sulphuric acid, and allowing flesh and bones to disintegrate until they formed a nauseous sludge. It was typical of Haigh that, after stirring the drum, he should have visited a local restaurant and lunched off tea and poached eggs. In the dock nothing disturbed his composure — his air of polite apathy and half-apologetic boredom; and, when he had heard the sentence of death pronounced and prepared to leave the court, I noticed he was faintly smiling, though the smile that glimmered beneath his moustache had a rather wry and doleful twist.

During the early summer of 1950, Frank's editorship reached an abrupt end, in circumstances about which many tales were told, some completely unfounded. He was succeeded by Guy Schofield, a

[9]   *The Sign of the Fish*, 1960.

well-read Yorkshireman and an author himself, more concerned with literature than Frank and, if less inclined to open a bottle of champagne, equally hospitable and sympathetic. I knew that, so long as he edited the *Mail*, I might remain its book-reviewer; but I feared that, once he had left his chair, despite the friendly support I received from Esmond, I should quickly be expelled. Meanwhile, I continued my own labours; and, some seven months before Frank's departure, in November 1949, I had published a new book on Ruskin, which was followed by a collection of essays and a minor travel-book, both in 1952, and in 1955 by *Hogarth's Progress*.

I had come to Ruskin by a strangely circuitous route. Many years earlier, when I was still at school, about 1915 or 1916, I happened to stay with a friend whom my mother had first met at her suburban art-classes, and who was now married to a peppery retired soldier, the occupant of a small estate, where I watched him shoot rabbits and pigeons, in the neighbourhood of Torquay. I loved South Devon's red-earth fields, tumbling hills and green coppices; and one afternoon, as we travelled home from Torquay, towards the pretty Georgian manor-house that the Colonel occupied since he had given up his family's neo-Gothic mansion deep in a deserted park, I had had a stimulating conversation. My mother's friend and I were seated on the top deck of a humdrum modern tram; and she said how much she wished that this dull but useful conveyance would take us a little closer to her door. I disagreed; already a lover of landscape and a devotee of times past – also, I am afraid, a natural prig – I declared that trams would spoil the view; at which a bearded old gentleman, who occupied the next seat, gently introduced himself, observed that, having heard me defend the country, he could only assume that I must have studied John Ruskin, and added that, half a century ago, he had met the prophet face to face.

Ruskin, he said, had brilliant blue eyes and wore a vivid azure stock. A cat was wandering around the room; but, when his hostess had tried to present it to her guest, it had declined an introduction, twitched its ears and tail with a show of feline disdain, and stalked away across the carpet. Its owners apologised; Ruskin, on the other hand, had remained completely unperturbed. 'Do not trouble yourselves! *Pussy will come*', he answered; and, sure enough, after circumnavigating his chair with sinuous exploratory steps and uttering a soft mysterious wail, it had slowly padded back again, sprung up in single flowing bound and taken possession of the prophet's knee. Subsequently, as often as I heard his name, I remembered Ruskin and the cat; and although my father's regard for *The Stones of Venice* (which I guessed that he had very seldom opened) would set me for a time against the great man, this encounter was probably the far-off starting-point of my long Ruskinian expedition.

I decided to produce a full-length 'Life', however, because I had first considered and then rejected a very different method of approach. As a sequel to *Four Portraits,* I had planned a book that would bear the title *Four Marriages.* I felt that the state of marriage – the mechanism that underlies it and the conflicts that may at length destroy or, as in the case of the Carlyles, miraculously strengthen and preserve it – was a subject on which, given my personal experience, I could write with some authority; and three of the couples I proposed to describe were William and Dorothy Temple, Thomas and Jane Carlyle, John Ruskin and his virgin consort Effie Gray. I have forgotten my fourth choice; but the others might have made an admirable series. Apart from poor Effie, each of the personages involved had a highly developed literary sense; each had loved and suffered deeply. Yet, the more I debated my plan and gathered fresh material, the more difficult it seemed to realise. The dignified Temples dropped out – I knew too little of their background; perhaps the unhappy Carlyles were already too familiar; and I was left confronting John Ruskin and his pretty, stubborn wife. Eventually, I decided that Ruskin's marriage would not form a satisfactory theme unless it were related to a larger survey that embraced his whole existence.

Here Proust gave me the help I needed. The novelist, I remembered, had often spoken of Ruskin as an 'intercessory spirit', an artist devoted to the pursuit of Beauty, for whom the Beauty he sought 'was no mere source of pleasure . . . but a reality infinitely more important than life itself, to which he would have gladly sacrificed his own. From that view of art (Proust concludes) Ruskin's entire aesthetic system springs'. When, in 1900, he paid his only visit to Venice – Byron's 'greenest island of the imagination' – during the train-journey his mother had read *The Stones of Venice* aloud to amuse her tired, restless son; and, once they arrived, he had spent his first evening, at work on his translation of *The Bible of Amiens* with Marie Nordlinger's assistance. Proust and Ruskin, incidentally, had shared many traits besides their genius and their love of art. Both had been weak children; both were brought up by anxiously devoted parents; both were attracted toward very young girls; and both carried the burden of an ill-adjusted sexual nature. Ruskin's nympholeptic passion for Rose La Touche – at their earliest meeting, in 1858, she was not yet ten years old, and had entered the room and given him her hand 'as a good dog gives its paw' – lasted until she died in 1875. This pathetic episode a biographer must somehow reconcile with the story of his intellectual progress. Didn't she find it strange, I asked a transatlantic blue-stocking, much addicted to psychiatry, that a deeply neurotic girl should have flown into the orbit of a neurotic middle-aged man? She answered that she thought it perfectly natural. Certain insects possessed a peculiar high-pitched hum capable of summoning another member of their species over many miles of swamp or jungle; and neurotics had the same ability to arouse and draw a counterpart.

The neurotic aspect of Ruskin's character presents an obvious temptation. One may seek to 'explain' him in terms of his weaknesses and failures; whereas it is the strength he developed under the pressure of weakness, and the war he waged against his hostile surroundings, that should form the basis of the story. Though his practical efforts usually miscarried, and the age he had hoped to reform very often disregarded him – so, at least, he thought himself – he had succeeded on another plane, the high plane of imaginative art where Marcel Proust acclaimed his genius. The conflict between art and ethics, between the visionary Beauty he pursued and the sense of moral obligation he had inherited from sternly virtuous parents, overshadowed his whole adult life. There were times, indeed, when, abandoning the rôle of artist, he determined to become a social moralist, and moments, too, when he recovered his childhood's faith, and declared himself an ardent Christian; but, despite his moods of confusion and indecision, the artist always re-emerged. 'The greatest thing a human soul does in this world (he had decided) is to see'; and, like Proust, he immensely enlarged our powers of seeing, enjoying and remembering. Unlike Proust's, however, the scope of his vision was comparatively limited; he paid little attention to his fellow men and women, whom, he confessed, he did not understand – 'I might as well have set myself', he informed a confidante after the breakdown of his marriage, 'to learn a new science, as to guess at people's characters and meanings,[10]; and he reserved his gift of aesthetic analysis for the visual arts and Nature. But, once a subject had stirred his imagination – Carpaccio's *St. Ursula,* Veronese's *Queen of Sheba,* a line of cumulus clouds arched across the sky[11], a wild cyclamen, even the bare limbs,

[10]   Ruskin to Lady Trevelyan; quoted by Raleigh Trevelyan in *A Pre-Raphaelite Circle,* 1978.

[11]   Ruskin's feeling for the beauty of clouds may be compared with that of Chateaubriand, who exerted a life-long influence on Proust.

admired at a distance, of a young Italian beggar-girl – he would concentrate on it with a passionate intensity of feeling that recalls Proust's ecstatic absorption in a single tree or flower. Whether he described or drew – the descriptive writer, of course, was also a superbly gifted draughtsman – Ruskin set out to record and preserve some ephemeral aspect of Beauty by 'translating pleasure into knowledge[12]'.

When my book on Ruskin, subtitled *'The Portrait of a Prophet'*, at length appeared in 1949, it received the usual kind reviews and had the usual rather laggard sale. I did not regret the time and trouble I had spent upon the great Victorian's features; my work had set me some fascinating problems and made it possible to examine much unpublished correspondence, among which I found a painfully detailed account of his long relationship with Rose La Touche[13]. I also met his last surviving disciple. In 1880 two young men, Detmar Blow and Sydney Cockerell, had accompanied him to Abbeville and Beauvais just before his final brain-storm; and Detmar, he reported, was 'as good as gold'; while Sydney (who had once been privileged to carry Rose's early letters, her 'rose-leaves', in a rose-wood box upon his lap) handled the Master's umbrella 'as if he were attending the Emperor of Japan'. In 1948 Sydney Cockerell had passed his eightieth year – he survived until 1962 – and, despite the infirmities that had now confined him to his room, still led an active social life. I visited him one afternoon at his quiet house near Kew Gardens; and there he showed me a stock that Ruskin had worn and a large handkerchief of the kind he generally used. The handkerchief's material, I remember, was a roughish yellow silk; and the stock, a beautiful unfaded blue, fastened with tiny hooks behind. I said, merely because I thought the detail odd, 'I see that Ruskin wore a made-up tie'; at which my invalid host looked surprised and offended, and, retorting sharply 'Don't we all?', put away his treasured relics.

This not altogether harmonious meeting had an unexpected sequel. In 1956 I opened a collection of letters addressed to Sir Sydney by his friends[14], and discovered a letter and a postcard from Bernard Shaw, written during the spring of 1950. He first announces that, although at the moment he has little time for reading, he has

[12] See Baudelaire's essay, *'Richard Wagner et Tannhäuser'*, 1860.

[13] This is contained in Ruskin's letters to Mrs Cowper Temple, afterwards Lady Mount Temple, which I was allowed to examine by courtesy of the late Mrs Detmar Blow.

[14] *The Best of Friends: Further Letters to Sydney Carlyle Cockerell*, edited by Viola Meynell, 1956.

somehow managed to get through 'Peter Quennell's life of Ruskin and Professor Oswald Doughty's life of Rossetti'. After this sentence three significant dots suggest that several lines have been omitted; and the printed version of Shaw's letter goes on straight to 'the Rossetti book', which, in Shaw's opinion, shows the poet-painter as a 'socially impossible and unpleasant untrustworthy and dishonest modern Casanova'. It is clear that whatever Shaw may have said about my portrait of Ruskin had prompted Cockerell to defend the Master and, simultaneously, excuse Rossetti. Shaw's characteristic postcard begins with the assertion that he and his correspondent do not really disagree, and concludes, again after three dots, with a couple of sentences that I found particularly provocative: 'I take P.Q. at his value, and allow for it. But his facts as an outsider seem fully documented and unquestionable'. Luckily perhaps, I have never admired Shaw, whose love of propounding an explosive paradox, whether his subject were Shakespeare or Stalin, was the symptom, I have often felt, of his Hibernian exhibitionism and inveterate self-esteem[15]. I decided, nevertheless, that his opinion of my own 'value' would undoubtedly be worth having, and wrote to the editress, Viola Meynell, begging for a private glimpse of the lines she had deleted. She refused my plea; the postcard was lost, she alleged — a reply that, considering the saleroom-value of Shavian manuscripts, seemed remarkably implausible.

Otherwise, none of Ruskin's admirers was offended by my portrait; and, in 1956, when I sent Sir Sydney a short pamphlet devoted to the Master's life and work that I had written for the British Council, his response was warmly generous. If I enjoyed my task, and the book developed more easily than many of its predecessors, that may have been due not only to the human appeal of my subject and the splendid qualities of Ruskin's prose, but to the fact that, between 1948 and 1950, I enjoyed unusual happiness, and had a single dazzling preoccupation that enriched my days and nights. I had kept no diary since Julia and I had parted; but, here and there, a small symbolic sign — an exclamation-mark or a bristling asterisk, both of them now completely unintelligible — would star a page of my engagement book. Another sign, a diminutive crescent moon, first makes its appearance on February 17, 1948; and, from that date until the

[15] I once persuaded Kingsley Martin, who naturally respected Shaw as a Fabian precursor of the British Labour Movement, to admit that a Shaw *sottisier* — a Flaubertian anthology of his more idiotic sayings — would make a solid and instructive book.

autumn of 1950, a succession of magical crescents continue to float above the scribbled entries. Then they vanish; and the last I can discover has been finely crossed through. Why I should have chosen a crescent moon I must admit I am not sure. Perhaps I was thinking of Cynthia, the moon-goddess, in whose honour the Elizabethan poets framed so many admirable poems; and whose effulgence the dramatist George Chapman likened to the 'tender moonshine' of a woman's beauty[16]. For whatever reason, I have always loved the crescent; and its association with the pleasures of that happy period gives it an added hold upon my feelings.

Naturally, even in 1949 — a year when my tattered engagement book contains the longest series of delicate lunar symbols — the sky was sometimes overcast. But my troubles were few; and, as I look back, I seem to have been granted a spell of almost undisturbed felicity, free from the doubts and fears and suspicions that had darkened earlier relationships. L. was not only a classic beauty but a gay, adventurous character, who managed her own life and temporarily managed mine — never permitting me to abuse my privileges, yet allowing me as large a part of her existence as she felt that I deserved — with instinctive skill and grace. Meanwhile, she had also allowed me to become an honorary member of her household. Besides her brother and her sisters, I met her two delightful children; and, although hitherto I had shunned domestic scenes, I now attended nursery tea-parties — Nanny's attitude towards the strange guest was, it is true, a little guarded — and once, I remember, accompanied L. to watch the performance of a school play. On the nursery-floor I was usually well-received, because, if I arrived for tea, I regularly brought a pineapple; and those pineapples have kept my memory green. My frugiferous visits I learn, are still remembered after nearly three decades.

[16] 'So women, that (of all things made of nothing)
    Are the most perfect idols of the moon,
    (Or still-unwean'd sweet moon-calves with white faces)
    Not only are patterns of change of men,
    But, as the tender moonshine of their beauties,
    Clears or is cloudy, makes men glad or sad'

Bussy d'Ambois. 1607

6

When I was still working on my biography of Ruskin, I had lost an old friend. Late in June, or early in July, 1948, I heard that Emerald Cunard had fallen dangerously ill; that she could no longer leave her room; and that, at a dinner-party held a little earlier, she had raised her glass and drunk a toast to death. I wondered how I could express my sympathy; I suspected that she would not welcome a visit, and would probably dislike flowers, to which she might attach some funereal significance. But then, I remembered that, on hearing me praise *Praeterita*, she had admitted that she had never read the book, and that from my account it sounded worth attention. Luckily, or unluckily as it turned out, I was able to buy a fine leather-bound Victorian copy, and sent it to the Dorchester Hotel. Her acknowledgement was characteristic — the only letter of hers that I possess, undated, written in a tremulous hand, yet strongly expressive of her bold and wayward character:

> Dear Peter,
> I hate that Ruskin book & you may have it again. He is such a dull, damnable bore. *How* can you write about him? He has added greatly to my suffering.
> See you soon perhaps — can not write.
>
> Emerald

That was her last message. Naturally, I was disappointed. But I was consoled to learn — my informant being her devoted Chilean admirer Antonio de Gandarillas, who had watched beside her bed — that, during the final hours of her life, after she had lapsed into a not unpleasant dream, she had imagined that she was attending a party, which she evidently enjoyed, and that Georgia Sitwell and I were among the guests she mentioned. So she had forgiven my sadly ill-chosen gift, and the suffering it had caused her. She died, attended by Tony Gandarillas and another close friend, Robert Abdy, on July 10, 1948. Her daughter, I believe, was not in England; they had quarreled, bitterly and conclusively, sixteen or seventeen years earlier; and when she asked me to read aloud to her, as she did one memorable evening, the large collection of romantic love-letters she had once received from George Moore[1], I had always carefully omitted Nancy's name. The novelist was said sometimes to have hinted that Nancy might have been his child. Certainly he had cherished her, encouraged her literary plans and often visited her at her Left-Bank flat in Paris; but he, too, had found her later extravagances both surprising and alarming.

After a brief, ill-fated marriage — she was the first fashionable young woman to be married wearing gold brocade — Nancy had had many lovers, among them Aldous Huxley, who, when he wrote his second novel, *Antic Hay,* had depicted her as Mrs Viveash, the epitome of heartless elegance, passionately and miserably adored by his ineffective hero; Michael Arlen, whose successful novelette *The Green Hat* glorifies that gallant lady Iris Storm; the Georgian sonneteer Robert Nichols, and the young Surrealist poet Louis Aragon, then flaming in the fore-front of the Parisian avant garde. Emerald would not have objected to love-affairs; indeed, she might have smiled on them; but Nancy possessed an unfortunate gift of confusing passions with ideas; and about 1930 she had become attached to the cause of racial freedom, enrolled a negro lover, and begun carrying him around Europe. I remember Henry Crowder well, and how much he disappointed me; for I had expected the kind of lean black leopard I had seen lunging across the stage in Diaghilev's *Scheherezade;* and what I saw was a large dark man, ceremonious, sententious, solemn, offering a huge parsonic hand and heavily, repeatedly shaking mine. Nancy vibrated beside this dusky pachyderm like a nervous antelope. It was not an equable affair; and Brian Howard, the one-time Oxford luminary, now a wandering bohemian, has given a vivid account of the difficult life they led together at some Austrian skiing-place — 'poor dear coal-black Henry being so good and patient', despite the horrid treatment that he suffered, her savage attacks and 'those awful snarling little yelps of self-assertion[2]'.

Meanwhile, Emerald had discovered Henry's existence and, stung

[1] See *The Sign of the Fish,* 1960. Moore's letters have since been published.

[2] Jacqueline Lancaster: *Brian Howard: Portrait of a Failure,* 1968.

into action by the sneers of her old antagonist Margot Oxford, had taken stern financial measures. That same year, 1931, Nancy issued a privately printed pamphlet, entitled *Black Man and White Ladyship*, in which she combined a defence of the negro peoples with a fierce and unpleasantly biased description of her mother's character and social tastes. It was a supremely foolish piece of work; not only did it enrage her mother and, no doubt, please Lady Oxford, but it saddened and alienated George Moore. Yet Nancy was a highly talented woman, in her own way almost as extraordinary a personage as the parent she reviled. Though taller, she closely resembled Emerald; she had the same acute and rather bird-like profile, the same slightly receding chin and rapid movements. Nancy's, writes Brian Howard, was 'the best woman's face of our time'; and he refers to her 'wavering perched walk' and her 'whispery, staccato, disjointed voice' – a trait that Huxley adds to the portrait of his fatal Mrs Viveash: 'her voice . . . seemed always on the point of expiring, as though each word were the last . . . faintly and breakingly from a death-bed – the last, with all the profound and nameless significance of the ultimate word'.

After the Second War, the period when I knew her best, she had still a weird attraction. She was alarmingly thin; and around her brittle arms she wore an armature of massive yellowed ivory bracelets. Her Kohl-rimmed eyes at once recalled Emerald's; and she had inherited her mother's diminutive, thin-lipped, slightly puckered mouth. But the *vie de bohème* was already taking its toll. She had developed the febrile gestures of a wire-drawn mannequin, and needed the constant support of alcohol to keep her mobile and vivacious. Her closing years were deeply sad. The lovers were more transitory and less respectable; her sponsorship of the various ideas she championed grew increasingly erratic; and, during a disastrous visit to England, she was arrested for some wild nocturnal escapade and eventually committed by a bewildered magistrate to an asylum near London, whence she wrote me a desperate letter, alleging that she was a victim of the American Secret Service, and particularly of John Foster Dulles, who knew the conspicuous part she had played in the Spanish Civil War. The typewriter is a dreadfully sensitive machine, which records all the anguish of the heart and nerves; every neurasthenic uses single-spacing, and the thinnest paper he or she can find; and Nancy's script bit deep into the surface of her smudged and overcrowded pages.

This, I think, was in 1964; but in 1957 we had had a happier correspondence. I had sent her some paragraphs about her mother and

George Moore, and my reading of Moore's love-letters, that I had written for a new book[3], and had decided that she ought to see. Emerald had been dead nearly a whole decade; and when, early in November, I received her response, I saw that the long and tragic breach had healed. Nancy's sketch of 'Her Ladyship' (whom, she said, I had '"got" . . . very well indeed') was appreciative, at moments, indeed, genuinely affectionate. True, there were qualifications:

> It shocked me that she did not keep all G.M.'s letters; I think she must have told me at some time that she had many, but . . . oh where are they by now? Dinner-parties and entertaining – the matters of the Opera[4] (always in a monumental tangle) took all her time. Although she would certainly respect the *making* of a work (especially when explained to her) she would, by nature not instinctively feel all that goes into it. Some things are durable, and others evanescent. She was more of the 'evanescent school'. And how creative in her way! What she did in transforming Holt[5] is unbelievable . . .

Nancy was also puzzled by her mother's reluctance, 'until he finally was able to give her *Ulick and Soracha*', to accept a dedication of any of G.M.'s books:

> As I cannot think it was prudery that made her 'sort-of' pretend G.M. (and T.B. later) were not lovers (if so they were?), this remains incomprehensible. I don't know how the majority of parents and children are nowadays, or even how they were in their relations before the twenties . . . Mine told me NOTHING, nor the hour of my birth, nor anything about family affairs, grandpapa, rents, money-matters etc. Possibly this is the root of my detachment from both.

About her father, too, she now had friendly memories. 'Although Sir Bache WAS considered "an ogre"' – by certain relations and most of Emerald's intellectual friends – and undoubtedly had 'loathed G.M.', he had 'personality, and much so'. After he had given up his mastership of a famous pack of hounds, he had become a devoted gardener, topiarist and craftsman, 'and spent hours alone in his

[3] *The Sign of the Fish*. 1960.

[4] Lady Cunard, at great cost to herself, assisted Sir Thomas Beecham, for many years her closest companion, to give London the kind of opera that both imagined it deserved.

[5] The enormous ancient house in Leicestershire that she had occupied as the young American wife of Sir Bache Cunard, a fox-hunting squire.

tower-workshop at Holt, making things in metal (silver leaves, cups, coconut carving etc. – and iron gates and furniture. An artisan, a born artisan with clever hands)'. Returning to her mother, she mentioned my statement that Emerald had disliked the open air:

> Her Ladyship seemed to hate it later on. In the days of Holt she would TACKLE fresh air in the middle of the afternoon. Dressed in Marienbad garb (do you know what this is? Maybe not) she would sally forth – tightly buttoned smart country coat, Homburg felt hat with small feather, muffled, gloves, elegant walking stick, and I would go with her, admiring the way she would pounce on the unpardonable piece of paper thrown on the ground, the empty cigarette container, and poke any such piece of rubbish neatly into the earth with her stick.

I have transcribed these unpublished fragments because they supply an agreeable footnote to the history of her mother's life and, at the same time, reveal the pleasantest aspect of her own gifted and unhappy nature. She has left no solid memorial. During her youth Nancy had belonged to a world that vanished many years ago. Whereas Virginia Woolf and her friends and relations have become literary household-gods, a contiguous section of Georgian society has been more or less forgotten; I mean, the High Bohemian world that, when I first reached London, could still be observed at the famous Eiffel Tower. This small restaurant, in Percy Street off the Tottenham Court Road, was run by a middle-aged Austrian named Stulik, who had covered the walls and a part of the ceiling with his favourite clients' canvases, and had commissioned Wyndham Lewis and his adjutant William Roberts to decorate a Vorticist Room upon the floor above. Stulik allowed his needier patrons an almost unlimited degree of credit; and, though I imagine that, while balancing his books, he sometimes over-charged the rich, the habit brought about his ruin.

Among the clients he may have occasionally despoiled were some very rich young men – Evan Morgan, for instance, heir to a Welsh peerage, the original of the brilliant, restless, seductive Ivor flatteringly portrayed in Aldous Huxley's *Crome Yellow,* but cruelly caricatured by Ronald Firbank in *The Flower Beneath the Foot* – and the fashionable dandy Napier Alington. At the Eiffel Tower they dined and drank and talked with far more genuinely bohemian guests – Augustus John, a rugged leonine figure, half Hyperion, half Silenus, and a constellation of lesser-known luminaries, including Tommy Earp and Nina Hamnett. In *Crome Yellow* Mary Bracegirdle, who has been put off by the hero's facetious declaration that the modern poets he prefers are 'Blight, Mildew and Smut', supposes that she must have misheard him, and that what he really intended to say was 'Squire, Binyon and Shanks', or 'Childe, Blunden and Earp', or even 'Abercrombie, Drinkwater and Rabindranath Tagore'. Her mention of Tommy shows that he had published interesting verses; but his chief distinction in Eiffel Tower days was that he had once promised to prepare a definitive biography of Stendhal and, after endless trouble and much laborious reading, had somehow never quite completed it.

Meanwhile, he gently conversed and dawdled, a true eccentric, his eccentricity being derived from the deepest recesses of his character. John painted his portrait; he had a lengthy pinkish face, bright cynical eyes, a round receding chin and a cockcomb-crest of stiff grey hair. His voice was high and faint, nearly as high as Lytton Strachey's; and, although inclined to philosophic silence, his conversational gambits were often highly unexpected. When asked the name of a young woman he had been seen dining with the other night, he replied, casually and vaguely, 'Oh, just *any* little bitch, you know'; and his interlocutor was taken aback to learn that he had suggested marrying her next day. Himself he was never astonished; his prosperous family detested him; and, when he learned that his mother had decided to destroy him my means of magic spells and conjurations, he remarked that, luckily she was not very well-informed — she didn't really know her subject — and seemed to be using all the wrong *grimoires*.

Tommy, I believe, had a modest private income; but Nina Hamnett was a poor relation of the rich bohemian world, a moderately talented but infinitely courageous artist, who battled her way through life from drink to drink, and from commission to commission. Osbert Sitwell bought her clever drawings; and so did many of his friends; but a moment arrived when they had all the Hamnetts — and her style showed little sign of changing — they could hang around their rooms. Nina was undismayed; her loud masculine laugh grew still louder and hoarser when she told of her misfortunes, and her gap-toothed smile broader. 'Jolly' was an adjective she often used; and she managed to keep the flame of jollity burning wherever she was tossed by fate. Once she explained she was sharing a prostitute's room, and occupied the single bed if her companion, a 'very jolly girl', happened to be out at work. On a second occasion I found her stranded in front of a

Parisian café, confronting a lofty pile of saucers that had accumulated hour after hour since she had arrived, and represented a formidable sum she hoped to be able to pay off as soon as she sighted a passer-by she knew. Having done my best, I was rewarded with a vividly detailed account of a nocturnal adventure she had just enjoyed. An apache had picked her up— ' terribly attractive chap; but, of course, a perfect *fiend*, m'dear!' And she raised her thin jersey to reveal her naked ribs and a large expanse of welts and bruises.

Even Nina's endurance had its limits; and, reduced to the depths of poverty, she finally escaped from her drunken last lover by hurling herself through the window of a Soho tenement. Before she vanished, the Eiffel Tower had gone; Stulik's credulous generosity had completed his ruin; and I remember a sad evening at the almost deserted restaurant some time in 1938. Lights were dimmed; the fountain of fresh green foliage that had once sprung beside the staircase had now shrunk into a dusty tangle; and two old waiters stood miserably flicking their napkins and gazing towards a door that never opened. Stulik himself, his pointed moustaches adroop, his fat round face a yellowish grey, paced to and fro, muttering half-audibly about his debtors and creditors, and the wrongs and woes of human life, with his hands behind his back, while his dog Chocolate (who also produced the impression of harbouring dark and anxious thoughts) walked slowly in the opposite direction.

Soon after he had sold his beloved establishment, Stulik disappeared and died; and, as 1938 was the year of the sale, the passages I have devoted to the Eiffel Tower may seem a little misplaced. But many of the restaurant's chief frequenters lived on into the post-war period; and there I often saw Richard Wyndham who later became a kind and hospitable friend. Our friendship developed slowly; and, during the great days of the Eiffel Tower, although we met, we seldom talked, until we found ourselves attending the same party at a Bloomsburian studio off Gordon Square. Many of the guests wore fancy dress; and I remember Beryl de Zoete, Arthur Waley's almost indestructible Egeria, in a jockey's stylish cap and silks. Dick and I happened to leave together – he had appropriated poor Beryl's whip; and, as we walked along the street, I asked him, with reference to the rather disappointing young women we had left behind us at the studio, if he hadn't noticed that, should an unknown girl, whom for a few minutes one had thought attractive, prove on closer inspection to be fairly plain, one often felt a secret sense of relief, when one considered the tribulations one would probably avoid by cutting one's losses and going home to bed.

Dick agreed. 'That's the first intelligent thing I've ever heard you say', he added in his gruff low-pitched voice; and from that hour we began to establish a sympathetic understanding. My new friend was then middle-aged — I suppose, about forty — and had a rugged, irregularly handsome face, with a short nose, a lengthy upper lip and a nimbus of waving greyish hair, into which he frequently rubbed some curious tar-scented lotion. He was tall and lean; and his whole frame produced an odd impression of physical disjointedness. His trousers corkscrewed up his legs; and he was apt to move across the room, dislodging an ornament here and there, in a series of uncoordinated giant strides. No stranger, meeting the bohemian artist, would have suspected that his bohemianism was a somewhat recent growth; and that he had started his adult career as a rich and conventional young *homme du monde*, heir, since his cousin Percy Wyndham's death to a large estate and a famous Wiltshire country house. Dick had married young, his wife being the debutante daughter of his commanding officer's last love, a worldly-wise Edwardian lady; but his marriage had scarcely survived the honeymoon; and a divorce had quickly followed. Perhaps it was this hurtful and humiliating experience that had induced him to break through the barriers of his previous social round — dancing at London balls, gambling, shooting, hunting, riding in point-to-points — and take a wholly new direction. Meanwhile, he happened to have become acquainted with a powerful modern prophet.

Wyndham Lewis receives little attention today; but in 1918, when he published *Tarr,* his splendidly entertaining first novel, the young T.S. Eliot had described him as 'a magician who compels our interest . . . the most fascinating personality of our time . . .' The artist, Eliot suggested, was at once more primitive and more civilized than his contemporaries; 'and in the work of Mr Lewis we recognise the thought of the modern and the energy of the cave-man[6]. Simultaneously, Rebecca West had called the novel 'a beautiful and serious work of art'; Ezra Pound had hailed the novelist as a 'master of design . . . a restless, turbulent intelligence'; and another reviewer had announced that its protagonists, Kreisler and Tarr, were 'two of the titanic characters' of twentieth-century English fiction; while Walter Sickert praised both his art-criticism and his memorably

[6] This eulogy appeared in an avant-garde magazine named *The Egoist.*

incisive drawings. His masterpiece, *Time and Western Man*, which appeared in 1927, and was succeeded by *The Lion and the Fox, Doom of Youth, Paleface, The Childermass* and *Men Without Art* (to name only a few of his bold and 'turbulent' productions) brought into the field of modern critical writing an unaccustomed fire and gusto. Pound has said that Lewis was 'a man at war'; and a warrior, though latterly a somewhat distracted warrior, he would remain throughout his life.

During the numerous campaigns he planned and conducted, his adversaries seldom varied. The stern champion of an 'austere and masculine art', he advanced — I quote from a current review — 'the governing function of the intellect', and derided the 'feminine sensibility', the wilful neglect of form he detected in so many much-praised modern books. Thus, he launched a particularly eloquent assault against Gertrude Stein's 'Gargantuan mental stutter' and, less justifiably no doubt, attacked 'the method of *Ulysses*' which, he claimed, 'imposes a softness, flabbiness and vagueness on its Bergsonian fluidity'. Lewis' chief defect, as novelist and controversialist alike, was that he rarely managed to distinguish between his rabid personal prejudices and his calmer intellectual judgements, and that the verdict he reached was far too often accompanied by an explosive burst of spleen. I saw him one evening, but for only half an hour, when Richard Hughes and I visited Edith Sitwell's flat to eat 'penny buns' and drink tea. Pallid, silent and remote, he occupied a dusky corner; and there was something about his expression and attitude — his thick spectacles had a sharply suspicious glint — that discouraged any hope of meeting him again.

Such were the qualifications of Dick's drawing-master and guide to modern art once he had entered the bohemian world. Lewis, I believe, cured him of his early affection for the English nineteenth-century landscape-painters, and taught him to cultivate the razor-sharp line that characterises his own technique. But master and pupil presently fell out. Lewis was a disputatious man, and quarrelled not only with Dick, but with the Sitwells, Roger Fry, his enthusiastic supporter Ezra Pound, even with the gentle and good-natured Eliot, each of whom, as their turn came, he reviled and ridiculed. Against Dick, however, the grudge he harboured was particularly personal. It concerned money; Dick was thought to be rich; and Lewis held that a prosperous amateur should supply the hard-worked artist's needs. His demands, Dick complained, were both incessant and exorbitant; and Lewis declared that his patron's laggardly response showed a mean and vulgar nature. He first retaliated by means of abusive postcards;

next, in 1931, published *The Apes of God,* where two long chapters are devoted to the leisurely demolition of a personage he called 'Dick' or 'Richard Whiddingdon', like the other 'Apes' he portrayed the type of deleterious dilettante, shown lording it *de haut en bas* over his subservient middle-class hangers-on.

At the risk of appearing disloyal to my old friend, I must admit that Lewis' caricature displays an Hogarthian comic verve. The caricaturist has missed not a single detail that could be used against his victim. I have already referred to Dick's air of disjointedness and the odd appearance of his trousers:

> Nonplussed (we read) Dick bucked slightly back with nearsighted alarm . . . then, his trousers cork-screwing, he plunged gallantly forward — he seemed in danger of falling as he dived after the escaping door-handle.

Still more offensive is the second chapter, which Lewis subtitled 'Ape Flagellant', where the dilettante is depicted in his studio, carelessly receiving the homage of a fellow artist, a 'mountebank marine painter', and the artist's jaunty little wife; and again 'the great studio-lord''s manner of crossing the floor is remembered and described:

> Darting his trunk round to the fireplace he swooped and struck it low down with the muzzle of his under-slung pipe . . . suede feet flung out to right and left, Dick went down the studio towards the kitchen. As he went his person was quaked . . . by a heavy hiccup.

In 1931 Lewis' paranoiac tendencies were reaching an advanced stage; but, although his grotesque portraits bear no more relation to the truth than does the image a distorting mirror reflects to the human face and body, they reveal, here and there, a ferocious acuteness of vision that infuriated Dick himself; and, when a reviewer announced that the dramatis personae of *The Apes of God* were distinctly recognisable, he threatened journalist and paper with a law-suit, and extorted an apology. Criticism did not usually trouble him; he was a stalwart individualist. He may have had several reasons for changing his mode of life; the strongest among them, however, was probably a sudden resolve to shed unwanted social baggage, and throw overboard the conventions and obligations that formed a tiresome part of his inheritance. Other Englishmen have felt the same need. Dick belonged to a section of English society that has always produced a magnificent crop of eccentrics and adventurers; and the Wyndham family has been particularly rich in adventurous men and women. Thus, his close relation Wilfred Scawen Blunt, dandy, sportsman, politician, traveller and accomplished minor poet, had bred Arab horses, founded the Crabbet Park Stud, ridden around the Middle East, defended Egyptian fellahin and the Irish peasantry against a conservative British government, done time in a British goal, alienated his wife — Byron's granddaughter — carried on an impassioned feud with his erratic daughter Judith, and been finally laid to rest, at the age of eighty-two, wrapped in white Arab robes, beneath the windows of his ancient house.

The feminine side of the Wyndham family were no less dashing and high-spirited. Sargent's famous portrait, 'The Wyndham Sisters', immortalises Dick's three aunts, one of them a renowned beauty, another a great charmer and celebrated blue-stocking hostess, long beloved by Arthur Balfour. The beauty, an elegant *poseuse*, was said to have broken many hearts; and in his autobiography[7] H.G. Wells describes how, as a very young man, having called on Harry Cust, then the editor of the *Pall Mall Gazette*, he was shown into a 'magnificent' office, which contained a grand piano, and resembled a drawing-room rather than an editorial sanctum. It appeared to be empty. 'Then I became aware of a sound of sobbing and realized that someone almost completely hidden from me lay prostrate on a sofa indulging in paroxysms of grief'. Wells considered that he had better cough. 'Thereupon the sound . . . ceased abruptly and a tall blond man sat up and then stood up, put away his pocket handkerchief and became entirely friendly and self-possessed . . .' Harry Cust was a well-known *homme-à-femmes;* and, when I repeated this story to Dick, and asked him if he could provide an explanation, he replied without a moment's thought: 'That must have been Aunt Pamela[8] . . .'

Among the Edwardian 'Souls', Percy and Madeline Wyndham[9], owners of Clouds, the house that Dick inherited, held an especially honoured place. Clouds had been built, between 1880 and 1886, by Norman Shaw, the most advanced of late-Victorian architects; and the Wyndhams had also commissioned William Morris to supply

[7] *Experiment in Autobiography*, 1934

[8] Lady Glenconner, afterwards married to the liberal statesman Lord Grey of Fallodon.

[9] Madeline Wyndham was the grand-daughter of the ill-fated Irish patriot Lord Edward Fitzgerald and his wife *'la belle Pamela'*, the illegitimate child of Madame de Genlis and Philippe Égalité.

chair-covers, wall-papers and carpets. From the crest of a gently rising hill, Clouds looked down over a wooded park, a big house with a broad garden terrace, planned on a nobly spacious scale. This was the first of his inherited possessions that Dick had decided to abandon; and it was already half-abandoned, and rapidly sinking into decay, some time before he shut its doors. Meanwhile, he had sold the Pre-Raphaelite pictures; and large bright patches, which marked the positions they had occupied, now chequered the surface of the faded Morris wall-papers, and broke up their cheerful arabesques of birds, pomegranates, flowers and twining leaves. Curtains and furniture had taken flight; naked floor-boards creaked beneath the tread; and to reach Dick's refuge, originally the house-keeper's room, his guests walked through a small concealed door – behind it hung long rows of neatly labelled household bells – descended a narrow staircase and traversed a gloomy basement.

In the shadows of the dark but comfortable house-keeper's room Dick pursued his new career. He seemed to have escaped regrets and eluded the phantoms of the past; though once, as we passed a vacant bedroom, he remarked quickly and bitterly, 'This is where I spent my honeymoon'; and one night, when we sat on the terrace above the park, and heard the crash of falling timber, he said that, since he had abandoned Clouds, or announced that he would soon abandon it, all the oaks and beeches had begun to die. But his last house consoled him for any sense of loss he felt. It was far smaller, a Sussex millhouse, flanked by a mill-pond and a shallow-lake, at the bottom of a valley, between a steep slope, covered with apple-trees, down which a reddish path and a rusty stream meandered – rusty because the soil of that part of the Home Counties, during the seventeenth-century a busy industrial district, is still rich in iron-ore – and a smoother ascent that rose beyond the lake towards a long old tile-roofed barn.

Cyril Connolly loved Tickerage; and, while writing *The Unquiet Grave,* he mentioned it, among other magical specifics, as a place whose quietly harmonious surroundings had helped him to keep Angst at bay –

the apple trees on the lawn, the bees in the roof, the geese on the pond, the black sun-lit marsh marigolds, the wood-fire crackling in the low bedroom, the creak of the cellar-door and the recurrent monotonies of the silver-whispering weir . . .

At Tickerage, if he had not gone abroad, Dick assembled his boon-companions almost every weekend – the painter Tristram

Hillier, known for his romantic seascapes, his gaiety and good looks and the picaresque stories he told about his love-affairs; John Rayner, then the cultivated Features Editor of Lord Beaverbrook's *Express;* Tom Driberg, a brilliantly gifted journalist, afterwards a Socialist politician, later promoted to the House of Lords; Ralph Keene, an adventurous maker of films; A.J.A. Symons, the erudite bibliophile, who suddenly achieved fame by publishing his memorable biography of Baron Corvo; and the epicurean art-dealer Freddie Mayor, who played the part of youthful Falstaff to Dick's lean and grizzled Prince Hal. Each was a great talker; each enjoyed wine; and Dick, a good listener, was also a generous host, particularly proud of his claret and of his admirable Crofts '08. A weekend at Tickerage was an occasion to which I always looked forward; we shared many friends; and a long procession of interesting young women flitted lightly through the mill. In Dick's sentimental life there were very few lacunae; one attractive face rapidly followed another; and it was said that, on his regular expeditions to the South of France, when he drew up at a wayside hotel, the proprietor, an old acquaintance, would invariably greet him with the same remark, *'Que madame a changé!'*, as he led his clients to their room.

Yet Dick was far from being the privileged amateur Wyndham Lewis had so savagely portrayed. He worked long hours, and was enough of a true artist often to mislike his own productions, and see the image that existed in his mind's eye floating just beyond his reach. Literature provided a secondary outlet; and during the 'thirties, after a New Year's party at Tickerage, impelled by a mood of black depression, he had flown off to the Sudan, where his friend Jack Poole ruled as District Commissioner over several hundred square miles of a remote province – the Bahr-el-Ghazal, popularly called 'The Bog', the home of the Dinka tribe, a tall and beautiful race, always completely naked except for a belt around the waist and, now and then, some towering head-dress, who usually stand on one leg and dye their hair a bright metallic blonde with the urine of their favourite cattle. Dick was happy among these dignified tribesmen; and his book, *The Gentle Savage,* published three years before the outbreak of the War, shows a rare descriptive talent. He had a 'painter's eye'; and, like Eugène Fromentin, the mid-nineteenth-century French artist, a lively recorder of North-African scenes – only Fromentin, George Moore once assured me, could paint 'the kink in an Arab horse's tail[10]'

[10]   See *'The Sign of the Fish'*

— he had developed a remarkable aptitude for writing prose. His impressions of the Sudanese landscape, of its refulgent sunsets and dawns, and of the huge storm-clouds that climbed into the sky above the flat, unending Bog, are always vividly distinct; and no less effective are his rapid thumb-nail sketches of the insects, flowers and animals he observed beside a forest trail — giant snails, slobbering millipedes, invisible monkeys that chased him through the branches, and the brilliant carpets of tropical butterflies, spread out upon the warm, moist earth, that lifted languidly at his approach, then, as soon as he had passed, quickly floated back again.

In 1926 standards of literary propriety were a great deal higher than they are today; and Dick was reluctant to inform his readers that he had acquired a native 'wife' or mistress — not a sculptural Dinka girl, alas, which might have embarassed his host, but Rafa, a Niam-Niam, member of a remote cannibal tribe, who had cost him two or three cows. Rafa was the perfect savage, and would tear to pieces and devour the little bird that she had been fondling a moment earlier. 'But her body was sublime, and with it she expressed all her emotions: when Rafa was sulky, every muscle and sinew sulked; when Rafa was tired, her head fell on to her arms — weighed down by the world's exhaustion . . . When Rafa slept, the earth seemed to nurse her as if she were a favoured child'. In Dick's narrative, she is merely the artist's model; and a description of her way of making love — or, rather, suffering the act of love — he attributed to a composite personage, an old official called Jameson. He, too, had had a native concubine, whose frigidity dismayed him: 'On her marriage night, she had lain quite still, picking the plaster off the wall with her fingernail'. Although she had paused for a second, 'her body had not even trembled; then she had continued to pick at the wall. She had spoken only once — to complain that she was out of sugar'.

The Gentle Savage received extremely good reviews; and to have succeeded in conquering a new medium pleased and reassured the author. Dick was a man who needed reassurance; he had a naturally restive and impatient spirit; and his restlessness appeared to spring from some secret disquietude, hidden deep below the surface, that he himself could never quite explain. Cyril Connolly's grateful description of Tickerage ends upon a gloomy note. What surroundings, he asks, could have been better calculated to defend the soul against despair and ennui? 'Yet always the anxious owner is flying from it as from the scene of a crime.' Perhaps the effort to simplify life, to divide his existence equally between creative work and pleasure, became more and more difficult in middle age. Dick, at that period, was constantly leaving Tickerage; and not every expedition turned out as agreeably as his visit to the Bahr-el-Ghazal. His map of the world was marked with 'cafard-centres', spiritual plague-spots that he carefully avoided, the worst and deadliest being a certain bone-white Greek island where he had hoped to settle down and paint, but, after a few days of drinking resinated local wine and scanning the hard-blue Aegean for a promised rescue ship, decided he might soon go mad.

Though Dick's love-affairs played a major part in his life, his attitude towards women, and, indeed, towards the whole business of love, remained perplexingly ambivalent. It was sometimes cynical, even harsh and callous. Yet he had a tender heart and warm affections; and, should he fall in love and meet an obstinate refusal, he pined and suffered like a true romantic. He was also the victim of strange phobias. Thus, having entered a second marriage – a far more successful alliance that his ill-starred early union – he insisted that he and his young wife must not attempt to live beneath the same roof, since the propinquity that a conventional marriage involved would ruin any chance of happiness. Despite his busily occupied existence, he was at heart, I think, a lonely man, who from the difficulties and disappointments of sexual love and the nagging problems of creative art found his best relief in friendship. But there he excelled – generous, affectionate, humorous, quick to respond, both completely unprejudiced and entirely undemanding. 'He was someone we shall miss so long as we live', said a woman friend, a platonic travelling companion, when she heard in 1948 of his sudden death abroad.

For Dick, the year that preceded his death had been particularly enjoyable. Through the good offices of a discerning newspaper-proprietor, a Sunday journal had appointed him their war-correspondent in the Middle East; and he had covered the beginnings of the Jewish-Arab struggle, the conclusion of the British Mandate and the full-scale hostilities that then broke out around Jerusalem. On his travels he piloted his own plane, as he had already done above the fields of Sussex; and he was evidently cheered and stimulated by the war-time risks he ran. I remember his brief return to London, and how – I believe it was our last encounter – I saw him stride into his club, hatless, wearing khaki trousers which exhibited the customary stains and creases, a heavy and not very clean bandage wrapped around his right thumb. 'What's happened to Wyndham ?' I heard an elderly member enquire. 'Says he's hurt his hand', replied a crony. 'Well, that'll stop the bugger painting!' remarked the first, and again lifted the copy of the *Times* that he had momentarily put aside. In fact, Dick confided to me, he had strained or bruised his thumb during a sharp difference of opinion with a tiresome Lebanese girl; and other tales he told me about his recent experiences sounded agreeably familiar.

The causes of his death, too, were highly characteristic; and soon afterwards I received a version of the tragedy that an eye-witness account (which did not come my way until I had begun this chapter) now exposes as a baseless legend. Dick, I was told, had been walking, early in June, 1948, along a trench beneath the ramparts of Jerusalem among a group of foreign journalists. They had agreed they must not show their heads; but Dick, who had adopted an Arab head-dress — he was a strong opponent of the Zionists — deliberately lagged behind, raised himself a little above the parapet and turned his camera towards the city's walls. The noise of a single rifle-shot brought his companions running back. He was still upright; his face registered an expression of intense astonishment; then he fell and quickly died. The astonishment seemed so typical of Dick — I could imagine his surprise at the sheer effrontery, the downright 'bloody cheek', displayed by an unknown Jewish sniper — that I thiught the story must be true.

The second and, I assume, more accurate version, though slightly less dramatic, is almost equally evocative. Dick, I learned from a letter dated June 6, 1948[11], had driven out with the eye-witness, an unnamed British officer 'attached and accredited to the Arab Legion', towards the area north of Shaf'ad, where the Legion was advancing. 'Dick said "How do you feel, David ?" I said I felt fine and excited. Dick said he was very happy and felt like a schoolboy'; and, as they approached the Legion's position, he suggested they should cross the ridge, so that he could photograph the Arab line. He rose, holding his camera — he wore a khaki uniform; and a Jewish Bren-gun opened up. 'I ducked but Dick didn't, and he got four shots in his chest. He must have died straightaway'. Evidently, his mood on the eve of death was harmonious and exalted.

Had Dick Wyndham happily survived, he would now be eighty-two; and I have attempted to describe him here not only as a friend but, in

[11] This letter, now in the possession of Richard Wyndham's half-brother Mr. Francis Wyndham, was sent from Egypt by a Mr. John F. Handford to Ian Fleming, then the director of the Sunday Times' foreign service.

some ways, as a social type, the representative of a period that outlasted the War, but by the sixties had already ended. Englishmen of Dick's kind need no longer divest themselves of their hereditary privileges; that the government will do on their behalf, whatever their own plans may be. But, before I leave the period, I must attempt two smaller portraits, each of a friend who, having inherited a heavy load of possessions and conventions, also elected to pursue art and separate everything he found most valuable in life from its superfluous appendages. I doubt if Dick knew Robert Abdy; certainly he did not know him well; but he, too, when he entered the adult world, had been a sportsman and a gambler, though, unlike Dick, he had already begun to reveal a decidedly eccentric strain. Should he visit a Leicestershire country house, he would take with him, besides his hunters, a pack-horse carrying his sheets; and at Biarritz, where he had hired a large villa, his servants wore green-and-gold liveries that he had personally designed. After dinner, I have heard, one of his Basque footmen would sometimes entertain his guests by executing the *danse du ventre*.

About this time, however, he suffered a severe financial set-back; an important London property, which his man of business had left uninsured over the weekend, caught fire and was reduced to ashes. The disaster transformed his whole existence; he decided he would abandon hunting and racing, and become an art-dealer and Man of Taste, and spent two years in Paris, visiting the Louvre every day, studying and handling the master-works of the eighteenth-century French *ébénistes*. At length he had made his first purchase. A good choice, said the expert he summoned; but perhaps not quite good enough considering the price that he had paid; and thereupon he had carried it out into the courtyard and beaten it to pieces with a poker. The episode illustrates his personality − a strange mixture of passion and taste and prejudice, of sensibility and strong self-will. As an art-critic, his judgments were often biased; surveying Wilton and Inigo Jones's magnificent Double Cube Room, he announced loudly that, whatever one might think of the room itself, he wouldn't give half-a-crown for any of William Kent's elaborate chairs and tables. Nor was he interested in Gothic architecture; while, at this stage, the arts of China and Japan completely passed his comprehension. Not until much later did I hear that a drawing by Utamaro now hung opposite his bed, and that, to protect it against the sunlight, he kept his curtains permanently drawn.

Later still, he made a sympathetic study of the lesser

nineteenth-century English draughtsmen. In one historical age alone would Bertie always feel a stranger — the barbaric age in which he lived. To say that he inhabited the past might be an exaggeration; but for him the past was effectively the present and the only temporal world he understood. His standards were still those of an Augustan connoisseur; and at our earliest meeting, when I lunched with him and his wife at a London house that belonged to Edward James, another rich eccentric of the period, he said that, as I was a writer, he would like to consult me about a literary problem. Diane was fond of poetry. He wishes to buy her a present, and thought the manuscripts of some of Donne's poems, accompanied perhaps by a couple of first editions, might form a not unwelcome gift. If I could give him the address of an intelligent book-seller, he proposed, since the weather was fine, to walk round there this afternoon.

Bertie built up his own collection on a similarly generous and ambitious scale. Before the War the Abdys had lived at Saint-Germain in an eighteenth-century pavilion near the Château; but, during the late thirties, once their son was born, they moved to the English West Country, where they occupied an ancient stone-built house called Newton Ferrers, high above a precipitous, bosky landscape through which a modest tributary of the Tamar flowed. It delighted Diane; and, so long as it pleased her, Bertie, who preferred France and regretted his elegant pavilion, was prepared to tolerate its rough-hewn fabric. Nevertheless, when I spoke of the house's architecture, he indignantly protested. '*Architecture* ! If it can be said to have architecture . . .' he exclaimed, pointing to its simple granite front and the sturdy balustrades, cut from the same stone, that lined the upper and the lower terrace. He distracted himself by digging a water-garden, and leading a small tributary of the main stream down the hill and in and out of the succession of pools that he surrounded with decorative aquatic plants, notably with huge clumps of *gunnera manicata*, no doubt because its spreading Baroque leafage has an amusingly un-English air.

Inside the house he assembled and gradually enlarged the collection he had brought from Saint-Germain. At the end of the drawing-room he had placed Winterhalter's superb portrait — probably the artist's masterpiece — of Princess Troubetskoy, painted on her visit to the court of Napoleon III, a seductive *femme du monde*, whose broad, slightly Slavonic face wears a faint half-mocking smile; and about it he had gathered some of his finest pieces of eighteenth-century French

133

furniture, Houdon's bust of Madame His, a bronze Horus, and such minor bibelots as a porcelain statuette of Madame de Pompadour's favourite little dog. Diane Abdy shared his preoccupation with the arts; she was herself both an assiduous painter and a diligent musician. Otherwise, in appearance at least, they were a somewhat ill-matched pair. Bertie, being well over six feet tall, often seemed too large and long-limbed for the space he occupied, while Diane, a delicately diminutive figure, was all grace and speed and lightness. To her father, nicknamed 'The Pocket Adonis' by Edwardian society, Diane evidently owed her charm; but her mother, an imposing *grande dame*, member of a formidable sisterhood known by their contemporaries as 'The Bossy Bruces', must have contributed her energy and strength of purpose. Like many small people she fretted against her size, which she attempted valiantly to disregard; and, during her youth, her adventurous way of life had sometimes much alarmed her parents. Besides driving fast cars, riding to hounds and, on one occasion, narrowly escaping death when her mount fell into a flooded stream, she had explored bohemian London, visited louche night-clubs and studied art at the Slade School under Professor Tonks' guidance. She had also, no doubt through Emerald Cunard, become the friend and confidante of George Moore, who had admired the poems she showed him, and paid her gently amorous court. In her own generation she had many devoted admirers; and her alliance with an eccentric art-loving baronet, an expatriate already once married, was an event her conservative family deplored.

At Newton Ferrers, between 1944 and 1948, the period of our friendship that I remember most distinctly, Diane still possessed a 'rage to live'. Problems beset her; servants and gardeners had vanished; she was doing her best to manage a nearby farm, superintend bee-hives and manufacture cheeses. Meanwhile, Bertie had returned from France a tired and disappointed man. On the outbreak of War he had rejoined his old regiment, but had found it difficult to adapt himself to modern military life. In the mess standards of conversation seemed nowadays absurdly low; and a dinner-party with his divisional commander, the future Field Marshal Lord Montgomery, proved particularly unfortunate. Bertie had talked at length; but the subject he chose had been the commerce of the sexes; and he had announced that human methods of reproduction struck him as inept and clumsy, and that the system of pollination employed by trees and plants was, he thought, far less uncivilised.

Having listened at first silently, afterwards more and more impatiently, the General had risen to his feet and, remarking 'Enough of this nonsense', had led his officers towards the map-room.

The army's decision that Captain Sir Robert Abdy would never make a modern soldier both offended and surprised him; and, although, when he returned to Newton Ferrers, he joined the Cornish Home Guard and, hung round with belts and holsters and cases, would spend whole nights defending the Tamar Bridge, he had lost his martial impetus. Bertie's disillusionment and war-time gloom were not the least of Diane's problems. But, whatever the problem she had to confront, she attacked it fiercely and determinedly. Diane setting forth to tend her hives, veiled and gloved, carrying a primitive smoke-machine to lull the bees asleep – the Newton Ferrers bees were an unusually ferocious strain – or, in a child's wellington boots, treading down a layer of black molasses into foul-smelling farmyard silage, was a spectacle that moved the heart. She did not appeal for sympathy and seldom asked for assistance; but, as the silage squelched beneath her feet or a mad bee sang around her ears, she had a look both of heroic resolve and of romantic desperation, which seemed to imply that, if the worst had not yet happened, we could expect it very soon now.

The Abdys had few neighbours; and those few, like General Montgomery, were often a little perturbed by their host's discursive table-talk. Among the most easily astonished was a retired diplomatist, a person of great height and impeccable gravity, with a long straight nose, a long stony chin and long beautifully starched cuffs, which added distinction to his sweeping gestures. Sir Robert was fond of teasing Sir Claud, who invariably responded; and I remember an afternoon when I heard Bertie unfold a curious Rabelaisian anecdote – the story of how a Spanish grandee had once been discovered in highly improper circumstances wearing only the Order of the Golden Fleece; while his victim continued to wave an arm and extend a supplicatory hand, as he ejaculated 'No more of this, Bertie! I must beg you to cease! Pray desist! Upon my word, you are going too far . . .'

A second neighbour was a fellow lover of art and himself the owner of a fine collection. The Colonel, a veteran of the First World War, had an extremely dandified appearance; his favourite term of praise was 'swagger', which he bestowed on every object that he purchased, from a Sumerian bas-relief to a waxen maquette by Donatello or an exquisite Renaissance drawing. He regularly visited Newton Ferrers;

and Bertie would often visit him at home; but they rarely agreed about the aesthetic worth or the commercial value of one another's acquisitions. Brusquely picking up the Colonel's Donatello — said to be a preliminary model for the famous equestrian statue of the *condottiere* Gattamelata — so brusquely that its owner feared he might dislocate the horse's tail, he would denounce it as a nineteenth-century fraud; and the Colonel, vibrant with indignation, would order him to leave the house. There were times, I think, when Bertie reversed the process; and the Colonel was expelled from Newton Ferrers. But their differences never lasted long; each respected the other's devotion to art and single-minded cult of beauty.

Newton Ferrers itself, always a beautiful place, grew more beautiful, and a great deal more urbane, under Diane's care and Bertie's guidance. Built near the river that separates Devon and Cornwall, it surveys a lonely wooded landscape that combines the traits of both counties — Devonian softness and warmth with Cornish strength and wildness. On the hilltops storm-winds have bowed and flattened the oaks into strange druidic postures; down the valley runs a broad tree-shadowed stream, where trout lie flickering against the current in a golden web of sun and shadow; and wide-winged buzzards drift far overhead with their faint, hoarse, mewing cries. At this distance I feel that the place I remember was already haunted by the tragic spirit. Diane asked too much of existence to be a very happy woman; but no disaster I might ever have foreseen could have outdone the hideous fate she suffered. She enjoyed speed and had long been a venturesome driver; and one day, as she hurried homewards, she met a hump-back bridge that hid an advancing lorry. The accident effectively ended her life; for, after prolonged anguish, she was condemned to a twilit world, far from any of the landmarks of her previous existence, that held her prisoner until she died.

Bertie tended her, while she seemed capable of recovering, with exemplary patience and devotion. When she vanished, he remained at Newton Ferrers, but occasionally appeared in London; and there we sometimes still met. He had scarcely changed, though his hair had whitened, his cheeks had grown hollower, and he now wore a wide black hat and large black cloak. Our encounters were often dramatic; he would spring up, as it were from the centre of the stage, like a Victorian demon-king, and immediately proceed to discuss some problem of art or life that he had recently been turning over. Once the background of our talk was the busiest part of Piccadilly; once in

Belgravia I found him standing alone on a doorstep and polishing a large brown shoe, which he laid down to take me into his flat and show me a collection of drawings and posters by the French cartoonist Chéret — his latest aesthetic *trouvaille* — that he had recently acquired.

Another meeting was with Gerald Berners, the third of the three rebellious Englishmen I am attempting to describe. It must have taken place late in the 1940s; Gerald, who died soon afterwards, was already very ill, and had left a nursing-home near London to entertain us at a local restaurant. It was not, I remember, an especially cheerful luncheon; and afterwards we walked through a neighbouring park, where Bertie inveighed against the deplorably vulgar taste that British municipal gardeners displayed. Both the Abdys knew our host well; he frequented much the same milieu; and he, too, had abandoned the oppressive surroundings in which he had been born and reared. But his ancestral heritage was considerably more cumbrous than that of either Dick or Bertie. Dick paid little attention to his ancestors, despite their long and interesting history; and Bertie, whose family had been founded by a seventeenth-century London merchant, was so ill-informed that when, having quitted the army, he applied for a post as King's Messenger and was asked to complete a questionnaire, giving, among other personal details, his mother's name and national origin, he had written down merely 'German, I think'[12], which, since Germany and Britain were then at war, disconcerted his examiners.

In the crowded pages of Burke, Gerald's ancestral line occupies nearly two-and-a-half columns, or some twenty-two inches of extremely small type, beginning with Sir John Bourchier de Berners, created first baron 'by summons to Parliament' about the middle of the fifteenth century, and his grandson and successor, another John Bourchier, who translated Marcus Aurelius, the *Boke of Huon of Bordeaux*[13] and Froissart's *Chronicles*. Except for the second baron, none of Gerald's ancestors seems to have had much to do with art or learning. Courtiers, soldiers, clerics, High Sheriffs, they had quietly performed the tasks expected of them by the society into which they had been born. Gerald's parents, too, were rigorous conformists. His mother, although, during her youth, she had shown some vague

---

[12] She had been christened, I learn from Burke's *Peerage & Baronetage*, Anna Adèle Coronna.

[13] Berners' translation, which Shakespeare used when he was writing *A Midsummer Night's Dream*, first introduced King Oberon to English readers. Chancellor of the Exchequer under Henry VIII, Berners was also a soldier and renowned diplomatist.

romantic tendencies, had become, after a somewhat unsuccessful marriage, a passionate devotee of fox-hunting, while his father, a sailor who spent most of his life at sea, moody, sardonic, unaffectionate, was 'essentially a man of action'. Gerald's paternal grandmother, Lady Bourchier – a baroness in her own right, but 'everything else in her own wrong' as his father once remarked – was a decidedly forbidding personage, 'not unlike Holbein's portrait of Bloody Mary', and 'intensely religious and violently low church'. She and her good-natured husband inhabited an ugly, much-restored Elizabethan house, encircled by a half-dry moat and a heavy grove of dark firs. But Gerald was brought up at Arley, the home of his maternal grandparents, a huge turreted neo-Gothic mansion, which bore a slight resemblance to Strawberry Hill; and it was there he had learned to adore music and had gained his first impressions of visual beauty from a picture-covered screen, where, beneath a film of yellow varnish, flowers and landscapes and exotic birds formed an enchanting labyrinth of shapes and colours.

When, in 1918, at the age of thirty-five, Gerald succeeded an uncle as the fourteenth Baron Berners, he had quickly settled with the past; and the decisive steps he took inspired Osbert Sitwell to write 'The Love-Bird', an ambitious long short-story, that, although it contains many imaginative touches, and the hero is a composite character rather than a personal portrait, was clearly based on Gerald's record. Sir Robert Mainwroth, we read, 'finding himself encumbered with houses and estates', had 'proceeded to divest himself of everything that did not appeal to him . . . either aesthetically or through his humour – and his sense of aesthetics and humour were perilously akin'. Thus he had broken up his store of awkward heirlooms, sold his ancestors' 'vast, draughty, machicolated mansions', and established a series of charming pieds-à-terre in different European countries. But thereafter fact and fiction diverge. Mainwroth, the author implies, was a frivolous dilettante, for all his moods of 'reasonless depression', who talked well, 'painted and wrote fluently', and under the polished surface of his work hid any trace of genuine feeling. The real Gerald, I am convinced, was at heart a feeling man; his autobiography suggests that, even as a school-boy, he was capable of deep affection.

Handsomeness he greatly admired in both sexes; and he could never have been called handsome. Short and, when I knew him, bald, he had a thin moustache, a tremulous eye-lid, an eye-glass, and usually wore a spotted bow-tie. His alert yet hesitant attitude had once reminded me of Lewis Carroll's White Rabbit; but the resemblance, I soon discovered, was entirely superficial. He might hesitate with an expression of wild surmise, his hands fluttering and his eye-glass flashing; but his pretended bewilderment was merely a part of the persona he had adopted many years ago, when he had been employed, as a young attaché, in the British Foreign Service. He had a clear head. Otherwise, during his leisured middle-age, he could scarcely have made so successful a use of his various creative talents. Diaghilev had recognised his musical gifts, and commissioned him to produce the score of a new ballet, *The Triumph of Neptune*, for which Sacheverell Sitwell wrote the libretto; and in 1934 he had published an autobiography, *First Childhood*, a highly entertaining and remarkably revealing book, and had painted many evocative landscapes that recalled the early Corot. If painters were apt to praise his books, and musicians tended to admire his pictures, he accepted their professional limitations without the slightest show of spleen.

As often happens, it was the persona, rather than the underlying face, that attracted his contemporaries. They saw him as a particularly gifted inhabitant of the *monde où l'on s'amuse*, a rich bohemian constantly seeking amusement, whose sense of humour, as Osbert Sitwell hinted, was closely associated with his sense of style. There is no doubt that Gerald, a natural lover of fun, always liked to be amused, and that some of the aesthetic causes he sponsored were chiefly recommended to him by their comic aspect — for example, the Surrealist Movement, which during the 1930s first erupted on the London scene. At the Surrealist Exhibition, looking especially fashionable and neat among Dali's limp watches, Ernst's spectres and lion-headed men and Magritte's hallucinatory nudes, he played the part of genial compère; and when Dali wilted and nearly swooned, while delivering a long speech from inside a diver's helmet, Gerald efficiently unscrewed the head-piece and brought the artist back to life.

In his own surroundings he assembled amusing objects and arranged fantastic episodes. Moti, Penelope Betjeman's half-arab gelding, once attended a tea-party at Faringdon, the eighteenth-century house, distinguished but not inconveniently large, that had replaced the draughty mansions of his childhood, and was photographed bending over the table with an air of perfect *savoir vivre*. At Faringdon, too, he dyed his white pigeons blue and green and rosy pink; and, now that his friend Robert Heber-Percy has inherited the house, a cloud of rainbow-coloured birds still sweep around the graceful pediment. Faringdon appeared to have been built for harmony; and there Gerald remained throughout the War, and the uneasy years that followed, until a mysterious illness wrecked his scheme of living. Specialists diagnosed a brain-tumour. But, whatever its origins, it was an illness of a peculiarly terrifying sort; whereas many other human maladies are in some degree external, this struck at the brain and nerves and threatened the centre of his being. Gerald put up a stubborn defence, and even from his invalidism derived occasional fun, wearing the wool skull-caps of a somewhat rabbinical design that a crack-brained admirer, the wife of an Oxford don, regularly knitted for his benefit. Our last meeting had a strange and impressive conclusion. He seemed old and tired and bowed by pain; and I suspected that he had given up hope. Our talk was desultory. Then he began to speak of certain friends — cultured, warm-hearted Catholics — who had set about converting him. They went on and on, he said, and never left him alone. It bored him, and did him no good. Finally, raising his voice with a flash of defiant courage: 'Why should I listen to them? It is all such *bosh* !'

7

Gerald died in 1950; and I doubt if he would have found the second half of the century quite as entertaining as the first; but a drama that occurred in 1951 would certainly have excited his imagination. On June 15th an evening newspaper announced that two young members of the Foreign Service had suddenly disappeared across the Channel; and the names Donald Maclean and Guy Burgess acquired a startling notoriety. They were names I had known for some years; and they belonged, though not to close friends, to familiar acquaintances. Donald I had first seen during the early 1930s at Bernard Penrose's riverside house near Falmouth; and, when I arrived, I soon heard that he had already managed to disgrace himself. 'Meeting him', wrote Cyril Connolly, 'one was conscious of both amiability and weakness . . . an outsize Cherubino intent on amorous experience but too shy and clumsy to succeed'[1]. At Lambe Creek he had attempted the seduction of a by no means puritanical fellow guest, and had been repulsed because his methods of approach were equally violent and ill-timed. He appeared to make little distinction between the sexes; his behaviour resembled that of an over-enthusiastic young dog; and I presently became involved in a ridiculous practical joke designed to teach him gentler ways. Slipping into his room, we propped against his pillow the realistic effigy of a brightly painted sea-nymph, the figure-head of a Victorian coastal-ship, that we felt sure must arouse his passions. Should he try to ravish her in semi-darkness, it was thought that contact with her teak-wood limbs might temporarily blunt his ardour.

We failed, of course; Donald smiled sulkily; and the subject was dismissed. Later, I learned that he had joined the Foreign Office, where his intelligence and industry were much esteemed. After serving in Paris and Washington, once he returned from the United States he was appointed Counsellor in Cairo. Now happily married

[1] *The Missing Diplomats*, 1952

and the father of two sons, he had come to be regarded by his official superiors as the white hope of the Service; but, during his stay in Egypt, an extraordinary transformation struck his character. He developed a manic strain, of which the most violent manifestation took place in the early part of 1950, when he and a boon-companion – a gifted friend of mine, whom I much preferred to Donald – broke into the flat of a young woman employed at the American Embassy and, like Beatrix Potter's 'Two Bad Mice', demolished every object they could find. Naturally, they had invaded the wrong flat. Both believed, however, that they were obeying the instructions of a demonic personage named 'Gordon', the name they have given to the wild boar portrayed on the label of a well-known gin-bottle, and that, with Gordon's help, they were discovering their true selves and releasing all their pent-up genius. My friend's account of the affair contained some strange details. He said, for instance, that what had particularly pleased them was the unexpected behaviour of their victim's looking-glass. Though they had attempted to smash it by hurling it into her bath, it had remained miraculously unbroken; while the bath had been reduced to fragments.

Invalided home, suffering, his good-natured superiors believed, from over-work and a transitory nervous crisis, Donald was granted six months' leave, and having undergone a spell of Jungian analysis, resumed his duties at the Foreign Office. With Cyril I saw him now and then; and it struck me that, since our early meeting in Cornwall, he had neither changed nor much matured. 'Silly but not stupid' was the description that I remember hearing Francis Birrell apply to a troublesome acquaintance; and through Donald's knowledge and sophistication and occasional gleams of charm I thought I still detected a stratum of juvenile silliness that, especially under Gordon's spell, might at any moment re-emerge. He had a fresh face with candid light-coloured eyes – a very English type of face – slightly spoiled by two large front teeth that projected just beyond their neighbours. Donald was a goose, often an amiable goose, despite his bursts of alcoholic rage, but not, when he talked and argued and proclaimed, to be taken very seriously.

Guy Burgess, on the other hand, produced a much more definite effect. While Donald's personality was irresolute and fluid, Guy's was tough and case-hardened and had a formidable cutting-edge. 'Grubby, intemperate, promiscuous', Cyril records in his pamphlet, he was also extraordinarily energetic, 'a great talker, boaster, walker, who . . . drank, not like a feckless undergraduate, as Donald was apt to do, but like some Rabelaisian bottle-swiper . . .' Donald's tendencies, at least during an alcoholic bout, were sometimes vaguely homosexual; Guy was an experienced inhabitant of the homosexual underworld, devoted to 'cottaging' and accustomed to the risks and hair-breadth escapes that formed the background of his dangerous pleasures.

In 1951, when we were first informed that Burgess and Maclean had fled the country, the news bewildered all their friends; it was as if a pair of moderately accomplished comedians should have stolen the tragedian's crown and robes. How were we to reconcile the solemnly drunken Donald and the crapulous, loquacious Guy with the desperate parts they had assumed — and had, we discovered, been secretly performing since the day they left Cambridge? Discretion was not a virtue with which we had felt inclined to credit them. Yet each had supported year after year the terrifying role of double agent, and only once or twice, usually in his cups, had hinted at the subterranean life he led. But then, neither heroes nor villains, observed from a private point of view, ever quite fulfil our hopes; and I have seldom encountered a widely famous or, indeed, notorious personage, of whom my original impressions were not faintly disillusioning. I admire the artist's or philosopher's gifts rather than the countenance he shows the world; and even an eminent modern thinker may reveal some childish traits. Bertrand Russell himself, whom I met with Julian Huxley, was less commanding than I had expected. True, he looked nobly staunch and virile, and instead of levering his torso out of his chair, as many younger men do, rose smoothly and swiftly to his feet like a taut steel spring uncoiling. But then he spoke. Huxley had lately visited Mexico; Bernal Diaz's wonderful account of the Spanish Conquest was a book that I had just read; and I happened to make some reference to the horrors of the Aztec faith, and to the tall white pyramids Diaz describes, the sacrificial shrines that surmounted them coated thick with human blood.

At this point the philosopher sharply interrupted me. The atrocities of the Inquisition, he said, had been equally appalling. It was useless to protest that, while the Inquisition's victims were relatively few, and they were condemned after lengthy legal proceedings,[2] the Mexican priesthood, at the dedication of Uitzilopochli's great temple, had slaughtered twenty-thousand

---

[2] In 1482 Pope Sixtus IV issued a bull, which declared that the heretic, like every criminal, were 'entitled to a fair trial and simple justice'.

prisoners of war, who formed, as they patiently awaited death, a queue that stretched across the city. Neither quantitatively nor qualitatively could their actions be compared. But Russell, a veteran antagonist of the Christian religion, angrily dismissed my plea; with his large beak, fierce eyes and long, withered, stringy neck, he resembled an indignant cassowary or some other gaunt, ill-tempered bird; and our conversation was abandoned.

Intellectual arrogance may be a product of public vanity; but elsewhere vanity takes on a different guise as a corrosive secret passion. At Oxford I had often heard from Robert Graves of his mysterious mentor T.E. Lawrence, whose *Seven Pillars of Wisdom* had not yet been published, but around whom legends were already gathering; and my single glimpse of the heroic adventurer was both bizarre and unexpected. Savile Row then terminated in a pretty Georgian archway, since replaced by the blank facade of a dismal modern police-station; and above the arch were a couple of big rooms that enclosed a picture gallery. Thither I went early one afternoon to visit an exhibition of Augustus John's works. The place was almost empty; but, as I explored the rooms and noticed that paintings and drawings of Lawrence's distinguished head covered an entire wall, I suddenly became aware of a new visitor standing just inside the entrance, making friendly talk — sometimes its friendliness seemed a little overdone — to a young woman who sat near the door, purveying catalogues and tickets.

Immediately I recognised Graves' hero — an outlandish figure, wearing a shabby oil-bespattered suit, a pair of metal clips about the bottoms of his trousers, his tweed cap turned back to front in the fashion affected at that time by proletarian motor-cyclists. I knew the head well from sketches and photographs — a splendid head, nobly proportioned, that bore the stamp of vivid energy. But the frame beneath it was meagre and ill-shaped, and so short that the mask of a powerful adult appeared to have been planted on a school-boy's shoulders. His attitude, too, was deprecatory; the eagerness with which he spoke to the ticket-seller provided an indication of his native shyness; and, anxious to conceal my interest, I glanced away again and turned towards the other pictures. During the interval, Lawrence changed his position. A further glance showed that he had removed his cap, and was standing opposite his own portraits. At first I hesitated to trust my eyes. Could that be 'Lawrence of Arabia', in this nearly empty room, lifting his chin, squaring his slight shoulders, exhibiting now one profile, now the other, for the benefit of all who cared to watch? But, however carefully I studied him, I received the same impression. He was obeying, I thought, a secret instinct, deeply rooted in his nature, the reverse side of the exaggerated diffidence with which he usually spoke and moved.

Later, I came to dislike his mannered and archaistic prose-style, and thought I detected an element of self-conscious artifice that made him, when he was describing his private experiences, a highly unreliable reporter. It may be that in every brave and adventurous man of action there is a certain touch of vanity; and historians tell us that Nelson, with his love of gorgeous uniforms and orders and decorations, was an inveterate exhibitionist. Just after the War I remember catching sight in Bond Street of another hero of our time, Field-Marshal Lord Montgomery. A huge motor-car drew up before a barber's shop; and the Field-Marshal rapidly dismounted. No photographers stood ready to immortalise the scene; there were no bystanders except myself; but his response was automatic. He paused, the famous beret he always wore cocked at the appropriate angle, struck a familiar pose, smiled to left and right, then dashed out of sight across the pavement; and, looking back on the careers of Burgess and Maclean, I wonder if the villain, too, may not share the hero's vanity.

Cyril Connolly's analysis of *The Missing Diplomats* is the shrewdest so far written. It was first serialised by the *Sunday Times*, which then published his weekly book-reviews, and later reprinted as a pamphlet by Ian Fleming, who asked me to contribute a foreword, under the imprint of the Queen Anne Press. Ian, I should explain, was one of the many friends I had made through Ann Rothermere; and the years 1951 and 1952 marked an important stage of his existence. Just before Christmas 1951 Ann left Warwick House, and joined him at his Caribbean home, where, with Noël Coward as *compère* and best man, they were subsequently married. Her departure was swift and unannounced, though not altogether unexpected; and from an old letter of mine I have copied some sentences that deal with the effect it made. 'Gossip about the Warwick House Drama', I inform her, 'has been brisk, but recently has tended to languish for want of anything to feed on. Public response is pretty evenly divided between "I think it's very brave of her", "I must say I respect her for it" and "What a pity – no more lovely parties !"' Ian and I had often stayed together at Wraxhall, the Rothermeres' country house, and on Monday mornings he had driven me back to London in his long, low, rakish car across Wiltshire and past Silbury Hill, the most mysterious and impressive of English prehistoric mounds, a steep green barrow covering a secret burial place that no archaeologist has yet unearthed, large enough to contain a whole regiment of Iron Age chieftains and their wives and followers.

Archaeology had little interest for Ian, and he always refused my time-wasting suggestion that we should stop and climb its slopes. He was a modern man, an addict of mechanical speed, who kept his eye on his road and his hands upon the wheel, though — a somewhat alarming practice — he occasionally drove with one hand while he lit an American cigarette or used a silver stick of lipsalve. During such a journey, I remember, he informed me that he meant to write a thriller — the Bond series had not yet been launched — and gave me a brief resumé of the plot, which concerned a cleverly executed murder and a lethal leg of lamb.[3]

Being no judge of the contemporary thriller, I must admit that I was unimpressed, just as, in later years, probably for the same reason, I found I could not take to James Bond. But Ian himself I liked; and he good-naturedly accepted me, no doubt because I was neither a wild bohemian nor a rampant homosexual. On their return to England, the Flemings occupied a house on St. Margaret's Bay between Dover and the Sandwich golf-course (the site of Ian's favourite club) above a pebbly beach and under the lee of a gigantic chalk cliff. I grew extremely fond of 'White Cliffs', though some of Ann's friends, remembering her previous houses, were apt to be critical of the long one-storeyed sea-side villa; and Duff Cooper, when he first approached it, had exclaimed in tones of deep astonishment, 'This, I suppose, must be how the poor live!' Lying abed, no sooner had I opened my eyes than I saw a strip of sea, uninterrupted by any reminder of the beach, beautifully filling half the window; and the vision brought back memories of Proust's Balbac and his early sojourn at the Grand Hotel. A radiator, invariably over-heated, diffused the acrid scent of scorching paint; and today that smell, should I encounter it, still recalls the colours of the sea and the sound of high tide on the shingle.

At St. Margaret's Bay, Noël Coward was the Fleming's nearest

---

[3]   Ian afterwards presented the idea to his friend Roald Dahl, who adapted and made highly successful use of it.

neighbour; and there, and afterwards at his elegant Jamaican retreat, I often drank his whisky and listened to his conversation. Noël's voice on and off the stage struck me as almost exactly similar. He was seldom definitely behind the scenes; and to every situation that occurred he gave a strong dramatic turn. A single episode may illustrate my point. Gertrude Lawrence, the actress who had seemed best to catch the spirit of his youthful comedies, and was perhaps the only woman for whom his attachment had nearly resembled love, died in 1951. That same day, two of his friends were motoring across Kent; and, as it had grown late and both were thirsty and tired, they decided they would visit him. Earlier, they had read reports of the great comédienne's death; but the news had slipped their minds; and they drove happily towards his door. They had reached their destination and were preparing to ring the bell, when the door was flung open; and, silhouetted against the light, there stood Noël, wearing a black or, at least, a very dark dressing-gown, his arms extended from the threshold. 'You *darlings*', he cried. 'I *knew* you'd come. . .' Not until several minutes had passed — minutes of speechless embarrassment — did they understand his tragic welcome and begin to fall into the dignified consolatory parts he had intended they should play. His own part — heart-broken but still hospitable — he enacted to perfection. With a few sighs and some faint autumnal smiles, he produced a tray and glasses; and, standing, they drank a silent toast in beloved Gertie's honour.

I do not suggest that his sorrow was insincere, but that sincerity and insincerity are relative terms as applied to any well-known actor, whose life is made up of the real and the unreal, the natural and the artificial, in extremely puzzling proportions. If the world is a stage, the stage is also a world, self-contained and self-secluded; and from that second world there is frequently no escape for the truly gifted mime. Off the stage, when did Noël act, and when was his private behaviour totally spontaneous? Given an audience, he seldom entered a room; he almost always made an entry; and I remember another occasion, this time at a house in France, where a number of English guests were assembled. Among them was the singer Olga Lynn — 'Oggie' to her large affectionate circle — a remarkably short and rather stout lady, inclined to wear a very broad hat, so that she had somewhat the appearance of a perambulatory mushroom. She was then recovering from a slight stroke; but of this Noël happened to be unaware. He arrived late and, a suitable entry having been made, moved genially around the room, distributing kisses and smiles and

bows, until at last he came to Oggie. 'Darling Oggie; and how are
you ?' he demanded. 'Thank you, Noël; I've been ill you see', she
replied in muffled accents and patted her poor flaccid cheek. Noël
dramatically threw up his hands. 'Not – a – tiny – *strokey* – Oggie –
darling ?' he enquired in tones of heart-felt consternation, carefully
spacing out the words and lending each a poignant emphasis. We
were all tempted to laugh, and quickly resisted the impulse; but
although the enquiry may perhaps sound brutal, it had the right effect
upon the sufferer, since it implied that a stroke was the kind of
harmless minor mishap, mildly ridiculous rather than really grave,
like tripping over a dog or tumbling downstairs, that might come
anybody's way.

Noël Coward was not the first famous theatrical personage I had
observed at close quarters. During my early youth, Eddie Marsh had
once taken me after the play to the small flat above the Aldwych
Theatre where Ivor Novello then held court. The brilliant *jeune premier*
of the 'twenties and 'thirties, adored by Eddie since Rupert Brooke's
death, was approaching middle age, but retained his youthful good
looks. Indeed, there was an aura of unspoiled youth, even a touch of
childishness, about himself and his entourage. Clad in a silk
dressing-gown – the kind of dressing-gown that has a scarf attached
and a decorative monogram embroidered on the breast-pocket – he
lolled gracefully back among his courtiers, a great friend, also
dressing-gowned, reclining familiarly at his side and his attendant
hovering around. I was reminded of one of the school-stories that had
amused me many years earlier. Ivor was the head boy, the handsome
'Cock of the Sixth', governing the school-world from his study
flanked by his chief favourite and by the troop of loyal prefects who
transmitted his commands. The effect was strangely juvenile, though
the neighbouring bedroom, I saw, enclosed a sumptuous double bed
which carried two separate pillows and two splendid pairs of silk
pyjamas. Our conversation was certainly innocent enough – it circled
round the last performance; and I remember that we played 'Snap' or
'Animal Grab' for extremely modest stakes.

In other theatrical households I have noticed a similar pattern –
current favourite, friendly factotum, charged with paying bills and
ordering travel-tickets, and miscellaneous hangers-on, among them a
tame female admirer, guaranteed sexually safe, and the devoted
one-time dresser, who, if the atmosphere clouds and a crisis threatens,
emerges bearing 'a nice cup of tea'. Ivor had simple tastes; and I have

been told that, at the end of a difficult day, having first proposed champagne, next burgundy or perhaps a restorative bottle of moselle, finally he would almost always decide that some good strong tea was what he and his companions really wanted. Noël was a more sophisticated host; but his regime was no less patriarchal; and the fact that his acquaintances called him 'The Master' helped to emphasise his dominant position. Both he and Ivor shunned bohemian excesses; they emulated David Garrick, the gentlemanly genius who had raised his fellow actors from the ranks of 'rogues and vagabonds'. Robert Newton, on the other hand, an actor I often met in convivial surroundings, was roguery and vagabondage incarnate, a blend of Falstaff, Pistol and Nicholas Nickleby's employer Mr. Vincent Crummles. Alcohol had bronzed and polished his face until it gleamed through the dusk of a night-club like a Victorian door-knocker; and above a huge mouth and a copper-red nose shone dark and wildly glittering eyes. A part he much enjoyed was the villain of *Treasure Island*; and, if he were sufficiently excited or enraged, he would borrow Long John's thunderous accents, roll his fiery orbs and gnash his teeth. An equally alarming moment occurred when the pirate became the Ancient Mariner and, having grasped one with a rough and puissant fist, sonorously rolled out his message.

For me the burden of his monologue was that I must write his life-story, which he proceeded to unfold. 'What a subject, dear boy !' Let him tell me of his childhood, brought up on the romantic Cornish coast, free as a sea-gull between two exquisite sisters as gay and carefree as young seals ! 'You must describe our midnight picnics' — and here, tightening his hold, he would begin to shake me back and forth — 'think of it; we are hidden in a coign of the cliff; the ruddy glow of our bonfire gleams upon smooth brown limbs; you catch the lilt of laughter, sometimes a secret whisper, and hear old Father Ocean murmuring below . . .' While he spoke, his face drew closer and closer until it was very nearly out of focus, and at every word he rocked me from side to side, with his free hand driving home some point that he found particularly effective; so that I could only escape by nodding vague encouragement and promising that I would start the book next day. Luckily, he soon forgot our plan; he was a self-destructive alcoholic; I have never known a more determined drinker. After a party, he said, he would grope his way downstairs and, as he wandered round the room, empty the dregs of abandoned glasses into a single large jug, and thus produce a monstrous cocktail, which he then swallowed in the hope — usually a vain hope — that his offended stomach would not reject the offering.

On the stage, however, through all the catastrophes of his private life, he remained a powerful presence, dominated and temporarily transfigured by any sympathetic rôle he played. The actor's gift of sinking his own identity in that of the personage he represents, has long astonished me as it astonishes most spectators. Garrick, who excelled in the part of Hamlet, also triumphed in the character of Vanbrugh's Sir John Brute; and his German admirer, G.C. Lichtenberg, writing to a friend at Gottingen[4], tells how his recreation of the part delighted an eighteenth-century audience. Brute is an ageing man of pleasure, comic yet also a shade tragic, whose large round face, when he comes home very drunk, though the upper half is hidden by his tumbled wig, and the remainder drenched with sweat and streaked with blood, wears a confusedly amicable expression. To Lady Brute's anxious enquiries about his present state of health, 'he replies, pulling himself together, "sound as a roach, wife"; but he does not move from the door-post, to which he stays glued as if wanting to rub his back. Then he becomes coarse again, and of a sudden is once more so tipsily wise and amiable that the whole audience breaks into a storm of applause'.

The part would have suited Robert Newton; but for the sober, well-conducted Garrick it must have involved a prodigious metamorphosis, a complete reversal of his tastes and feelings. It is just such a change that only the born actor can apparently achieve at will; and, in a recent article on the greatest actors he has watched[5], Sir John Gielgud describes Lucien Guitry playing the part of an elderly roué who has taken his young mistress to a sea-side hotel, and stands above her as she lies upon the bed. During the last scene he is destined to strangle the girl; and now she shrinks away from him, struck with a prophetic sense of doom:

> For a few moments . . . he seemed suddenly to grow inches taller and become a towering and terrifying creature. Then, suddenly breaking the tension completely, he resumed his normally charming manner for the rest of the scene . . . I am convinced that in fact he did absolutely nothing, moving neither his face, his hands nor his body. His absolute stillness and the projection of his concentrated imagination, controlled and executed with con-

---

4 See Lichtenberg's *Letters from England*, 1774-1775, translated by John Nowell, in 'Impressions of Garrick', *History Today*, March, 1972.

5 *The Times*, 26 February 1977

summate technique, produced . . . an extraordinary and unforgettable effect.

Few tragedians or comedians seem ready to explain the process by which they discard their own identities and assume an alien set of features; and my attempts to question a great Shakespearian actress proved ludicrously unsuccessful. I had admired Dame Edith Evans in a dazzling variety of parts; and, when Cecil Beaton heard that I had been commissioned to produce yet another book about Shakespeare and was seeking expert guidance, he put me beside her at his table. I had high hopes. The actress, I thought, who had embodied so many of the poet's creations must understand his genius well, and would help me to examine its imaginative workings from the performer's point of view. I was disappointed; she could not or would not respond. Perhaps she very much disliked being expected to 'talk shop' at dinner; perhaps she found me a presumptuous bore; but every question I asked, and every idea I put forward, met the same barrier of nebulous incomprehension. Her appearance, too, was strangely baffling; on the stage active, alert and graceful, she had become a small and shapeless woman, short-legged, thick-ankled, clad in filmy draperies, with a large lymphatic face and heavy drooping eyelids, which she slowly raised and lowered. While I blundered on and her impatience grew, she reminded me more and more of Lady Bracknell; and, as often as she consented to speak, she adopted Lady Bracknell's haughty gobbling tones. Was that *my* opinion ? – her eyelids rose and descended. She had never heard it said before. . .

I began to suspect then that the basis of a great performer's art might not be primarily intellectual, and that beneath the technique acquired through long experience there might lie something more mysterious, a gift of self-transformation and of imaginative self-projection once possessed by the magician and the soothsayer. Perhaps because he had more talent than genius, Noël Coward, whether he was on or off the stage, or, as frequently happened, afloat between the two, provided a far simpler problem. Though like every talented man resolutely egocentric, he had a warm heart, an extensive knowledge of the world and a keen appreciation of his fellow mortals. His attitude towards Ian Fleming, for example, and Ian's dark moods and passionate prejudices, was always subtly understanding. He humoured, scolded, occasionally derided, yet somehow never did the smallest damage to Ian's ticklish *amour propre*. His victim, indeed, seemed positively to enjoy being teased and even ridiculed.

151

Ian was one of those Englishmen who, though they sternly condemn homosexuals, and the idea of homosexuality fills them with repugnance and alarm, are seldom altogether insensitive to the admiration of their own sex. But, while most of his devotees expressed their admiration in the language of jocular companionship – the kind of masculine badinage he enjoyed at his favourite golf-club – Noël's took a very different shape. He treated Ian as he might have treated a difficult social beauty or a wayward prima donna, and often criticised the extremely unfeeling use to which he put his great attractions. Had he forgotten how he had invited poor Rosemary, a defenceless woman novelist, to spend a week or two at Goldeneye, and then, after flinging a dead octopus into her bedroom, almost immediately turned her out again ? 'You, my dear', he proclaimed, hissing through clenched teeth, jutting his angular chin and pointing an accusatory cigarette-holder, 'You are just an old . . .' But his exact phrase, which would look far worse in print than it sounded viva voce, I will not transcribe here. It startled his audience. Ian, however, merely shook his head, smiled and uttered vague reproving noises. Otherwise this back-handed tribute to his charm left him wholly undisturbed.

As the Flemings' guest, I spent three memorable holidays at Goldeneye, their small Jamaican house; and I have already written of its splendid background[6] – the romantic half-tamed garden that ran down to a rocky cliff, and, under the cliff, the shallow pellucid lagoon and its crescent-shaped beach, where the rosy conch-shells its wavelets rolled up lay drying on the hard white sand. In Jamaica Ian seemed perfectly at home, if he could be said ever to be really at home in any place that he inhabited; and there he had the benefit of an absorbing occupation. He was now a busy novelist; *Casino Royale*, published in April 1953, had proved remarkably successful; and James Bond was fast becoming a twentieth-century folk hero. During my visits, he worked every day from an early breakfast until nearly one o'clock, shut into his bedroom and protected from the outer world by wooden blinds, through which the rattle of his typewriter, like a burst of machine-gun fire, regularly swept across the terrace. Two thousand words a day was his prescribed quota; and he evidently enjoyed his work. Although James Bond is not a portrait of the artist, but the kind of *alter ego* we sometimes evoke in an euphoric day-dream to make the bold speeches and execute the brave deeds that lie beyond our waking reach, there seems no doubt that the intrepid secret agent incorporated certain sides of Ian's character – his passion for speed, his

6 See *The Sign of the Fish*, 1960

taste for mechanical devices, his masculine hedonism and restless energy. Ian, however, was a far more complex man that the belligerent hero he created. Bond's self-esteem and unquestioning self-assurance were qualities he altogether lacked.

When his acquaintances identified him with his personage, or, in a teasing spirit, even addressed him as 'Bond', he felt understandably annoyed. Despite his contempt for highbrows and for the elusive sicknesses of the soul that disturb so many modern writers, he was himself a natural melancholic, subject to bouts of gloom from which he desperately sought an escape by plunging head over heels into the life of action. He was a puritan, too, at heart perhaps an ingrained Calvinist. Grandson of Robert Fleming, an upright Lowland Scot, founder of a famous private bank, and second son of Major Valentine Fleming, member of parliament and country gentleman (killed on the Western Front in 1917), he had been brought up to respect the simple virtues. As a biographer I have noticed that clever children are usually the product of an incongruous or inharmonious marriage; and Ian's mother was a dutiful and affectionate, but flamboyant and self-centred woman, whom Augustus John, an old and dear admirer, had very often drawn and painted. After her husband's early death, she assumed a matriarchal rôle; and, besides bidding her sons never to forget their Scottish heritage, she preached the gospel of success. This doctrine her eldest son Peter followed confidently and easily; but Ian, though, before he left school, as twice *Victor Ludorum* at Eton he had already made his mark, both ran away from Sandhurst and failed in his subsequent attempts to join the Diplomatic Service.

These mishaps, and the effort of keeping pace with his exemplary elder brother, would appear to have a strong effect upon his later evolution. Black Mount and Nettlebed are the somewhat forbidding names of the places in which he spent his childhood; and at the former, the family's Scottish home, the Flemings were devoted to all the most exhausting pastimes of Caledonian country life, endlessly wading through icy burns and trudging across savage moors. As a group, it struck an English observer, they looked curiously muscle-bound; so that, during a meal, when one of them turned to speak, he moved not merely his head, or his head and shoulders alone, but his whole tweed-coated torso. I myself noticed this odd habit on the single occasion I met Peter Fleming; and about Ian there was a touch of the same rigidity, which grew more pronounced should his temper have been aroused or his spirits happen to be low.

Throughout the years I knew him, Ian always took life strangely hard, except in Jamaica, where he worked and played according to a prearranged schedule that nobody might interrupt; and even there the complete contentment he sought now and then eluded him. I have said that Ian was a puritan; he was also a perfectionist, and carried around with him a picture, like the coloured plate attached to a jig-saw puzzle, of his surroundings as he felt they *ought* to be; but in Ian's puzzle some pieces were missing, others obviously defective; and the pattern he managed to build up seldom entirely realised his hopes. Again and again some jarring detail spoiled his imaginative composition. One of his pleasures, for example, was to lie abed soon after dawn, and observe the morning freshness of his garden. Then suddenly I would appear and cross his view on my way towards the beach, leaving a dark track over the dew-silvered lawn; while against the tropical foliage my garish towel made an ugly blotch of colour. Ann was therefore instructed to suggest that I should change my irritating habit and, so as to remain invisible from Ian's bedroom, take a longer path behind the house.

In England Ian's strain of perfectionism became particularly obtrusive. He did not enjoy Christmas and detested large parties; but, since at home the feast was inescapable, he tried his hardest to accept it. His sense of tradition, however, frequently conflicted with Ann's deep-rooted sense of fun; and yet more difficult to bear than the festivities themselves were some of the guests she had invited. Once again, he had a very definite picture of what the celebrations ought to be; and he would describe the example set by his valued colleague Robert, whose domestic organization showed a rare mixture of propriety, economy and savoir vivre. I forget if Robert and his wife attended church; as a rule, I think, they did. On their return, two or three neighbours arrived, bearing small but nicely chosen presents, to drink a glass of fine sherry; and, when they had gone, a family luncheon was spread, some bottles of a sound claret having already been decanted. Next came a conjugal siesta; and at six o'clock the waits appeared, and duly sang their ancient carols . . . So Ian unfolded the ritual of a perfect Christmas Day, which he then compared with Christmas in his own home, where people drank too much and sprawled and fell asleep, and, even worse, the most inappropriate topics were noisily discussed at dinner. I was myself a culprit. He had heard me, on Christmas Eve, discussing the Oscar Wilde case with Ann's delightful father Guy Charteris, and asking him whether he had encountered many 'bi-metallists' in Edwardian high society.

Ian's character, his biographer remarks[7], had a distinctly histrionic side; and he was always inclined to dramatise the problems of his personal existence, now that he had become a married man. At one moment, before he had published his first novel, he would adopt the persona of a much enduring wage-slave, bearing his burdens 'with crotchety fortitude and working doubly hard [he told his wife's brother] to keep Lucian Freud, Peter Quennell, Freddie Ashton *et al*. in champagne during the coming months and years'; at another, he was a contemplative solitary, beleaguered by the 'Mayfair Jezebels' and loquacious highbrows who hung around Ann day and night. Peace, he proclaimed, was all he needed; and '*Pace*, Annie, *pace* !' he would beg, if the tide of conversation rose too high or he discovered further 'mischiefs' she was planning.

Ian had a keen regard for success – Somerset Maugham, Simenon, Roald Dahl and Raymond Chandler were among the few modern novelists he whole-heartedly respected; and it was interesting to see how he dealt with his own success once it finally descended on him. I have sometimes thought that, given talent, industry and strength of mind, any ambitious man will ultimately achieve his ambition, but almost always – a very important proviso – at just the wrong stage of his career, or under a slightly diminished and faintly disappointing guise. Perhaps Ian's successes had arrived a little too late. Not until 1958 could he inform a well-wisher that he had definitely conquered 'fame and fortune'; but as early as 1955 he was already growing tired of Bond, and feared that he had 'exhausted his inventiveness' and needed a fresh supply of themes. True, his public loyally disagreed. In March 1961, *Life* magazine printed a list of ten books that President Kennedy had recently admired, and that had even 'helped him to shape his life', where *From Russia, With Love* occupied the ninth place, between a new translation of *Le Rouge et le Noir* and (I was flattered to see) the last of my Byronic studies. Ian, however, was then in the midst of an embittering lawsuit; and a month later he suffered a 'rather major heart-attack', and the gradual breakdown of his health began.

I had now known him, and, despite all our differences, we had remained good friends, for some twelve or thirteen years. We had found many subjects to discuss. Though we seldom talked of books, and Bond was a subject that we generally avoided, I remember

[7]   John Pearson: *The Life of Ian Fleming*, 1966

offering him unasked advice, and suggesting that he should tell us more about his hero's private habits — how Bond's martinis were prepared, and how his speckled breakfast-eggs were cooked — and less about his tremendous feats of physical endurance, such as his climb up a red-hot metal tube, carrying in his arms a naked girl. There was an occasion, too, when he unexpectedly appealed for help. Bond was soon to be nearly boiled alive at a satanic nursing home; but the place still lacked a name. I proposed the name of a horrid suburban house my parents once inhabited, to which he willingly agreed.

That Ian should ever have sought advice was perhaps a bad sign and, alas, he had no Indian summer. As his illness developed and the claws of 'the iron crab' tightened around his heart, he seemed slowly to abandon life — a process I was also to observe during the sad decline of Cyril Connolly. Words reached him; he listened and replied; but one felt that he was listening from a certain distance. Meanwhile courageous, defiant, aloof, he dismissed all the chances of recovery that his doctors offered him, and refused to give up alcohol and tobacco, which had become his only sensuous pleasures. I remember him not many days before he set out on his last journey and paid his last visit — a fatal exertion — to the Sandwich golf club. He was sitting beside a lake in the garden of Littlehampton, the house he and Ann had lately bought and reconstructed, holding a tall glass and obstinately chain-smoking. Weed had begun to obscure the surface of the lake; but he asserted that it must be sewage. There was English country-life for you!

8

I envy the autobiographer who can mould the story of his life into a smooth ascending climb, from achievement to achievement, or adventure to adventure. My own method, I needn't point out, has been very much less straightforward; irrespective of their proper sequence, I have followed a long series of varying characters and themes; and, while I pursued the subject of Ian Fleming, I have taken him across the years, as far as his death in 1964. Now I must return to January 1951, when my professional existence underwent a sudden change, and I became once again an editor. This was not entirely unexpected. My friend Lord Drogheda, then Garrett Moore and the Managing Director of the *Financial Times*, had already told me that I might be offered the editorship of a new historical monthly magazine, which Brendan Bracken, his remarkably independent and vigorous Chairman, was determined to produce; but, since paper supplies were still rationed, the project had been temporarily shelved. It was revived in 1950; and I was joined by Alan Hodge, Brendan's original choice, who, during the War, had worked with him, as his private secretary, at the Ministry of Information. The magazine was entitled *History Today*; and the opening issue appeared under our joint editorship on January 1, 1951. We continued to edit it for almost three decades.[1]

Ours was a rewarding alliance. Though Alan and I shared many interests, sympathies and affections, we were very different characters. Alan, for example, having read history at Oxford, was a genuine historian; I remained an historical littérateur, who had an inconvenient habit of forgetting dates and names, and a somewhat more slapdash attitude towards our editorial problems. I must often have annoyed him, I fear, by heavily revising any article that I considered ill-written, and by paying somewhat excessive attention to the aesthetic aspect of our work. It was I who usually chose our covers

[1] *History Today* was taken over by a new editor in October 1979. Alan Hodge, alas, died on May 25 of the same year.

and selected many of our illustrations; while he was more preoccupied with the scholarly content of the magazine, and with ensuring that no article we published should fall below a certain standard. But, if my dilettantism sometimes irked him, he was far too good-hearted a man to let his irritation show; and, during those busy twenty-eight years we had few serious disputes. We respected one another's preferences and prejudices; and the tenor of our office-life was calm. Nor were we completely submerged by our labours; we had extraneous occupations. Alan, at an early stage, worked for Brendan Bracken and Sir Winston Churchill; and I continued my regular hack-work as a weekly book-reviewer.

When Ann left Esmond Rothermere, I had half expected that my link with the *Daily Mail* would very soon be cut short; but I had under-estimated both Esmond's good nature and his steadfast sense of justice. As I have recorded, I remained his employee until October 1956; and I was then expelled not by the proprietor himself but by certain ill-disposed subordinates. Between them they hatched a machiavellian plan of campaign, and then unwisely debated it in a crowded Fleet Street bar, where they were overheard by an old Oxford friend, who reported back to me. His story confirmed my vague suspicions. I had noticed that the reviews I submitted were now often rigorously cut down; that out of eight hundred or a thousand words only four or five hundred were usually permitted to appear; and that they were then printed near the end of the paper in some inconspicuous nook or cranny. The object, I assumed, was slowly to sap my morale; I decided, nevertheless, that I would not resign, and week after week persisted in posting my copy. It was an odd experience casting my envelope into the box, although I knew the pages I had enclosed probably dropped straight into oblivion; and my relationship with the unwilling recipient soon became a trial of strength. Which would tire first ? – he of seeing my weekly envelope arrive; I of feeling that, for all the impression I made, I might have been dancing in the dark or declaiming under water.

The *Daily Mail* had just emerged from one of its recurrent crises; and a new editor had been suddenly promoted to the chair, just as an American vice-president may unexpectedly achieve the White House, and sat behind his desk looking bewildered and alarmed, fearful perhaps that, should he take any over-decisive action, he might find that he has woken up and was back again amid the 'subs'. Thus, when I spoke to him, he strongly denied that there was any question of discarding me. But, as the campaign continued and my reviews, if they appeared at all, now rubbed shoulders with the 'Gardening Notes', I finally appealed to Esmond, who said that the editor must take a hold on himself, and either make up his own mind or seek the Feature Editor's advice. This he did; and Mr Pontifex, a stout, saturnine personage I had long distrusted, must have gladly given tongue. No contribution of mine, I imagine him announcing, had sold a single copy of the paper; and the reviews he had unwillingly printed were so much journalistic dead-wood. Esmond, however, though he did not dissent — he understood my journalistic shortcomings — generously cushioned my departure; and I bade goodbye to Northcliffe House, after my thirteen years' service, somewhat more prosperous, or less heavily overdrawn, than I had been in 1943.

My friendship with Esmond survived. During those thirteen years I had seen him often, and in many different settings, in London, in English country houses and in his curious little villa, originally the first Lord Rothermere's pleasure dome, a kind of Art Nouveau swallow's-nest plastered against a precipice on the verge of Monte Carlo. Surrounded by Ann's guests he was seldom very talkative — that he left to accredited intellectuals; but, when we were alone together, as once, for example, on a journey homewards from the South of France, he talked freely and amusingly, and discussed among other subjects his powerful father and his prodigious uncle Lord Northcliffe, the two men, so unlike himself, who had overshadowed and controlled his youth. Esmond was a reluctant tycoon. Power, though he may sometimes have enjoyed his position, was not essential to his happiness; and, given the choice, he would probably have welcomed a sober middle-class existence, in a small comfortable house — the kind of house where he had spent the war-years — with a good tennis-court and a first-rate suburban golf-course just beyond his garden. It was the death of his two brothers, remarkably promising young men, both dead before 1918, that had raised him to the rank of Heir Apparent; and meanwhile he had been brutally bullied at his private school and at Eton nearly killed by an attack of mastoiditis. He had begun life as the weakest and least conspicuous member of a brilliant and dynamic family.

Clearly, Esmond had made strenuous efforts to realise his father's hopes; and the stories he told about his unsuccessful attempts showed an engaging sense of the ridiculous. In 1927 the first Lord Rothermere had boldly plunged into European politics and, having campaigned against the post-war Treaty of Trianon (which had much reduced Hungarian territory), was himself offered the Hungarian throne. He accepted it for his only surviving son; and Esmond, then almost thirty years old and a rather silent member of the House of Commons, dutifully travelled out to Budapest. Having inspected the Iron Crown of Hungary, he agreed that he would try it on; but it was cold and hard and 'too damned heavy', he said; and soon afterwards members of the Hungarian ruling class threatened him with immediate assassination; whereat he decided he must change his plans and sensibly re-crossed the frontier.

Less alarming but equally disappointing were Esmond's early experiences in the journalistic field. His father had suddenly given him control of a London evening paper; and Esmond, who liked the stage, elected to launch his editorship by writing and publishing a review of the latest musical comedy that included some sharp criticisms of the sadly miscast leading actress. She happened, alas, to be Lord Rothermere's new favourite; and the critic-editor was there and then removed. Although Esmond remained staunchly loyal both to his father's and to his uncle's memory — the only occasion I got into serious disgrace was when I selected, as the 'Daily Mail Book of the Month', a volume of reminiscences by his old friend Lord Vansittart that I had quickly glanced through, and that included some unforseeably caustic references to his father's political ideas and aims — he did not disguise their private foibles. Until he reached middle age Lord Rothermere was chiefly devoted to the pursuit of power and fortune; but, once he had gained his objective, he abruptly took to pleasure; which he organised through his confidential assistants with the same businesslike efficiency. At Monte Carlo, the aide-de-camp who had been instructed to see off a departing mistress would almost always be expected to await the Blue Train that was bringing her successor.

In the Casino the *richissime* English lord made a formidable appearance; and there alone did he give any sign of temporarily neglecting women. While he gambled, a long jewelled claw very often touched his sleeve, and a husky voice demanded 'you remember *me*, of course, Lord Rothermere?' But his pretended acquaintance had chosen the wrong moment; and, never looking round or taking his eyes from the table, he used to pick up a *mille plaque*, pass it over his shoulder and stubbornly continue playing. Otherwise, the range of his tastes was catholic; and Serge Diaghilev, exasperated because he had insisted that a very thin and not very agile young woman should become a *prima ballerina* if he financed a new ballet, remarked bitterly in Constant Lambert's hearing, with a heavy Russian sigh, *'Elle ne sait pas danser. C'est un cadavre — Mais, que voulez-vous, il y a des nécrophiles !'*

Here I recollect an anecdote, told me by Esmond during the journey I have mentioned, about the adventures of a Christmas holiday they had shared at St. Moritz. Lord Rothermere had recently been much annoyed by an avaricious foreign harpy; and Esmond thought that he needed a more respectable woman friend to console him for his tribulations. At their hotel was staying an elegant Austrian countess, with her little daughter and an English nanny; and, having sought her acquaintance, Esmond cleverly contrived a meeting between the lady and his father. It was vastly successful; every day, beneath his bedroom window, he watched a decorous quartet leaving the hotel — Lord Rothermere and his companion arm-in-arm, the child and nurse-maid several steps behind — quietly traversing the snowy garden and vanishing among the trees, and felt that he could now congratulate himself on a seasonable good deed well performed. That, however, was not the end of the story. When the morning appointed for his father's departure came, Esmond decided that, as the countess would almost certainly accompany him, it might perhaps be tactful to remain upstairs and eat a solitary breakfast. But no sooner had he descended than he observed Lord Rothermere's friend, dragging her bewildered child by the arm, rush angrily across the hall. In passing she cast him a savage glance, which surprised and disconcerted him until he learned that, like a predatory Olympian god, his father had carried off the youthful nanny. Esmond added that he had never seen the pair exchange a single word or smile — the young person, he remembered, was a modest, unassuming girl; yet his father had wafted her away to Paris, where he quickly installed her in her own apartment.

It is a story that might have pleased Tchekhov; and Esmond told it with considerable verve. He enjoyed talking of his father and his uncle — Lord Rothermere, a tough belligerent dynast methodically carving out his empire; Lord Northcliffe, a feverishly imaginative spirit, whose talent for dreaming and planning, allied to 'a certain admirable greatness of mind', had once fascinated H.G. Wells.[2] Esmond himself, beside these two ancestral giants, seemed a strangely gentle character. Except in moments of acute crisis, when, I have heard it said, he might become both firm and shrewd, he almost always

[2] *Experiment in Autobiography*, 1934

shunned a conflict, and walked through life, a tall and handsome figure, not so much opposed to his immediate surroundings as vaguely, benevolently detached from them. He rarely showed surprise; and I never saw him genuinely shocked.

Although an attentive guardian of his papers' financial health, Esmond took relatively little interest in their editorial content. Since he disliked bother, he avoided bothering his staff; and his peculiar blend of virtues and defects made him, at least for my purposes, highly agreeable employer. Under his auspices, it now strikes me, I led a remarkably untroubled life, doing my own work, seldom visiting the office and arranging holidays to suit myself. If I look back through old engagement books, I am often astonished to see how regularly I left London, and how many good-natured friends in the country invited me to stay with them. The names of their house occur again and again; but very few of those once-loved houses and gardens now play any part in my existence. Some have been sold; one a beautiful amalgam of Gothic stone and eighteenth-century brick beside a smooth, swift-sliding river, is today a National Trust property; others, deserted by the friends I knew, have passed into the hands of a younger and much more spartan generation, who prefer the kitchen to the dining-room, and frequently depend, as their only domestic support, on a pair of sturdy housewives from the village.

The social climate has changed, and, unmistakably, is still changing. Talleyrand's phrase, *'la douceur de vivre'*, applied to the charm of life before the Flood, has become a literary commonplace; but, although it would be foolish to suggest that I had quite so much to lose as Talleyrand, I, too, have felt the air grow colder, and watched the horizon slowly darken. At this distance the 'fifties and early 'sixties, the period when a learned Prime Minister, with unexpected slanginess, assured us that we had 'never had it so good', begin to seem a halcyon age. Our movements were certainly less restricted; in addition to my pleasant English week-ends, carried by the still-buoyant wings of the pound sterling I often took long holidays abroad; and during 1950, I see that, having made two separate journeys to Paris, I visited Somerset Maugham on Cap Ferrat. The days I spent there were always interesting rather than consistently enjoyable. Maugham was a severe host. He imposed a regime and demanded a standard of behaviour that his guests neglected at their peril; and a single ill-judged remark or minor mis-step might plunge them into permanent disgrace. Thus, a friend of mine, a thoroughly good-hearted and unmalicious man, who had been invited to remain a week, or several weeks, happened, very soon after he arrived, to tell a story that annoyed his host – it involved a joke about stuttering; and Willie, before he retired that night, bade him a decisive farewell. 'I'd better say goodbye now', he remarked; 'you'll have gone, of course, before I get up'.

I was luckier or, possibly, more cautious; Willie was always kind to me, even flattering and encouraging. But I was never wholly at ease in his company; and his sombre mask, with its deep, despondent furrows and its saurian folds and creases, had so strange an effect that, once, in the mid-fifties, when he heard that I had re-married and offered his congratulations, enquiring 'H-h-happy now, Peter?', I remembered the legend of the Evil Eye and, thinking it was probably dangerous to assent, answered 'Not *un*happy, Willie'; which elicited the gloomy response: 'Well, that's *s-something*, isn't it?' Another odd trait was his habit of discovering the plot of a Somerset Maugham tale in any current situation. He explained, for example, a mother's efforts to please her adult children by hinting that, as years earlier she had been involved in a slightly scandalous law-suit, one of them might perhaps be blackmailing her.

Willie's opinion of the human race was low; and he found little to say about its virtues; but, although he was eminently successful himself, he applauded both his fellow writers' successes and their gift of making money, and à propos of a popular young journalist, a frequent visitor at the Villa Mauresque, asked me if I knew that, before Godfrey reached early middle age, he had already put aside some £50,000, safely invested in the soundest stocks. Nor was he unimpressed by social rank; and, after a dinner-party, where his guest of honour was a fat and raucous foreign lady, who, while she described her recent quarrel with an offensive American neighbour on the Coast, had remarked cheerfully, 'I hear she says I'm just an old German bitch; *et, après tout, je suis certainement princesse de Schleswig-Holstein*', he sent his devoted secretary Alan Searle to fetch the necessary reference-book, adding how pleasant it was to be able to look up a departed guest in the *Almanach de Gotha*!

The deep-rooted unhappiness that pervaded his life had had many different causes. The death, during his early childhood, of a mother he adored; his lonely youth; the loss of Gerald Haxton, the companion of his middle years and the only human being he had ever equally admired and loved; and, throughout his existence, the humiliating stutter that often throttled him and left him nearly speechless – each had contributed something to the shipwreck of his soul. At the Villa Mauresque one could not escape its effects. Planned for a life of well-earned ease, his house and gardens had a haunted air; I was perpetually conscious of their master's presence, and of the clouds he spread around him. His pictures, too, though highly valuable works, bought to replace the magnificent collection of dramatic canvases by Zoffany with which he had endowed the British National Theatre, resembled a rich man's shrewd collection rather than the lively and variegated record of his private tastes and feelings.

The Villa Mauresque stands some distance above the sea, amid a labyrinth of much more modern houses, built since Willie's first arrival, in the least attractive part of Cap Ferrat. Traffic is heavy there and hurtling cars and lorries often drive a pedestrian off the road. But then, just beyond St. Jean, still a pleasant village, a narrow promontory leaves the Cape; and on the rocky point that Vauban fortified — huge fragments of his bastions cover its slopes — I stayed during this period of my life, nearly every spring or summer. La Fiorentina, sacked and half destroyed by the Germans when they abandoned Southern France, had been rebuilt by its owner's son as a faithful facsimile of one of Palladio's Venetian villas; and its classic porticoes lie open to sun and air and to the winter storm-winds that sweep the Gulf of Beaulieu. My friend Rory Cameron, the creative spirit of the place, had also lovingly re-designed the garden, and bought and re-planted forty-year-old cypresses to line a noble avenue running down towards the sea. Here, as in so many Southern landscapes, the early morning was always the happiest hour; and while the Mediterranean became a flood of light, the mountain-range across the Gulf assumed the aspect of a couchant lion, dark valleys ribbing its bare flanks, sunshine on its massive head. Later, as the sun climbed and humanity began to arrive, this beatific vision faded; one returned to the social world, and heard what had happened at the Casino last night and the latest gossip of the Coast. Rory and his mother Lady Kenmare entertained innumerable guests; though both of them, I think, might sometimes have preferred a much more solitary existence, Rory writing a travel-book, Enid adding another twenty feet, accurately repainted by herself, to the gigantic Chinese wall-paper she had hung around her dining-room. Like many beauties, she was at heart a shy character; and it was probably her shyness, coupled with a certain natural dilatoriness, that made her late for almost every meal. When she appeared, however, her pe hyrax, an odd little thick-furred beast distantly related to the elephant, which she had brought home from a Kenyan forest, gingerly balanced on her left shoulder, her youthful carriage, blue-white hair and brilliant azure eyes produced a dazzling impression. Conventional courtesies having been got through, she was often gravely silent; but, if I were lucky enough to sit beside her, she would treat me, now and then, to a refreshingly scandalous remark, delivered *sotto voce*, in a style that recalled some lively conversation at the Boar's Head Tavern, Eastcheap, rather than twentieth-century table-talk. As a hostess, though always solicitous for her guests' welfare, she had a single disconcerting habit. When we had gone to bed, we were frequently aroused by the sound of loud hammering, which reached us through her bedroom door. Enid was an insomniac, who usually slept, she told us, about two or three hours; and she devoted some portion of the night to her favourite arts and crafts. Painting wall-papers was one of them; another happened to be toffee-making; and the noise we heard was that of Enid breaking up a sheet of newly-baked toffee with a kitchen hammer on her marble hearth.

Before La Fiorentina went the way of other houses I have often visited, it occupied an important place in my affections; but even there a shade of disquietude would occasionally blot the landscape. The South of France is a region that, as a whole, I have never learned to love; modern entrepreneurs have so cruelly disfigured it; and its bland climate exerts a curiously unnerving effect upon an Anglo-Saxon constitution. I could have almost too much leisure, I found, too much of the *'luxe, calme, volupté'* to which I had eagerly been looking forward; and the Coast was crowded from Menton to Cannes with energetic fellow hedonists – French bourgeois families scorched and blistered by the sun, but determined they would get their money's-worth, plodding silently along an asphalt road; rich American expatriates reclining beside the pool and discussing where they meant to spend the next few months; card-playing lesbians and decorative English wanderers, among whom I remember a blonde Antinous, said in early life to have been the footman of a well-known peer, who usually displayed a pair of golden sandals cross-gartered up his handsome calves.

Their proximity tended to discourage my own interest in a life of ease and pleasure; and then, there was the vague, insidious melancholy that, near the Mediterranean as on Caribbean islands, the descent of nightfall often brings. Beyond the grove of wind-bent stone pines with which the formal garden ended, under a grass-plot just above the sea, the remains of Paganini, denied Christian burial by the unfeeling Bishop of Nice, lay between 1842 and 1844. In *Florentine Nights*, the marvellous series of dreams and recollections published five years before the great musician's death, Heine describes him first stalking through a public garden at Hamburg, his long neglected curls framing a 'pale, cadaverous face, on which sorrow, genius and hell had engraved their indestructible lines'; then, on the concert platform, wearing a 'black dress-coat and a black waistcoat of horrible cut, such as is perhaps prescribed by infernal etiquette at the court of Proserpina, his black trousers drooping anxiously around the thin legs'. When he bowed low, he nearly touched the ground; 'in the angular curves of his body there was a horrible woodenness, and also something absurdly animal-like. Had he learned these complimentary bows from an automaton or from a dog? Is that the entreating gaze of one sick unto death . . .' or had he already died, but recently left the underworld, 'a vampire with a violin'? If ghosts indeed walk, Paganini, so phantasmal during his troubled earthly existence, must surely have hung around his seaside tomb. The pine-grove and the lawn behind it had a hushed, mysterious air; and one of Rory's guests claimed to have met there a little dripping female spectre, which he thought must be the wraith of an unhappy young woman, said to have vanished overboard while her millionaire husband's yacht was moored opposite the point far out at sea.

I saw no ghosts myself; and the touches of malaise that I occasionally experienced may have had something to do with the sedentary life I had been leading for the last ten or fifteen years. At La Fiorentina, though every morning I took a leisurely swim up and down its large salt-water pool, and Rory Cameron and I sometimes climbed through the limestone hills above Roquebrune, I carefully avoided exercise, and usually ate and drank too much. In the spring of 1953, however, I made a formidable resolution — I would undertake a walking-tour; and, after a few days at La Fiorentina, I put Lotus Land behind me, flew to Pisa and, on 22nd April, joined Patrick Leigh Fermor at Siena, where I discovered him already happily established. I could not have chosen a better walking-companion. *The Traveller* is a poem I have long admired; but Paddy, whose memorable odyssey began when he was only eighteen and journeyed on foot from Rotterdam to Athens and Constantinople,[3] is the exact antithesis of the eighteenth-century vagrant as Oliver Goldsmith describes him in his melodious opening line. 'Remote, unfriended, melancholy, slow' are epithets that could never be applied to Paddy. He possesses both a splendid gift for friendship and an enviably euphoric character; and he moves, I very soon learned, at an extremely rapid pace.

I wish that I had kept a daily journal; all I can now fall back on is a list of pencilled place names: Chiusi, Perugia, Assisi, Spello, Spoleto, Todi, Gubbio and, once more, Perugia, together with a catalogue of Umbrian spring flowers: 'Wild cyclamen, iris, primroses, forget-me-nots, yellow orchis, white anemone, celandine, dwarf snap-dragon, bell-shaped flowers v. pale yellow'. To Assisi we travelled by train; and not until we were leaving that sacred city did we at length become pedestrians. My earliest attempts to carry a knapsack aroused the loud derision of a file of German tourists. But I disregarded them; and presently we reached a forest-girt hermitage high on the flanks of Mount Subasio, whither, at the beginning of the thirteenth-century Saint Francis and his earliest followers had retired to lead a life of solitude and contemplation. There we talked with an aged monk; or, rather, Paddy, an efficient linguist, talked, and I sat and tenatively took off my shoes. Those shoes, heavy and hob-nailed, were the worst I could have brought. Old, wrinkled and designed for a different wearer, they might have carried me comfortably enough down an English woodland path or country lane; but against rugged Italian mountain-trails they registered a violent protest, and proceeded to torture every inch of my feet, from the skinned heels to the battered toes, with atrocious pertinacity.

Before we had finished our walk the expression 'foot-sore' had acquired a fresh meaning; and sometimes the sulky complaints of my injured feet were apt to spoil the pleasure of the eyes. A yoke of milk-white oxen crossing a steep brown slope, and swinging their noble horns as they paced along a furrow, would look more sluggish, more mindlessly and maddeningly bovine than, I knew, they should have done; and sometimes I paid more attention to pebbles and boulders than to the sweep of the surrounding landscape, the forests above us and the olive trees beneath. Paddy was usually a hundred yards ahead, leaping from rock to rock, and chanting a wild Greek song, like Byron on the field of Waterloo. One such descent from the mountains — or perhaps this may be a composite picture — comes back

[3] See one of the most original and entertaining travel-books of the decade, *A Time of Gifts*, 1977

today with especial vividness. We are approaching the ramparts, seen through a dusty golden haze, of an ancient Umbrian city; at the gate a battered country omnibus, which itself might have been built in the Middle Ages, is depositing its passengers; and up the rutted path stream a wandering procession of goats on the heels of their long-bearded chieftain, who constantly rears and stretches his lean neck to snatch a pendant leaf or twig. The lane is deeply sunk between banks of reddish soil, over arched by olive-branches, and to the right, among the olives' silvery roots, spring the blue-purple spikes of a clump of wild iris. I stand aside to watch the herd pass with that strange meandering, side-stepping movement peculiar to the Mediterranean species; then follow Paddy through the gate. But here we pause; we have not yet reached our goal; for Paddy is determined to find a restaurant perfectly suited to our tastes and needs. Thus he accosts a citizen: '*Senta, signore . . .*' we are Englishmen, students of art and life, devoted to architecture and history, yet also to good food and wine; and we seek a restaurant, preferably on or near the city wall, commanding a view of the sunset, where we can drink out of doors beneath an arbour. No gimcrack modern place, of course. Its fabric should embody mediaeval arches, though a Renaissance colonnade would be almost equally appropriate . . .

Paddy's patient investigations very often proved successful. The first citizen he stopped to question might turn away and shake his head, murmuring sadly '*pazzo, pazzo* !'; but then a second and a third appeared; and, while I shifted uneasily from foot to foot — each was now a solid block of pain — an interesting debate continued, until we had found an agreeable trattoria that bore at least some slight resemblance to the heavenly restaurant we were seeking. Once we had settled there, I immediately received my reward. Paddy is a rare example of a twentieth-century man — indeed, almost the only man I know — who has never allowed himself to be harnessed to an occupation that he did not more or less enjoy; even his wartime servitude at Caterham Barracks he found amusing and instructive. His capacity for enthusiasm, one of his greatest gifts, is supported by a huge supply of miscellaneous knowledge; and, when we talked of buildings we had just seen, his conversation would revolve at dragon-fly speed around a vast variety of favourite subjects — now the difference between Guelf and Ghibelline battlements; now the use of the acanthus leaf, particularly the 'wind-blown acanthus', in the sculptured capitals of Byzantine churches. Umbria, he reminded me, was the dark-green motherland of the mysterious Etruscan people and, although modern Etruscologists assert that they are apt to seem mysterious merely because we cannot read their language, having examined their painted tombs and the strong, severe masonry of an Etruscan arch, we concluded we must disagree. Etruria, after all, had been regarded by the inhabitants of parvenu Rome as the *genetrix et mater superstitionum*, whence they derived both the diviner's magic rites and the hideous galdiatorial games; and Umbria has a far more sombre and solemn beauty than the graceful man-made landscapes that lie further south.

At the restaurants we chose we were sometimes inspired to drink a loyal toast to the Etruscan wine-god *Fufluns*. Our expedition had a frivolous, occasionally a Bacchic side; and in Perugia, where it began and ended, despite the city's gloomy past – the splendid main square was once so drenched with blood, during the armed conflict of two patrician factions, that a series of altars were set up all around it in an attempt to purify the site – our existence took a pleasantly social turn; and we met an English-speaking country gentleman, a friend of Paddy's friend the novelist Rex Warner. Count R. had a town-house near the market, grandiose but dim and shabby; the cavernous main room, decorated with many-branched family-trees and sinister ancestral portraits, was traversed by a long black stove-pipe that ascended crookedly towards the roof; while in the country he occupied a vast imposing red-brick castle, once the fortress of an ancestor nicknamed 'Robert the Dog', a fierce medieval robber-baron. From its donjon we looked out over his olives and vines, and the tile roofs of his peasants. They were mostly Communists, he said; but, since deception was their second nature, and, he supposed, they did not actively dislike him, they did their best to spare his feelings. A framed photograph of Lenin often hung beside the fire, above the head of the black-shawled grandmother who sat there silently all day; but, if he attempted to catch them unawares and quickly pushed the door open, they had seldom failed to see him coming, and had managed to reverse the photograph, which bore on the opposite side a brightly coloured picture of the Infant Jesus or the Virgin Mary.

Our last expedition, before we returned to Perugia, covered the *Alta Valle Tiberina*, the Tiber's sluggish upper reaches, where it loops through a quiet, smiling plain – a *'ridente pianura'*, says the guide-book – thick and chocolate-brown with silt. We parted on May 5; and, while I regained La Fiorentina, to rest my feet and change my clothes, Paddy joined an English journalist, with whom he had promised to attend a little-known festival in the Abruzzi. The origins of this pagan feast that has entered the Christian calendar can clearly be traced back to primaeval snake-worship. Hundreds of snakes, both dangerous and harmless, are collected by the celebrants, paraded up and down the streets and encouraged to wreathe around the sacred images.[4] Some fall and are trodden underfoot; and Paddy, a natural lover of life, rescued one ill-treated snake, slipped it into his coat-pocket and carried it away to Rome. In a Roman tramcar, as he went from the station to his lodgings, it inexplicably escaped; and Paddy, fearing that its appearance might cause alarm, and still uncertain whether its sting were lethal, decided he must report his loss. The Roman police are accustomed to mad foreigners; but his opening announcement when he entered the police-station, 'Ho perduto un serpente !' left them utterly bewildered.

Paddy was very soon to plan a much more adventurous expedition. Myself I remained in England, busily writing and cheerfully rusticating until the second week of September, when I revisited Cap Ferrat and, after seven days, went on to Venice. There I stayed with Elizabeth de Breteuil, one of Rory's most devoted admirers, at an apartment close to the Salute; and it was then I dined at the Palazzo Labia and admired Tiepolo's incomparable representation of Cleopatra's famous banquet. Meanwhile, in London, I had just exchanged my unpleasant flat off Baker Street – the grimmest and darkest I had inhabited since the end of World War II – for less disorderly surroundings. Few male companions, as I think I have already explained, had ever crossed that gloomy threshold; but once, during Coronation Week, I lent my keys to Georgia and Sacheverell Sitwell and their younger son Francis; and, although they wrote me a charming letter of thanks, I heard they were profoundly shocked and puzzled – by the simple squalor of my sitting-room with its dingy matted walls and the discovery that, to reach my bathroom, which had a leaking glass roof, they were obliged to open an inner front-door and venture down a dog-leg passage.

Happily, certain of my women friends were brave enough to climb my stairs; and the name Bakers Mews – I have now forgotten the number; and even the site long ago vanished beneath a concrete office-block – evokes some pleasant and beguiling memories. Among my visitors were two young women, Mary and Betsy, whom I had not

[4]   My fellow-traveller published a vivid account of this festival, which is held at the village of Cucullo near Sulmona, in the *Spectator*, 5 June 1953

known very long, and who would occasionally walk round to see me after I had finished work. With neither of them was I at any stage in love; but each was an oddly original character; and, as both enjoyed talking, particularly about themselves, and one of my favourite amusements is being told strange stories of other people's private lives, the more detailed and unsparingly candid the better, I was always glad to listen. Both had difficult families; Mary's father, formerly a sergeant in the Irish Guards, was a gambler and a race-course tipster. She was fond of him, but she did wish, she admitted, that his clothes were less outlandish, and that, if he *must* wear worn-out canvas shoes, he would not wear shoes of different colours, black and brown or white and blue. Mary had had a wandering childhood; and when she was still a fifteen-year-old virgin, and her father took her to the South of France, presumably following the horses, she had been seduced by a member of a local race-gang — later he stabbed her in a jealous passion — and had given birth to an unwanted baby, which was quickly spirited away and she had never seen again. This separation was the only event in her life of which I heard her speak with bitterness.

Since that episode Mary had entered a world that the ordinary middle-class observer very seldom penetrates — where nothing is stable, security has ceased to exist, and the police are natural enemies. One evening, at an East End night-club, she had accepted a lift from a casual acquaintance she did not know to be a 'villain'; but, during their journey home, the police had stopped his car, and found that the boot was full of stolen goods. At the police-station, while she sat on a bench outside, she had heard him being beaten up. Presently she asked a constable if she might go; she was in the clear, wasn't she ? ' "You stay there, you dirty cow !' he said'. At the time I met her, Mary was a kind of amatory free-lance — 'prostitute' is too harsh, 'courtesan' too elegant a word— whom a sharp professional, walking a regular beat, would have heartily despised. My total ignorance of her own world astonished and bewildered her. She attracted eccentric clients; a sober businessman enjoyed pelting her with cream-buns as she walked naked round and round his garden; and a strange recluse wished her to pose for the picture he pretended he was painting of a Grecian goddess. He had made her promise that she would never examine his work; but, when he left the room, she tiptoed towards his easel and saw a large square of unblemished canvas. He must have gone off, she conjectured at the time, to have a quiet 'Arthur J'. What was that, I enquired. 'Don't you know *nothing* ?' she indignantly

171

replied. 'Can't you understand a bit of rhyming slang ? "Arthur J." means Arthur J. Rank. Rank rhymes with "wank", doesn't it ? And I expect you know what "wank" means'.

Mary, regarded from any aspect, seemed an entirely frank and undesigning character. Lies she may have told for practical purposes; but of the pretensions and evasions with which middle-class talk abounds she was altogether innocent. Of her part-time trade she was neither ashamed nor particularly proud; vanity, snobbery and self-esteem were weaknesses that she scarcely understood. Yet her friendship, despite her many virtues, had certain obvious disadvantages. Once I suggested that I should take her out to dinner; and we walked up Baker Street to an old-fashioned Italian restaurant where I had often dined before. Mary's appearance was somewhat startling — her dark viperine locks were uncombed; and she was wearing a thin brown dress over very little else. The kind-hearted waiters could scarcely deny us admittance; but they produced a screen, which, with rather too deliberate casualness, they unfolded round our corner table.

Betsy and Mary were remarkably different characters; for Betsy, unlike Mary, was the essence of tidiness, cleanliness and preparedness; and, if she thought she might be asked to stay the night, and felt inclined to accept the invitation, she had every accessory she might need carefully packed into her handbag. Her father, too, was much more respectable than Mary's — 'something on the railways' at St. Pancras. His exact function she would not immediately describe; but, having thought it over, she said she supposed you might say that he was 'a sort of liaison-officer between the engine-drivers and the station'. 'Officer' was evidently the key-note; while Mary remained splendidly unconscious of any social world beyond her own, Betsy, who was employed by an international oil-company, and sometimes accompanied one of the directors when he travelled round the kingdom, nursed a passionate determination to improve herself. Her accent bothered her; her voice had a Cockney lilt, and she found it difficult to shake off the Cockney habit of fracturing her vowels. Between Betsy's lips 'spoon' became 'spe-une', and, however hard she tried, the superfluous second syllable had a way of creeping back. She was also annoyed that she could not memorize verse, and occasionally appealed for my assistance. As my flat was not far from Manchester Square, I suggested she should learn Tom Moore's poem, or, at least, the opening quatrain:

O let us repair to Manchester Square
To see if the lovely Marchesa[5] be there,
All gentle and juvenile, curly and gay,
In the fashion of Ackermann's 'Dresses for May' . . .

But she never quite succeeded; and even the first line usually defeated her. After two or three abortive attempts, she would give up the struggle and begin to laugh; Betsy's untroubled sense of humour was a particularly engaging trait. She laughed about everything – for example, about her lack of sympathy with her colleagues at the office. An experienced young woman, she accepted physical love as a highly pleasurable and completely proper exercise; but they, who belonged by birth and training to a more suburban social milieu, always implied that they judged it a slightly embarrassing, indeed, a rather 'common' business, which a married woman must be prepared to tolerate at reasonably long intervals, but need not pretend she ever much enjoyed. Over the eleven o'clock coffee cups they would exchange ludicrous descriptions of a husband's unexpected efforts: 'There was I, dear, like a fish on a slab! Naturally, he was good for nothing next day; and I had to 'phone his office, and tell them he thought that he was getting 'flu . . .'

Betsy, for all her social anxieties, had a sanguine, easy-going nature; and in appearance – she was fair-haired and clear-skinned, with a pleasantly tip-tilted nose – she resembled a sleek young nymph by Lucas Cranach. She was a sensible girl, too; and, during the latter stages of our friendship, she made a very wise decision. Since the English class-system baffled her, she accepted the hand of a Scandinavian executive, employed by the same firm and not much older than herself, and left snobbish, ghost-ridden London for an egalitarian northern city, where questions of class, vocabulary and accent never raised their stupid heads. I have been told that she had a happy marriage, and bore a number of fine-looking children. At first she sent me Christmas cards, which I punctually acknowledged; but, after a year or two, she sent no more.

Mary would also vanish. Some family friends, she told me, were anxious that their eldest son should settle down. He had been 'inside'; now that he was out again, they hoped a wife might keep him straight; and, though she seemed scarcely cut out for a moral reformer's rôle, Mary had agreed to marry him. She departed

[5]   The third Lady Hertford, one-time mistress of the Prince Regent and, when Moore wrote, a fairly venerable person, who occupied the present home of the Wallace Collection

173

abruptly. One morning she was still at her window exactly opposite mine in Bakers Mews, from which she paid close and critical attention fo any visitors who rang my bell; the next evening, it was dark and empty. The cretonne curtains had gone, and her pair of potted plants; and I felt unreasonably hurt and disappointed that she had not found time to say goodbye.

Before I deserted Bakers Mews myself, I had launched a strenuous literary campaign. It was there that I began my last attempt to become a modern novelist; but, having completed some thirty or forty pages, I put them away into a drawer. *Hostile Transaction*, the interesting title I had chosen, I owed to Byron's correspondence. In November, 1822, he wrote to Lady Hardy, widow of the officer who had watched Nelson die, giving her his views on sexual love:

> I have always laid it down as a maxim . . . that a man and a woman make far better friendship than can exist between two of the same sex; but . . . with this condition, that they never have made, or are to make love . . . Lovers may be, and indeed, generally *are* enemies . . . I rather look upon love altogether as a sort of hostile transaction, very necessary to . . . keep the world going, but by no means a sinecure to the parties concerned.

Under this title I intended to write a story for which my recollections of my second marriage would provide the subject-matter, and to open my narrative with the help of a tale that Isabelle had once related. When she was about twelve, she and her German grandmother had spent a summer holiday in Alsace Lorraine, at a hotel near a busy saw-mill on the banks of a cascading river. A young engineer, who worked at the mill, regularly ate his dinner in the restaurant; and, after one meal, with his hands about her legs, he had suddenly lifted her up towards the glass behind her seat, and, saying 'Look how pretty you are, mademoiselle !' bidden her contemplate her own reflection. She was pleased, of course, but still more keenly pleased when, in the depths of the glass, she saw an alien face appear— that of the girl who used to wait at their table, and whom the engineer had teased and flattered. An attractive pink-cheeked face, it was now distorted by a look of savage jealousy. That glimpse, Isabelle told me, gave her a feeling of pleasure and pride that she had never known before.

To Isabelle's tale, which had always stuck in my memory, I devoted many working-days, while I did my best to extract from it the last precious drops of imaginative significance and bring into dramatic relief every detail of its background – the river beneath the trees, the heaps of fragrant saw-dust surrounding the riverside mill, over which she often climbed, the sombre dining-room and the strip of discoloured glass that lined the walls above the velvet benches. Isabelle herself I visualised very clearly – a fair-haired child, who had a pretty mutinous face and large blue, widely separated eyes. In my mind I had arranged the whole scene. Now I must focus it within a frame of words: and here my fanatical regard for the English language, and the anxious attention I paid to problems of style, frequently distracted me. What had become of the image I had meant to evoke, while I was building up a stylish sentence, and balancing sentence against sentence to produce a well-constructed paragraph ? Life had escaped through the crevices of my narrative as I struggled to impose a form, until all that remained was an elaborate network of phrases, carefully disposed around a central void.

So, at least, I often suspected when I re-read my opening chapter; and gradually I lost hope. I could describe, no doubt; but the great quality my descriptions lacked was the sense of life and movement. Nor had I the genuine novelist's gift of first observing, then combining characters – the method employed by Proust, whose major personages, Monsieur de Charlus, Madame de Guermantes, Madame Verdurin, Robert de Saint-Loup, were each evolved from his painstaking observations of several different men and women. My own heroine, so far as she was not Isabelle, seemed no more than a literary wraith; beyond the frontiers of my personal experience I found it difficult to go. Thus, after a few weeks, I abandoned *Hostile Transaction*; and, perhaps because I had now at last decided that I could never join the novelists, I enjoyed again becoming a biographer. *Hogarth's Progress*, which appeared in July, 1955, was certainly a work of love; and I was surprised and delighted to see that Evelyn Waugh – I still valued his professional opinion – had given the book an extremely kind review. Though he had long ago enrolled me among his favourite *têtes de Turc*, together with lapsed Catholics, journalists, atheists, socialists, cowardly companions-in-arms and miscellaneous modern upstarts, the only defect he pointed out, besides my Whiggish view of history, was a crude suggestion that Hogarth might sometimes have felt attracted, at the Rose Tavern or Tom King's, by a London woman of the town; whereas it was perfectly clear that, like the reviewer himself, he had always 'maintained the status of a respectably married man'.

Once more I had entered a rich field; for Hogarth, if not the greatest of English eighteenth-century artists, was undoubtedly the most original, and had boldly set out to absorb and recreate the whole period through which he lived. Since his early youth he had had a passion for the theatre; and he had determined, he said, to 'compose pictures on canvas similar to representations on the stage', choosing his themes from 'that intermediate species of subjects . . . between the sublime and grotesque . . .' The 'pictorial dramatist' was ostensibly a moralist; but, unlike the average moralist, Hogarth loved his fellow men, and was as much stirred by the beauty and diversity of life — the charm of the human face and the splendid structure of the human body — as by the moral virtues and vices that his characters exemplified. He loved the inhuman world, too; and, in the last episode of his final dramatic series, *Marriage-à-la-Mode*, the furnishings of the old-fashioned room near London Bridge, where the unhappy Countess dies, seem hardly less significant than the actors they surround. Close to the moribund Countess lie the remains of an unfinished meal; and 'with almost equal delicacy and zest Hogarth has depicted the apparatus of the merchant's meagre breakfast-table — the sheen of the plates, the glitter of a polished knife, the oily lustre of an earthenware jug and the flaccid texture of boiled meat'.

About Hogarth's personal career comparatively little is known. Married to a calm and stately woman, daughter of the prosperous 'history-painter' Sir James Thornhill, he led a sensible domestic life, devoted to his relations, to the orphan girls, Susan Wyndham and Mary Wollaston, he had adopted and employed, and to the household pets he kept, his pug-dog Trump, who occupies the foreground of his best-known self-portrait, and to the bull-finch, whom he buried in his Chiswick garden under the simple epitaph '*Alas poor Dick* !' But the 'strutting consequential little man', with his red 'roquelaure cloak' and hat 'cocked and stuck on one side', and his air of cockney bravado that enlivens Roubiliac's bust, made a single grand mistake: once he had discovered his true genius, he felt that he must invade and conquer new territories, and emulate Thornhill by becoming a 'history painter' and adopting the traditional heroic style. He failed repeatedly; although the huge paintings he executed, free of charge, in 1736, for the main staircase of St. Bartholomew's Hospital, were 'esteemed a very curious piece', they added little to his fame; and when, in 1761, he painted his *Sigismunda* — he had hoped, he said, that the figure of Boccaccio's heroine weeping over her lover's heart would enable him to exhibit his expressive powers — it was generally

176

derided. The last scene of *Marriage-à-la-Mode*, where the Countess's crippled, probably syphilitic child is lifted by the old nurse to kiss her mother's livid face, had already shown his gift of rendering pathos. But Sigismunda, Horace Walpole declared, was a bathetic apparition, 'exactly a maudlin whore, tearing off the trinkets her keeper has given her, to fling at his head . . . Her fingers are bloody with the heart, as if she had just bought a sheep's pluck in St. James's Market.

His rash expedition into political controversy, and the terrible revenge exacted by John Wilkes and the poetic bruiser Charles Churchill, also saddened Hogarth's life, which came to an abrupt end on October 25 1764. But, eleven years earlier, he had published the wonderfully whimsical and suggestive book he called *The Analysis of Beauty*, written, he announced, 'with a view of fixing the fluctuating IDEAS of TASTE', the earliest work in European literature, says its modern editor,[6] 'to make formal values both the starting point *and* basis of a whole aesthetic theory . . . a novel and original attempt to define beauty in empirical terms'. Hogarth was both a self-made artist and a self-instructed theorist; and his main theory he seems to have derived from his use of a kind of artistic short-hand he had worked out long ago — a method of recording any object that impressed him, any face or gesture he was anxious to preserve, by means of a series of hieroglyphs that refreshed his 'technical memory', and were so neat and compact that he was once observed fixing a miniature portrait of a coffee-house acquaintance on his left-hand finger-nail. While practising this system, he had very soon perceived that angles and bulges were best suited to grotesque or comic objects, but that smoothly rolling and expanding curves expressed his recognition of the beautiful; whence he concluded that two particularly attractive curves, which he called 'the Line of Beauty' and 'The Line of Grace', should weave their way through every picture, since they not only delighted the human eye but struck a secret chord in the imagination.

I had many good reasons for becoming attached to Hogarth — the greatest social historian of a period that particularly interested me, and, after Dickens, the keenest and most passionately involved spectator of the London landscape and its people; and I was also fascinated by the steady evolution of his genius. The painted versions of *A Harlot's Progress*, which Hogarth sold to William Beckford's father, were destroyed during the mid-eighteenth century; but the originals of *A Rake's Progress* show that, when he executed them, at the

[6] See *The Analysis of Beauty*, edited with an introduction by Joseph Burke, 1955.

age of thirty-seven, his talents were still immature. Each scene resembles a separate peep-show, theatrically lit and neatly fitted into the confines of an eighteenth-century picture-stage. Not until, in 1743, he produced *Marriage-à-la-Mode* could he completely break these bounds and release the 'Line of Beauty'.

I notice that I completed *Hogarth's Progress*, and delivered the typescript to the publishers on October 18 1954; and, next February, invited by Ann Fleming, who, with her usual impulsive generosity, had also volunteered to pay my passage, I visited Jamaica for the first time. I was at Goldeneye that I corrected the proofs of my book, while Ann painted flowers and fishes and shells, and Ian hammered out his latest story. Then, after three calm and unusually happy weeks, I flew from Montego Bay to Nassau. I disliked the Bahamian background as much as I had loved the rich and various Jamaican landscape. New Providence seemed a dull and barren island, a short flattish strip of coral rock, of sharp-leaved palmetto-scrub and pestilential mangrove-swamp. Native flowers are few, though delicate spider lilies often grow in sandy places; and I missed the iridescent humming-birds that often flashed through Ian's garden — when I enquired if there were any local species, I was told that a hurricane had blown them all away. My host and hostess could not have given me a friendlier reception or put me into a much more comfortable room; but, apologetically, I had to admit that I had never learned canasta, which they began playing an hour before noon and only put aside about six or seven o'clock. Deep depression presently swept down and I remember how I walked along Cable Beach, amid a crowd of bright-shirted American holiday-makers, beside a pallid brilliant sea, and reflected that, had I been asked to choose between spending the rest of my life here and earning my livelihood as a bank-clerk in a London suburb, I should certainly prefer to stay at home. Such was my despair that I opened my engagement book and started feverishly crossing off the days.

These dark clouds, however, soon lifted. Nassau, during the nineteen-fifties, had one beautiful inhabitant, whom I had already met in London; and the hope of seeing her again had helped to bring me on my present journey. Byron was convinced, he wrote, that the Goddess Fortune — a divinity the dictator Sulla worshipped — had determined every turn of his career; and I have noticed myself that 'the Good Goddess' grants us an occasional hint of what, some years hence, she means to do, but may immediately afterwards point in another direction, so that we lose sight of the prophetic gesture. I had encountered M. at Warwick House, where, as it happened, we were both lunching; and Ann, who had not yet left Esmond, said that she had given me a neighbour I was bound to find attractive. The first impression I received was principally of youth and elegance. Those were the days when Christian Dior's 'New Look' still survived, though under a slightly altered form; and my neighbour wore a thin grey woollen dress, with a very small waist and an expansive, many-pleated skirt, surmounted by something that was neither exactly a hat nor quite an ordinary veil. Her husband, whom she had married two or three years earlier, had once introduced me to her at a party; but we had not met again; and I began with a direct question — a way of opening a conversation that, although it may provoke a sharp snub, often produces excellent results — and asked her to tell me what she was doing in London, where she was going next and the kind of life she led. She responded willingly, told me of her house in Nassau, where she spent the winter months, and of a series of summer journeys that took her, at jet-plane speed, across the United States and Europe, from Miami to the Lido. With an impertinence that still shocks me, I said, 'it sounds a dreadful life'; and, to my surprise, I had for a moment the impression that she did not altogether disagree.

Our colloquy was presently cut short by an absurd domestic mishap. Before M. lay a plateful of delicious out-of-season raspberries, and Esmond's major domo had just brought round an impressive Georgian sugar-caster; but, when she had used it and began to eat the raspberries, she gave a sudden startled cry — some malevolent downstairs demon had filled the caster to the brim with salt. Thus our personal dialogue was broken off and only resumed, after a longish pause, in Nassau. She seemed at first not very pleased to see me among her rich Bahamian friends; but our relations slowly improved; and it was with M. that I spent the evening of my fiftieth birthday. From a small nightclub, where, outside the plate-glass window, a decrepit model liner bobbed up and down a choppy pool, we visited the scene of a horrific crime, committed in the early 'forties. A local tycoon had been murdered and hideously mutilated — a frieze of blood-stained hand-prints marked his death-struggle as he groped around his bedroom — some said for sexual, others for commercial reasons, apparently by a gang of hired assassins, savage 'out-islanders', who had slipped into New Providence under cover of darkness. Through the trees we examined his deserted seaside house. The beach was a hard, dead white; the huge moon had a dead unearthly glare; and the fact that I was now fifty years old, and had covered probably three-quarters of my life-span, appeared completely unimportant.

Had I reviewed my record on that ghostly moonlit beach, I might have asked myself some painful questions. How much or how little had I accomplished during the previous five decades; and how should I distinguish between my profits and my losses ? Though I could not remember a period of my life when I had been altogether satisfied with my work or completely at ease in my surroundings, I had had many long moments, I might have claimed, of calm contemplative exhilaration;[7] and for most of those moments I had been indebted to the celestial sense of sight. That, no doubt, was why I had felt particularly drawn towards Ruskin, Byron and the artist-dramatist Hogarth. Each was a passionate observer, a man who loved to use his eyes, and who had taught himself to see. I have already quoted Ruskin's description of seeing as the 'greatest thing' a soul can do; and, although Byron's visual sensibility was, of course, much less acute — none of the long letters he wrote during his Venetian period contains a single reference to a church, a palace or a statue — he was never weary, he told Lady Melbourne, of studying his fellow men[8]; while the splendours of the natural world — a thunderstorm sweeping across the Alps, or a summer day 'dying like a Dolphin' above the distant heights of Friuli — always fired his imagination. Hogarth, again, was an exquisitely observant spirit, devoted, not to Nature as a whole, but to the endlessly absorbing details of the human face and body. He constantly pursued impressions; 'pursuing,' he wrote in the *Analysis*, 'is the business of our lives;' and it became especially enjoyable if 'waving and serpentine lines' should 'lead the eye a wanton kind of chace,' which, through the pleasure it affords the mind, entitles the object we observe 'to the name of beautiful.'

A quarter of a century has passed since I visited Nassau; but I still believe that the pursuit of truth and beauty, wherever they may be recognized and in whatever shape, is the noblest human occupation, and that the shock of recognizing them is a deeply joyful experience, beside which most other joys seem relatively valueless. Here, for example are three incidents, selected at random, that I shall never

[7] 'The only thing is all my experience I cling to is my coolness and leisurely exhilarated contemplation:' Walter Sickert, quoted by Cyril Connolly in *The Unquiet Grave*.

[8] '. . . Anything that confirms, or extends one's observations on life and character delights me . . .' *Byron to Lady Melbourne* October 1 1813.

quite forget. Once, motoring in South-Western France – this time I was accompanied by my rebellious friend from the Bahamas – we reached a point on the road to the Dordogne, where it is not so much the landscape as the light that changes, where the solitary poplar tree first begins to resemble a Mediterranean cypress, and distant defiles are full of grape-blue shadow. At a sudden turn of the road we entered a small valley, a rocky tree-clad slope on the right and, on the left, a steep green field. Down the field leapt three vigorous streams, which joined below to form a cheerful brook. Each, in its swift descent, made a separate ribbon of brightness; each had the splendid strength and gaiety of some brave young living creature just set free. Wonderfully clear and cold, they dashed down pebbly channels under banks of thick green turf, and through shallow pools rimmed with forget-me-nots, king-cups and clusters of diminutive yellow flags.

Having climbed the field and retraced the stream's course, we felt that we had left the ordinary world behind. I had not yet read Rousseau's *Rêveries du Promeneur Solitaire*; but, having opened it many years later, I came to the passage in which he describes his experiences beside the Lake of Bienne, and tells how, while he watched the rhythmic movement of its waters, and listened to the monotonous ripple and splash of wavelets that regularly broke against its shore, past and future appeared equally meaningless; an eternal Present ringed him round; and an ecstatic awareness of his own existence obliterated any other feeling. There Rousseau, the most tormented of mankind, thought that he had been truly happy – '*non d'un bonheur imparfait, pauvre et relatif . . . mais d'un bonheur parfait et plein, qui ne laisse dans l'âme aucun vide qu'elle sent le besoin de remplir.*' Something of the same mood was inspired by the pastoral landscape we explored that afternoon. We were both happy and conscious of being happy – a sensation that momentarily left no crevice through which a disturbing thought could worm its way.

The second episode has often reminded me of one of Tchekhov's most poetic tales. In Constance Garnett's English version it occupies less than thirteen pages – a straightforward account of how the narrator, travelling across the Russian steppe, sees two beautiful girls, briefly enjoys their presence and the atmosphere they diffuse of youth and unselfconscious grace, then reluctantly leaves them behind him as he continues on his humdrum road. *The Beauties* evokes the note of sadness, of regret and nostalgic longing, that haunts Tchekhov's finest plays and stories. There can be no possible link between the young narrator and these elusive apparitions. The

Armenian beauty, a sixteen-year-old girl who flits bare-footed through her father's threshing-yard, is utterly unaware of his existence:

> I felt sorry both for her and for myself and for the Little Russian, who mournfully watched her every time she ran through the cloud of chaff to the carts. Whether it was envy of her beauty, or that I was regretting that the girl was not mine, and never would be . . . or whether I vaguely felt that her rare beauty was accidental, unnecessary, and, like everything on earth, of short duration; or whether, perhaps, my sadness was that peculiar feeling which is excited in man by the contemplation of real beauty, God alone knows.[9]

Her counterpart, a fair-haired Russian girl, seen from a railway carriage, late one afternoon, walking down a wayside platform, is an equally remote figure; and she, too, when the carriage leaves the station, thanks to her gaiety, mobility and 'exquisitely sly smile' provokes a poignant sense of loss. My own beauty seemed all the more elusive because I never saw her face; so far as I was concerned, her extraordinary phsyical appeal resided in her neck alone and in the slender shoulders that supported it. The scene of my experience was a London bus, a No. 11, travelling from Chelsea to the Strand. Just before we had reached Westminster, while we were threading the gloomy canyon of newly modernised Victoria Street, I noticed that a young foreigner and his wife — I assumed they must be married, and guessed they were South American or Spanish— had occupied the seat in front of mine, and that he was pointing out the Abbey. Then I became aware of her neck, a smooth, straight, golden column that bore a neatly rounded head. Her dark short hair had been brushed up; but a single wisp, as small as a blackbird's under-feather, had escaped her brush and drifted free. She did not turn her head; nor did I hope she would. The pleasure I experienced, sitting behind her, is doubly difficult to analyse, since, although it may have had a sentimental, even a slightly sensual colouring, it originated primarily in the architectural balance of her well-poised neck and shoulders, in the divine symmetry of the whole construction and in its look of perfect *rightness* — an effect that we associate elsewhere only with the greatest works of human art.

For the heroine of the last episode I have this evening left the window open. A keen explorer and intrepid Alpinist, she makes the

[9] Constance Garnett's translation

whole garden, most of the gardens beyond, and the ancient red-brick walls that divide them, her own jealously guarded feudal domain, over which she fights incessant battles. The old house we both of us inhabit, and particularly the garden-side, covered with the rampageous foliage and, for a week every year, the big champagne-coloured blossoms of a climbing shrub named *actinidia chinensis*, also belongs to her by right. Sometimes she may leave or enter through a convenient door; sometimes she departs through one window and, after dangerous peregrinations high above the ground, decides to slip home through a second. A favourite route is along a fragile ledge, only a couple of inches broad, whence she ascends the leaded roof of a built-out modern bathroom. Here she is obliged to pause; even a young Burmese cat cannot leap before she looks. Beneath her lies a thirty-foot gulf; the window-sill she intends to alight on is situated four or five feet beneath the level of the bathroom roof, at right angles to her present position, and itself is fairly narrow. She must attempt a transverse descending leap across a chasm where nothing could arrest her fall.

"Whatever appears to be fit, and proper to answer great purposes (writes Hogarth in *The Analysis of Beauty*) ever satisfies the mind . . ." Her sense of purpose and intense determination lend my heroine a marvellous courage, and invest her, at the same time, with an almost supernatural charm. Paws contracted, she quietly sinks down, examines the distance ahead and the terrifying depths below, assembles her powers, stretches her long legs, and rises to her full height. Her plunge is perfectly executed, superbly elegant; and again I think of Hogarth's treatise, and of the paragraph in which he distinguishes between the Line of Beauty and the more magnificently waving Line of Grace: 'It is known that bodies in motion always describe some line or other . . . Whoever has seen a fine arabian war-horse . . . cannot but remember what a long waving line his rising, and . . . pressing forward cuts through the air . . .' The line that Suki describes is a graceful flowing curve that exactly suits her aim. She reaches the window-sill, takes up a securely comfortable position, and next addresses herself to a further interesting task. Today the window is closed; and the giant shadow behind the panes must be prevailed upon to open it. As a rule the triangular dark face that surmounts her sable-brown body is totally expressionless; now she utters a faint imploring wail; and her lucent eyes — a clear pistachio-green — reflect an air of doubt and sorrow. Dogs often parody human emotions; a cat's occasional display of feeling is all the more effective because it is so obviously histrionic, and seldom followed, when it has achieved its end, by the smallest show of gratitude. Once the window is pushed up, Suki bounds across the ledge, and lightly drops into the room; but, after a few minutes devoted to rest and reflection, marked by sinuous movements of the tail, a faraway household noise attracts her notice; and, head low-slung like the head of a stalking leopard, she glides off delicately down the stairs.

Each of these very different episodes brought me much the same degree of pleasure. 'Beauty' and 'truth' are vague words; but, as I followed the three streams, studied the perfectly balanced proportions of an unknown woman's neck, and watched a cat's display of grace and courage, I felt I understood their meaning. Such glimpses, and, on a far loftier scale, the marvellous revelations accorded by the work of great artists, are the nearest I have come, and, I suppose, shall ever come, to spiritual enlightenment. I have always lacked faith and, since I grew up, have ceased to believe either in a Christian God or in the possibility of a future life. Far from believing that God created Man, I assume that the human consciousness has given birth to God; though the fact that God is mankind's bold creation need not make it less inspiring. Today, now that a personal God has receded, Art, which has strengthened and enriched the legend, and surrounded it with splendid images, seems more and more to take its place. At seventy-five, my own belief in Art remains as passionate as fifty years ago.

Here and elsewhere, I am often surprised to notice, the landscape of my life shows comparatively little change. I love the same pictures and, generally, the same books; and, both in painting and in literature, I admire the same qualities. Human existence, the Etruscans maintained, was divided into seven-year periods; and, when the tenth had passed, the individual, having run through his allotted span, need expect no further signs from heaven. This, happily, I have so far found untrue. Flashes of illumination still descend; yet a single change has certainly occurred; as soon as one enters that ominous eighth decade, the prospect of one's own death becomes, if not a morbid obsession, a regular preoccupation, obstinately lodged at the back of the mind, even though the foreground may continue to be peopled with amusing and distracting fancies. What chiefly haunts one is less a primitive fear of death, the medieval *timor mortis*, than a problem that defies solution – how to accept the idea of nothingness and of one's future non-existence. That idea, like the 'black holes' modern astronomers have located in the fabric of the universe, totally baffles the imagination; and, should one attempt to build up a detailed picture of some familiar friendly room – books, chairs, eighteenth-century prints, a large window surrounded by broad leaves, and the window-sill on which a cat alighted – but then deliberately exclude oneself, one feels a sudden touch of horror, so difficult is it to think of the world surviving without one's own invaluable aid.

I have long collected evocative 'last words' and the philosophic pronouncements of great men when they felt that death was drawing near; and my friend Alan Hodge, now himself dead – he died, alas, while I was halfway through this chapter – used to describe a revelatory conversation that, about 1955, he had had with Winston Churchill. Alan was then assisting him to produce his *History of the English-Speaking Peoples*, and often spent a working holiday at a villa in the South of France. His business was to prepare a series of drafts, on which the great man would then impose a fine sonority and Churchillian dignity; but, when that had been accomplished, they often dined together and, after dinner, sat beside the fire. The great man had passed his eightieth year, and his heroic life lay far behind him. His mood was sometimes pensive; and, one evening, the logs in the fire were damp, and spat reproachfully and hissed and smoked. The spectacle aroused him from a lengthy silence. 'Curious', he said, 'to imagine oneself a log – reluctant to be consumed – yet obliged *eventually* to give way . . .' Further than that his reverie did not go; but the effect it made was deeply solemn.

Sir Winston had still ten years to live; and among memorable last words, pronounced under the shadow of death itself, I particularly admire the farewell utterance of the Emperor Antoninus Pius, Hadrian's adopted son, father-in-law of Marcus Aurelius, and one of the 'good emperors', the virtuous and industrious Antonines we were expected to admire at school. Gibbon, however, with his usual flippancy, makes gentle fun of Antoninus. At least, he remarks that, whereas the life of Hadrian had been 'almost a perpetual journey', and he had 'marched on foot, and bareheaded, over the snows of Caledonia, and the sultry plains of the Upper Egypt', his successor seldom left home;[10] 'and, during the twenty-three years that he directed the public administration, the longest journeys of that

[10] This may not have been entirely true; by some Roman historians he is said to have visited Syria and Egypt.

amiable prince extended no further than from his palace in Rome to the retirement of his Lanuvian villa'.

Yet Antoninus, Gibbon freely admits, was a by no means idle ruler; at home he codified the Roman legal system; beyond the Italian frontier, he 'diffused order and tranquillity over the greatest part of the earth'. Nor was he a grim ascetic; 'he enjoyed, with moderation, the conveniences of his fortune, and the innocent pleasures of society'; and Gibbon adds, in a footnote, that he 'was fond of the theatre, and not insensible to the charms of the fair sex'. He also appreciated the pursuits and pastimes of a Roman country gentleman; and, on his estate, especially when the grapes were gathered, he liked attending rustic feasts. A tall, impressive man, he had a loud but pleasant voice, and was renowned for his *civilitas*, his unwillingness to take offence and his easy-going courtesy. The Emperor was even prepared to tolerate Christians — or so Christian writers themselves declared — although, if they were judicially accused and convicted, he might allow the law to take its course. His own religious faith was quietly conservative; he built and restored temples, and did his best to encourage the worship of the ancient Roman gods. Still practising this calm and temperate philosophy, Antoninus reached his seventy-fifth year. Then, in the spring of 161 A.D., he, too, recognized the approach of death, and retired to his country house near Rome, where, at supper, he ate some Alpine cheese, and woke up feverish next morning. On March 7, the tribune of his body-guard asked him to give the watch-word for the day. *'Aequanimitas'* he firmly answered, and withdrew into his private apartments, from which he never reappeared.

INDEX